Ian Ridley, co-writer on this book with Paul Merson, is Football Columnist for the *Observer*. His most recent book *Addicted* – a collaboration with Tony Adams on the Arsenal captain's critically acclaimed autobiography – was shortlisted for the William Hill Sports Book of the Year award and was the bestselling sports book of 1998. Ian's other books *include Season in the Cold: A Journey Through English Football*; *Cantona: The Red and the Black*; and *Tales from the Boot Camps* with Steve Claridge.

HERO AND VILLAIN
PAUL MERSON
WITH IAN RIDLEY

CollinsWillow

An Imprint of HarperCollins*Publishers*

First published in hardback 1999
by CollinsWillow
an imprint of HarperCollins*Publishers*
London

First published in paperback 2000

New and revised edition

The HarperCollins website address is:
www.harpercollins.co.uk

A CIP catalogue record for this book is
available from the British Library

ISBN 0 00 218896 1

Printed and bound in Great Britain by Clays Ltd, St Ives plc

Photographic acknowledgements
Allsport colour plates pages 6b, 9, 11, 16b;
Empics 3, 6c, 7tl, 10b, 12tl, 12tr, 14b, 15t, 15c, 16t;
Popperfoto/Reuter 1t, 1b, 2tl, 4, 13b, 14tl;
Press Association: 2tr, 2b, 5t, 5b, 7tr, 7b, 8t, 8b, 10t, 12b,
13t, 14tr, 16c; **Solent News** 15b; **Tim Sonnex** 6t

Contents

Introduction

Believe it or not, football has been more popular than it is currently; or at least, attendances were higher in the forties and fifties when it wasn't considered dangerous to stand on the terraces, in the days before compulsory seating cut down on capacities. Never, however, has the English game been so wealthy – at the top level, that is – or so superficially healthy.

The arrival of satellite television and the consequent creation of the Premiership have spawned riches beyond the wildest dreams of those Brylcreemed post-War heroes. Now the modern hair gel set can command transfer fees that boggle the mind and, with Bosman a factor when contracts run out, annual salaries of £1 million and more. With the apparent glamour and that sort of sum come some serious occupational hazards, however.

For this new generation of elite footballer is under a perpetual media microscope. With the increased rewards comes an intrusion that expands with each explosion in the amount of programming on television, air time on radio, and extra sports pages in newspapers.

Not forgetting, these days, each website on the Internet or added minute on club telephone lines. And, yes, the growth area of football books. It is a close call as to whether this latter-day Tower of Babel is responding to public demand or fuelling it for profit-chasing ends.

It is not just the sports outlets either. Tough as the sports press can be, it is the news reporters of the Sunday papers whom players fear most. Their private lives are fair game, it is assumed, given all this money they are receiving via supporters forking out ever increasingly for season tickets, merchandise or television subscriptions.

Players no longer know if that nice girl wanting their autograph and a picture with them is a reporter, a plant, or just some chancer who will later be selling the story of their encounter with a soccer star. Indiscretion is worth a bundle. Jim Carrey thought he had it bad in *The Truman Show*. For these multi-million pound prisoners, staying indoors with a takeaway and video is sometimes the best alternative.

In many ways, Paul Merson is the epitome of this new voracious culture that has grown up in the nineties and threatens to develop into an all-consuming monster as we enter even more high-pressured times in the Millennium. Merson has benefited hugely from the amount of money washing about these days. He has also paid a high price for that money. On the field, the story and the glory and the public acclaim are there for all to see. Off it, there can be a private pain and pressure that baffles young men who simply wanted to play football, who in their awesome youth believed themselves and their created persona to be indestructible.

Merson was a gifted, outstanding schoolboy striker who developed into a versatile creative player of touch and technique. He added rich subtlety to the intense power that was the Arsenal of George Graham, for whom he won two championships as well as FA and League Cups in the late eighties and early nineties. He also played for England. Like Icarus, however, Merson flew too close to the sun.

Behind the glamour was a sordid world that became too much for him. In December 1994, so much misery was enveloping him that he just had to admit that he was addicted to gambling, alcohol and drugs. Football was shocked. The lads always knew he liked a bit of a bet and a few lagers but this was stunning. The more so when he entered a clinic specialising in addictive illness in Hampshire.

After that, shock turned to sympathy for the first active player to own up publicly to such a problem, though a few, most notably Jimmy Greaves, had come to realise their own alcoholism when their playing days were over and that other crutch in their lives – football – was removed. Merson's bravery was widely applauded. He was admired, even revered. And that was that. Everyone lived happily ever after.

Actually, no. Football is not like that. Life is not like that. *Hero and Villain* confirms it and reveals the reality of recovery from this most damaging and deadly of illnesses, from which more people die every year, directly or indirectly, than any other disease.

The footballing year of 1998/99 often saw Paul at his highest professionally and his lowest personally. With addiction classed as an illness by the World Health Organisation, so his sporadic forays back into gambling (three times) and drinking (twice) are classed as relapses. Potentially, they could have been fatal.

As anyone who has ever sought to arrest addictive illness by abstinence one day at a time will tell you, once you solve the gambling, drinking or drugging problem, you are then left with a living problem. All the issues and feelings that caused the addict to use their activity or substance of choice in the first place resurface once the issues of life and one's own personality intrude to interrupt the first flush of enthusiasm for the new way of living.

'Do you still need to go to those meetings?' the addict is often asked after some time in recovery. The answer is yes, because the need is to maintain an emotional sobriety. That is best done by continuing to communicate – at meetings of Gamblers, Alcoholics or Narcotics Anonymous – with people whom the addict relates to and can offer help and support. In addition, the addict who has been around a while is needed to help a newcomer, who needs the encouragement. Anyway, it is called alcohol*is*m, not alcohol*was*m.

It is the main reason for this book, as well as – let's be honest – attempting to capture the politics, personalities and drama behind the scenes that seem so intriguing to writers and public alike these days.

The aim at the outset was to check how Paul's recovery was bearing up after three years without a bet, drink or drug; to show the pleasures and pitfalls of recovery away from the public gaze. Often, the picture is of a smiling man enjoying his football. It is genuinely one aspect of him. The rest of the time, it is about dealing with the anger and sadness, fear and jealousy, joy and pain of recovery.

About coping with life, in fact. Other footballers have since followed Paul into recovery. Tony Adams, notably,

Alex Rae of Sunderland and Shane Nicholson, now of Stockport County, have all bravely faced up to their own addictions. They would undoubtedly say that having found the courage to stop using, coping these days is infinitely easier than during their addictive phase, but celebrity – or notoriety – brings its own problems. Bravely they have endured it though. Paul Gascoigne, meanwhile, has used it as a reason for failing to sustain his own recovery from alcoholism.

Sympathy keeps addicts sick, but Paul Merson has great empathy for his old friend Gazza, having, too, an instantly recognisable face and a history well known to all amid this climate in which a footballer is very public property. The self-help fellowships may be anonymous – with their strict code of confidentiality in meetings – but their credo and traditions were established long before the media came to resemble the mythological Argus, with his one hundred eyes.

The idea was that *Hero and Villain* should be recorded day by day, because that is how recovering addicts live; one day at a time. And each day they manage without using, they equal the world record for length of sobriety. Recovery from the illness is seen as a daily reprieve. Sadly, Paul was not always reprieved.

The idea, too, was that it should chart Middlesbrough's attempt to stay in the Premiership and the daily lives of its colourful characters, including the manager Bryan Robson and that man Gazza. It changed, though, as Paul moved for £6.75 million to Aston Villa and it seemed he had swapped a relegation battle for a championship challenge, though the characters were no less rounded in John Gregory, Mark Bosnich and Stan Collymore. They say change is the only permanent thing in life.

It was the best of times, it was the worst of times, as someone else wrote.

We begin in June of 1998, as going to the World Cup with England was a high point of Paul's career. It was also a difficult time, since he would be away from home for six weeks – the longest period of his life – and away from the network of support that the addict comes to rely on as life's safety net. In that, he was fortunate to have Tony Adams around.

The picture for most of us was of a colourful festival of football; the reality was often a gloomy and tedious experience, fitfully punctuated by excitement and enlivened ultimately by that amazing match against Argentina, during which Paul scored in the penalty shoot-out.

He had won promotion with Middlesbrough after his adventurous – some would say foolish – move from Arsenal for £5.25 million at the beginning of that season. It was not all a smooth run back to the Premiership, however. As the going got tough back in the winter, and the feelings of loneliness and being isolated in the North-East grew ever stronger, he resorted to gambling again.

It passed, thankfully. He could see the danger within him, though, and tried to communicate as much to his Boro' team-mate Gascoigne, with whom he shared a house after the latter's move from Rangers, and vainly he tried to help him.

First, there was La Manga, with Paul revealing for the first time that the then England coach Glenn Hoddle told him that Gascoigne had definitely been earmarked for a squad place before his notorious weekend drinking binge. Then there was Gazza's brief stay in the Priory in London, where Paul made several visits, along with another well-known recovering addict from the world of show business.

In between, it was Merson himself who needed help, however. On his return to Middlesbrough after the World Cup, there was another bout of gambling and a drinking binge in Gazza's company. His index finger hovered on the self-destruct button. It provoked him into a transfer away from an environment he feared could prove damaging to him on a more regular, long-term basis.

At first, all went well at Aston Villa as he scored on his debut against Wimbledon and revelled in the team's record-breaking unbeaten start to the season that saw them top of the table for four months. He was recalled to England colours by Glenn Hoddle, whose subsequent departure amazed Paul along with many others, and he scored against the Czech Republic.

The problem with changing locations, though – 'doing a geographical', as addicts know it – is that you take you with you. By his own admission, Paul was not taking care of his sobriety and it caught up with him. It may have been a mega-money move but he had no cash in his spiritual bank, no resistance to the depression that would set in over the winter. Enduring a six-week lay-off with a back injury proved too much for him.

Over Christmas he gambled again. And a little more in January. Then for the whole of a blurred February during which he could remember only the details of his failed betting that cost him £35,000 in one three-week period alone. It was a reckless, frightening period, during which he also, controversially, escaped on a long weekend in New York to raise his own spirits, only to find himself criticised by all and sundry, not least his manager at Villa John Gregory, who had not been informed of his whereabouts.

The gambling spree of that winter finally overcame Paul's wife Lorraine, who, in the latest chapter of their turbulent marriage story, insisted on a separation that Paul accepted regretfully. He sought refuge in the bottle one more time, though. This time, having hitherto kept his escapades largely private, he was finally caught out by a prying camera lens as he left a London nightclub in the early hours of a Sunday morning.

His form on the field dipped as Villa's title tilt faded and Paul was dropped. It was just the motivation that he probably needed. All the things he held dearly – and when he is well, no one loves playing football more than Paul Merson – were being taken away from him. Hurting acutely again, he had no choice, unless he was to follow the path of his ultimate destruction, but to look again at himself and his addiction. Twice he considered going into treatment again. Once he felt suicidal. He could not go on as he was, he knew he had to do something and to do something different.

In the nick of time, he went back to the basics of recovery. He spat out his pride and returned to Alcoholics Anonymous. He got in touch once more with his old counsellor from treatment, Steve Stephens. He started reading AA literature once again and phoning up his friends in the fellowship. It worked. He arrested the gambling, stopped drinking before the cocaine could get to him again – as he admitted it probably would – and sank himself anew into his football.

Paul spent a large part of the winter looking forward to the end of the season. When it came, he wished the season could continue. He had rediscovered his appetite for the game. And for recovery. Where he had seen gloom in the dark days of January and February, he saw optimism for 1999/2000 as spring arrived.

For the first five months of the following season, however, that optimism appeared misplaced, as Villa went on a roll and he was unable to gain a permanent place in a winning team. But then came the FA Cup third round tie against Darlington in December, a match which would prove to be the turning point in his season. Five months later Paul was playing in the FA Cup final and had won the club supporters' and club players' Player of the Year awards.

All the more puzzling, then, when he discovered that manager John Gregory was willing to sell him.

Hero and Villain is the undulating story of two years in the life of Paul Merson, of two years in the life of a recovering – sometimes not recovering – addict. At times, there are large inconsistencies in Paul's attitudes towards the game, his team-mates and his family in the course of it. But that is how he was, how his season and recovery was.

What emerges is a man deeply in love with football and with his sons Charlie, Ben and Sam; a man who is willing to put his head above the parapet and offer forthright opinions on all the *dramatis personae* of English football.

At international level, Kevin Keegan replaced Hoddle, about whom Paul has much to say. At club level, after the at times acrimonious departure from Middlesbrough that upset Bryan Robson and Paul Gascoigne, came the soap opera that was Villa Park, what with John Gregory's first years as a Premiership manager and Stan Collymore's own excursion to the Priory and his eventual transfer.

Sometimes Paul does not emerge in as good a light as he might, but then he has always been willing to accept an honest opinion of himself as well as giving one of other people. There might have been a temptation to modify in hindsight some of the material but he never fell prey to it. It is as it happened and as was said, whether he was proved right or wrong.

Quite often – he might well agree – his criticisms of others are actually about himself and the way he felt at the time. They say that when you point the finger, three more are pointing back towards yourself.

It is one of Paul's many endearing traits, a willingness to own up to his mistakes, accept his faults and try to do better next time. He got knocked down and got up again in the course of a turbulent, scary year. In AA, they say that the 'How' in 'How it works' stands for Honesty, Open-mindedness and Willingness. In which case, it is no surprise that Paul got himself back into recovery after a painful, at times nightmare, twelve months. It was a touching relief to witness.

Ian Ridley
St Albans, June 2000

1998

JUNE

The End of the World?

Monday 1 June

We flew home today from our training camp at La Manga, near Murcia in Southern Spain. It's good to be back with my wife Lorraine and sons Charlie, Ben and Sam, good to be one of England's World Cup squad of 22, but a part of me is still feeling sorry for Paul Gascoigne after one of the most controversial episodes in the national team's history.

And feeling guilty, too. Gazza's a better player than me. Better than anybody, in fact. Why am I going and not him? I just can't understand any of it, but then I never have been able to understand fully the illness of addiction. I didn't with my own and I don't with his. Because I believe he is suffering with it, too.

It has been a hell of a weekend, one that I don't think any potential England squad member should be put through just ten days away from the start of a World Cup. We should be going to France relaxed, not wound up. I need to sleep on it. Perhaps the craziness will make more sense after a night's rest.

Tuesday 2 June

Gazza is telling his story to the *Sun*. It makes sad, sometimes sick, reading as he wallows in the details of how Glenn Hoddle told him that he would not be going to the finals. As someone who was in the thick of the whole controversy involving my Middlesbrough team-mate – and house-mate for three months of last season – it is not particularly uplifting to recall it all, though since we don't meet up until Friday, I've got plenty of time to think about it.

Glenn had said the squad could have a few drinks on the Saturday night. I suppose it was a reward at the end of the intense training camp we had endured for a week, during which we had twice made the one and a half-hour flight over to Casablanca and back for warm-up matches against Morocco and Belgium. Or maybe it was respite. Still, I didn't see the need for it, contriving some jolly piss-up. For Gazza, it was like a red rag to a bull.

My old Arsenal team-mate Tony Adams kept me company that night. Like me, Tone is a recovering alcoholic and we didn't want to be part of any drinking session that might develop so we just wandered around the hotel for a while, having a coffee and sandwich here and there.

We did look in at the private bar – where all the windows had been covered with paper so that other hotel guests could not see what was going on – at about 9pm. Gazza was on the piano and a few of the players were laughing along with him. It was all quite childish, I thought, both in the way we were being treated and the way some were behaving.

Gazza had had a few beers and gone way beyond that time where you could say anything constructive to him that he might listen to. He was yelling at me and Tone to come and have a drink with him. We knew we couldn't stay.

The next time I saw him was on the Sunday afternoon. I had been to play bowls with Dion Dublin while Gazza had been golfing with David Seaman, Ian Walker and Paul Ince. We were all supposed to see Glenn individually, starting with Dave Seaman at 4.15pm, with a list having gone up on the board in the morning.

Mine was one of the last times, at 6.15pm. I was assuming that it meant that I would be one of the six from the 28 out there who would not be going to France. Most of the Sunday papers were saying that I would be one of the unlucky ones and I thought they were right.

We all met for tea and scones on the terrace of the hotel at 4pm and Gazza was drunk, no doubt about it. He had apparently had some cans of beer on the golf course, against all orders, though when you've got a drink problem, it's hard to stop once you've started, which Gazza had done on the Saturday night. Some of the boys were laughing, but I didn't find it funny.

'This is shit. I've gone,' he was saying. 'I can't do it any more.'

He had played well at the golf, despite the drinking, I was told but now he had stopped it was all kicking in.

Tony and I decided to take him down to the swimming pool to try and liven him up, or at least sober him up, before his meeting with Glenn. We just took off his clothes and threw him in. Holidaymakers sharing the complex were staring, but he just swore at some of them. Luckily most people didn't take any notice, but how it didn't all get out I will never know.

We sat with him by the pool for half an hour and he

was saying: 'I won't go. I'm finished.' He seemed desperately sad and sorry for himself and he had had a lot to endure as he was going through a bad time with his wife Sheryl and divorce looked on the cards.

I told him not to worry, and that I would probably be the one not going. I had been joking all week: 'I'm going to smash up the room if he tells me that,' and I said it again. To this day, Gazza blames me for putting the idea in his head for what happened next.

Soon after he had gone up to see Glenn, the FA Press Officer Steve Double came down and said that he had heard Gazza wouldn't be going. It annoyed me that a press officer knew before the player himself and the rest of the squad. Soon after, someone came down to say that something had kicked off in Glenn's room and that Gazza had hurt his leg. I dashed up to Gazza's room to find out what was going on.

Dave Seaman and one or two others were already there, telling him not to worry, that he was still a great player. It was stuff he didn't need to hear, in my opinion. What he needed now was tough-love reality; to hear the truth about himself so that he could wise up and do something before it was all too late. He was not in the mood for anything like that, though. There was nothing much I could do or tell him, so I just went to fetch Gary Lewin, the physio, to attend to the leg he had cut in kicking out at the furniture in Glenn's room after being told the news.

Gary told me that I was in the squad but I didn't dare believe it yet. When I went back to my room, I found out that I must be.

There, in the adjoining room, Dion Dublin was packing to go home. There was a plane home for the unlucky six, he said, and they had to be down at reception in another ten minutes. I told him that my appointment was not for another fifteen minutes – after all the Gazza stuff everything was behind schedule – so he said that I must be in. I commiserated with Dion and wished him all the best with Coventry City for the coming season. I spent a lot of time with him that week. He is a smashing lad, the sort you'd like on your team.

'What do you think about your mate?' Glenn asked me when I went for my meeting.

'I'm gutted,' I said. 'I hope I'm not going just because he's out.'

'No,' he replied. '*You were both on that plane.*'

I think Glenn changed his mind following events on the Saturday night and Sunday confirmed to him that he had made the right decision. Why else would Glenn have told Gazza on the Sunday morning to walk off the dead leg that he sustained on the Friday night against Belgium?

It was the Belgian game, in hindsight, that I think confirmed me in the squad. Most of the players thought that to be in the team that night was just a token gesture, a way for Glenn to say: 'Thanks for coming.' But I thought I had one of my best games for England, playing up front with Les Ferdinand. I got a lot of the ball and used it reasonably well, even though it was a 0–0 draw.

Even Graeme Le Saux found a reason that night to convince himself that he wouldn't go to France. And he was the only natural left-footer in the squad. It felt like school trials. No-one seemed to be a banker. Graeme wondered why he was playing against Belgium when he had already proved himself.

I didn't think this was the way to do things. It was all

very childish and stressful. I got on alright with Glenn, I thought he was a good bloke, and he had recalled me to the England squad, so he was good for me in the same way that Graham Taylor had been. But this trip had not been enjoyable. The facilities and the weather at La Manga were magnificent, but everyone was a bag of nerves when we should have been more confident before a World Cup. Glenn had never really spoken to us individually, so you didn't know where you stood.

In my meeting with him I felt like giving up my place for Gazza. It was strange that I felt guilty about going. And I thought the lads would think, 'Why is Merse going when Gazza isn't?' That's the kind of paranoid personality I have.

Today I am just glad that the worry about my place is over at last. I am going to a World Cup. I know what my summer holds, starting on Friday when we meet up again at Burnham Beeches, the hotel near Slough that England use. Not so Gazza. I wonder what the summer has in store for him – what his future will bring, in fact.

Friday 5 June

All I did really for the last few days before joining up with the squad for France today was sit around the house, play with the kids, go shopping and watch television. Ah, the glamorous life that footballers lead sometimes.

I took the boys to school and said goodbye to them for at least three weeks, which was very sad. I've never been away that long before. I was also very nervous and excited by the prospect of the World Cup, which may be why I was in and out of the toilet all morning.

At Burnham Beeches, the first thing I was requested to

do was take a drugs test. I had become so used to taking them over the last few years that I knew more about taking the urine sample than the testers seemed to. Of course it was negative.

The atmosphere at the hotel was immediately much more relaxed over lunch than at La Manga with nobody worrying about their place any more. On the way to training I got talking to Teddy Sheringham about his last few days in Portugal, a story which the papers have got hold of. They have pictures of him in a nightclub in the early hours of the morning in the company of a blonde, with a cigarette in his mouth.

I don't think it's much of a story really. He's a single bloke letting his hair down before what is going to be a tough month, but in the absence of anything else it's the big news. The problem is that Glenn had told us that we were still on England duty and that we should keep our heads down to avoid any scandal or controversy before we go to France. Ted can expect an earful from the boss.

I did alright in training after a poor start and when we got back to the hotel I rang Lorraine. The boys were already in bed asleep. I told Lorraine how much I loved her and, with wives and girlfriends being allowed here tomorrow, how much I was looking forward to seeing her.

Saturday 6 June

Had a headache after breakfast – not surprising because the *Sun, Mirror, Express* and *Mail* are all banned and we're only allowed to look at the *Independent, Guardian, The Times* and *Telegraph*. All those big words do me in. Thirty days of reading them and I should be one of the best Scrabble players in the world.

Even the broadsheets are full of Ted. He has been daft, but I can't condemn him. Four years ago it would have been me. In a way I envy him. He hired a private jet and got away – who's to say that isn't better for him than vegetating at home? And who was he hurting? Glenn has made him apologise for his behaviour to the press today but I think that's a joke. The only person he needs to apologise to is his son Charlie, who is likely to take some stick now from other kids about his dad.

One eerie thing does come into my mind. Before we went to the La Manga training camp, I went to see Eileen Drewery, the healer in whom Glenn places a lot of faith. I must say, I do feel I get some benefit from her too. With some players she can help with physical injuries by laying hands on to the calf, hamstring or wherever, while with others like me it can be more spiritual as she puts her hands on your head. Then, you can sense a healing sensation both mentally and emotionally as she banishes negative spirits.

Anyway, she was telling me that she wanted to see Ted but that he didn't want to come and see her. 'Something will happen to him before the World Cup and I think he'll have to come and see me then,' she said.

Training was hard and we played a 10 vs 11 game. I was in the 10 and we did well first half, even though Alan Shearer missed a penalty for the 11. Then Tony Adams swapped sides, from the 11 to the 10 and the game ended up 2–2. Tone and Paul Ince had a big disagreement about tactics at one point, Tony telling Incey to shut up. The boss was quite shocked at first but it's probably just the first of many rows over the next few weeks, I'm sure. Anyway, they made up on the coach back to the hotel.

Tonight the whole squad went to the musical *Chicago*,

which I enjoyed, and afterwards for a meal with our wives or girlfriends. Ted was in a group of half a dozen lads who didn't have partners and we joked that he should have asked the girl from Portugal to come. On the coach home, John Gorman sang a couple of songs on the mike. He was surprisingly good.

Sunday 7 June

Ordered tea and toast in bed for Lorraine and me which was a treat for her as she usually has three kids to see to in the morning. It was hard to say goodbye to her after lunch. I am going to miss her because I love her so much and I rely on her in my life. She is a rock to me.

We went training and didn't get back until 8pm. Any later and we would have hit Monday morning's rush hour. I rang Lorraine to thank her for the weekend and said hello to Charlie, then played snooker with Martin Keown and thrashed him. I asked him if he wanted to go outside and play 50–50 tackles because at the moment that is the only thing he's going to beat me at.

Monday 8 June

I felt really good this morning seeing as I stayed up late and watched the NBA finals, which the Chicago Bulls won easily.

At training, the way the teams were setting up, it looks as if Michael Owen will be playing in place of Teddy for a friendly we have in Caen tomorrow. Towards the end of what was a hard session, some bloke dressed as a large pepperami ran on to the training pitch for at least a minute. It was quite funny, done for a publicity stunt I think, but it did make you wonder about the security around us.

In the afternoon, I went to see Eileen Drewery one last time before we left for France and it did me good. She makes me feel good and fresh. In the evening I rang Bryan Robson and he has given me only three weeks off, which has upset me considering that I have just played 61 games in the past season and will only have had four weeks off all year.

I lost 2–0 at table tennis to Tony Adams and took it out on Martin Keown by beating him 3–0 at snooker. Also beat Paul Ince. He was the man at snooker, so now I'm the man.

Tuesday 9 June

All the training is done, all the preparations made, and today we left for the World Cup. I am 30 years of age, but I don't think I have ever felt fitter. It began, of course, with stopping drinking and taking cocaine four years ago and reached new levels under Arsène Wenger at Arsenal, with his physical regime of carefully monitored training and dietary regime.

That involves vitamin and iron supplements, Creatine for muscular development and caffeine tablets, which are taken on match days with lunch and then an hour before the game, designed to improve concentration and stamina. A lot of players swear by it all but some can't take the palpitations that the caffeine – equivalent to drinking some eight cups of coffee – gives them. Some also find that it gives them diarrhoea so stop taking it.

Having played under Arsène at Monaco, Glenn is a great advocate of all these scientific methods and even uses the same French doctor as him, Yann Rougier, who advises on all the dietary and conditioning methods.

About two months ago we were all blood-tested on individual programmes to see which supplements we particularly needed. I didn't need much, given that I had been familiar with them anyway. Though at Middlesbrough, I was still in touch with the Arsenal and England physio Gary Lewin who let me have the caffeine tablets.

Lorraine rang at 7.30am to get me out of bed, because we had to be down in reception at 8am to check in our bags. On the coach to the airport, I sat next to Tony Adams, telling him how excited I was by the whole prospect. The amazing thing is that over the next few weeks, someone is going to emerge as a star of the world game. Who will it be? I reckoned the candidates on this coach this morning were Paul Scholes, David Beckham and Michael Owen.

After having scored the winning goal against Morocco a fortnight earlier, Michael was given a game against Caen, who we stopped off to play in a practice match on our way to our headquarters at La Baule. It was an important game in many ways for team tactics and understanding, as the team that will play the first game against Tunisia has never played together – if Owen plays, that is.

He is such a nice lad, Michael, and I can't get over how young he looks. I suppose that's a sign that I am getting old, when footballers look young. He is also so cool about everything. There is no fear in him. I try to think back when I was that age – still over three years from being named the PFA's Young Player of the Year – and I guess I was similar, though probably not as relaxed. I suppose it only happens when you mature in the game, when you realise how difficult it really is.

We beat Caen with a goal by Paul Scholes but it was not very convincing stuff. We could be home after the first phase if we don't do better than this. It was a strange atmosphere playing behind closed doors, as Glenn wanted. Completely different – we hope – from the hothouse atmosphere we are soon to be in. At the end, journalists outside the ground were trying to get information about the game from us. All very weird.

From Caen, we made a short half-hour plane hop to St Nazaire, the nearest airstrip to La Baule, the Brittany resort where we will be based for the duration of the tournament. I was assigned a room adjoining Tony Adams's, with a kitchen between us. It all seems very comfortable. Straight to bed after dinner. Finally, I am at a World Cup. That is some feeling, some achievement.

Wednesday 10 June

Slept badly, I think because of the anticipation of the tournament starting today, though we are still nearly a week away from playing. Can't drink the breakfast coffee, so tried the tea, which was not much better, to wash down the cereal and pastry.

The facilities here at Escoublac just outside La Baule are excellent. In the car park, a games arcade has been constructed, with a pool table, pinball, jukebox and driving machine installed. There is also a golf course so everything is spot on. With a morning free, I played pinball, then Tony at pool. He beat me, so I'll have to find something else to take him on at.

Before lunch, we had a meeting with Dr Rougier about all the various dietary supplements. The boss says the tablets are all geared up for the final, but for me the most important game of the tournament is against Tunisia next Monday. Lunch is pasta and later dinner is meat, often chicken, with two veg. Chips are off. Thus is set our routine for the next month. It's good food but I hope it doesn't get too boring.

We watched the opening game of the tournament, Brazil beating Scotland 2–1. I can't see Brazil winning the tournament, but then if I was a good judge I wouldn't be in Gamblers Anonymous, would I? I thought Scotland deserved a draw. Gordon Durie was brilliant in the way he ran up front and always showed for the outlet ball while Colin Hendrie and Colin Calderwood hardly gave Ronaldo a kick.

After dinner we watched Norway – more like Wimbledon than Wimbledon these days – draw 2–2 with Morocco. Norway look to me as if they will be going home very soon. I feel I'm overdosing on football already, so tomorrow I will go to the weights room when Austria play Cameroon.

Thursday 11 June

Massive shock before training this morning when the boss named the team. David Beckham wasn't in it. He looked very hurt. A lot of the lads think it is a joke, because even though David hasn't set the world alight in the centre of midfield, where he has been playing just lately, he appeared to have cemented his position at right wing-back. Also, Darren Anderton hasn't really done much in the last three games as he's still recovering from injury, but he is in the final XI.

I just hope Dave keeps his head up. The boss didn't pull him aside before training to tell him why he isn't in, which in my opinion is bad management of a young player. After Glenn named the team, the reserves played them – outplayed them, as usually happens by the law of Sod – and Dave was very down. It lasted only about twenty minutes because the rain started chucking it down then. A bit different in weather to La Manga but much the same when it comes to Glenn making shock decisions.

Played Owen at pool and lost 6–1. He's good at everything, this boy. It makes you sick.

Friday 12 June

Played golf this morning with Darren Anderton against Dave Seaman and David Batty. I was terrible and didn't get much help from Darren, who is the worst putter I have ever seen, though he is a bit of a bandit off a handicap of 12, to my 18. Then played pool against Michael Owen and beat him. Then he beat me. Back to normal.

Today I was going to the games arcade a lot because all the lads were betting on the outcome of matches on the television and I felt I needed to stay away from that sort of thing. It has become wearing over the last couple of days. I can't stop them, and wouldn't want to, so the only thing I can do is remove myself from the situation. There's a saying in Alcoholics Anonymous that if you sit in the barber's chair long enough, you'll get your hair cut; which means that if you're around drink, or gambling, for too long, eventually you'll get sucked into it.

Anyway, Teddy Sheringham and Alan Shearer are the tightest bookmakers in the world. They can't lose with the odds they are offering. BBC's *Watchdog* might be over to investigate next week.

Saturday 13 June

The weather is a bit like Middlesbrough on a bad day and I got saturated just running across the courtyard for breakfast. Talked to my dad, then the boys on the phone. My eldest Charlie, who is now seven and a half, had his first proper football match today for his team in St Albans – Larkspur – and I was very proud of him. I told him just to enjoy it, which is what all youngsters should be told. If you don't enjoy this game, it really is not worth playing.

Later after training, at which we just worked on a few set pieces in the rain then had a short game, I spoke to Charlie again. His team won the tournament and he scored the winning goal in the final. I was delighted for him but sad that I couldn't be there.

Today was like *Groundhog Day*. I just played all the machines while the football was on the television – I'm top man on the driving machine and also beat Tony at pool – and I'm feeling bored and depressed. This is not how I expected a World Cup to be. The picture back home is of colour and drama and excitement. For us it is about greyness, loneliness and isolation at the moment. I like the idea of having all the teams in one location, like an Olympic village, which should be feasible in a country like France where every venue is only an hour's flight away. That way, you might get the carnival feeling of the event a bit more.

Perhaps it is just this phoney period before we play our first game. I will put it down to that. I have to hold on to the fact that I am very lucky to be out here and that I have Tony Adams to talk to. He understands the addict's moods and mentality.

My tip to win the tournament, Spain, have lost their opening game to Nigeria 3–2 in nearby Nantes, which was a big shock to me. With Holland only drawing later 0–0 with Belgium, it is a bad day for two big guns. I'm just glad to have got through it without having a bet. For me, that is the bottom line.

Sunday 14 June

Still waking up early, feeling tired and low. Just have to tell myself what they say in AA: 'This too shall pass'. Phoned Lorraine, then phoned back fifteen minutes later to tell her I love her. We flew down to Marseille for tomorrow's game. It was another good flight – I think I'm starting to like flying now – but the hotel we are being put up in at the airport is like *Prisoner Cell Block H*.

We trained at the Stade Velodrome, which is a fantastic venue, and the boss and his assistant John Gorman seemed very nervous to me. It's understandable, I suppose, because tomorrow is a big, big day when everything they have been working towards comes together, but there's no laughing, which I think you need. Glenn had a right go at Martin Keown for some lack of control or something, which I thought was out of order. I think it's getting to the boss. The lads seem very calm, though.

You always have worries at this stage. My concern for the team is about Alan Shearer. I know he says he is just the same player as he was before his serious injury, but I am not so sure. He used to create a lot of his own chances by making runs down the channel and cutting in to go for goal. Now you have to put the ball in the box for him more often, which is also why I am amazed David Beckham has been left out. As a finisher, Alan is up there with Ian Wright but he has lost some of that dash that used to be his trademark around Euro '96 time. I hope he comes good but in warm-up games and training I have seen nothing to suggest he will, I'm afraid. Prove me wrong Alan, eh?

Monday 15 June
England 2 Tunisia 0

I felt good today, excited about the whole thing. It's right what they say in all the self-help fellowships, that bad feelings will pass and if you go through them, rather than round them with the help of a drink, drug or bet, you learn something from them. They make the good times seem better, too. Today I could savour the whole occasion.

It was some occasion too. The mood was good in the camp. We were raring to go. As a substitute you're in a strange position – part of it and ready to go on but without that edge of nervousness that comes from being a starter – so you sit in the dressing room observing it all. The lads were confident and keen. I knew, and I think we all knew, that we were much better than the Tunisians, though no-one dared to say such a dangerous thing.

The atmosphere was quite fantastic. We were lucky to be in the shade but it looked like there were 30,000 English fans baking out there in the afternoon sun. How could we not respond to them and for them?

It took a while but gradually we got on top. And Alan

proved me wrong by heading the opening goal. That's why he's worth so much money, I suppose. Not many would have come back from the injury he's had but he is as strong as an ox and he is a man for the big game.

Paul Scholes might have had three goals but for good goalkeeping and finally completed the formalities by scoring the goal of the tournament so far with a curling shot. Two-nil. Job done. We were on our way and at last I felt we were a part of this tournament.

The FA flew down wives and girlfriends and it was great to see Lorraine for a short time before we had to get the plane back to La Baule. After dinner I played Owen at pool. Lost 10–9, so I needed some consolation. I played Martin Keown on the driving machine and won 5–0.

In the evening we watched Romania beat Colombia 1–0. Now our game against the Romanians becomes massive. We have a week to prepare for it, which in many ways is a good thing, though it would have seemed the longest in the world if we hadn't won our opening match. Now it should be a good week.

The fixtures for the Premiership are released today and Middlesbrough's have been faxed to me. We have got Leeds at home in our first game back. Can't wait for that. Not. Because it's George Graham, Leeds are bound to man-mark me.

Tuesday 16 June

Woke late, then rang Lorraine. We were married eight years ago today and I forgot to say happy anniversary. At lunch we were given our post and my day was brightened by a lovely card from Lorraine.

We trained hard today and the boss had a little go at a couple of the lads, which I thought was counter-productive. Tony Adams has a foot injury. People say that England will struggle if Shearer isn't playing but I think we would miss Tony more than anyone. He is the leader of this squad, captain in all but name, and I haven't seen a better central defender at this tournament. We – that is the reserves – got thrashed by the first team. Glenn had a go at Steve McManaman behind his back for not doing his sit-ups but it turned out that he had.

Everyone in the tournament has now played one game and I can't say I've seen anything that has really impressed or frightened me. The standard has been very up and down. I still think that Spain are a really good team but losing their first game has shown to me what I think is a flaw in the format of the tournament. You can lose one game in a freak result and be virtually out of the World Cup. If the groups were bigger, I'm sure the cream would rise to the top over more games and you would get the best teams in the last 16 or last eight.

We watched Scotland draw with Norway and I was pleased for them. I really hope they qualify. Brazil all of a sudden were unbelievable in beating Morocco 3–0. Not as good as me in beating Martin Keown 14–0 on the car machine, though.

Wednesday 17 June

The weather has changed and it is beautiful now. We trained in the afternoon and the midweek team – the second XI that is – played the first team and hammered them. We finished with shooting practice and Keown was unbelievable. Didn't know he could finish like that.

I feel very sharp in training and I just hope I get on in a game and can say I played in a World Cup.

I'm first choice on the car-driving machine, mind. I beat Les Ferdinand 5–0, Martin 4–0 and Seaman 2–0, though Paul Ince was a tougher nut and I only won 3–2. He is very competitive, Incey. Some people say he is flash, just like Ian Wright, but you couldn't meet two better blokes. I have known Incey since he was 10 and always got on well with him. He is a winner and that's his attitude.

David Beckham was sent to do a press conference today and by all accounts was very honest about the disappointment he felt at being dropped. That's the only way to be but I don't think he should have been put through the ordeal. It smacked of cruelty to me.

Thursday 18 June

A day off. My Middlesbrough colleague Nigel Pearson rang this morning, which was really nice of him. He is such a great bloke. He is hoping to get the Sheffield United job, which would be good for Nigel and even better for Sheffield United.

Special treat this afternoon. We were allowed out of the compound to go down to the sea front and did some sunbathing. Then the boss took us all to a restaurant, though the lads who had played golf in the afternoon weren't too happy as they were tired and wanted to stay in the camp and watch the French playing Saudi Arabia.

The way the squad divides up is quite interesting. We are all more gregarious now we know each other better, unlike when we were coming back from Morocco when it seemed like a collection of Los Angeles gangs. Groups inevitably form, though. The Manchester United lads will stick together while Alan Shearer, David Batty, Gareth Southgate and Rob Lee are forever playing a memory game together.

I stick close to Tony Adams who is a winner in football and in life and I also enjoy the company of Michael Owen and Rio Ferdinand, young lads who are keen to hear and learn from your experiences.

Nigel P rang back tonight with some bad news. Our coach at Middlesbrough, John Pickering, has cancer. Had a lovely letter from Charlie, Ben and Sam. I do miss my boys.

Friday 19 June

Quiet day, the hottest so far. I felt good in training, after which the boss talked to me like a little boy, telling me I was doing a press conference. I do think you should have a choice in the matter. As usual, I answered the questions honestly to the best of my ability, but I don't think they really wanted to speak to me and I can understand why. They're sending out someone who isn't even playing. Who's going to be interested in one of the 'nuggets'?

Gareth Southgate damaged an ankle towards the end of training and Glenn was furious, which I thought was out of order. Gareth is gutted. He didn't mean to do it; he desperately wants to play against Romania. It's like with your son. There's no point having a go at a little boy who dropped a cup of milk, is there, if it was an accident?

Spain could only draw with Paraguay and look like they are out. Owen beat me 10–6 at pool.

Saturday 20 June

The boss named the team for Monday's game against Romania today; one change – Gary Neville for Gareth. I would have played Keown. Gareth was still sent to a press conference and instructed to say that he is 50–50 even though he's got no chance. He's not happy about that and I can see why.

The second team played against the first team again today and they were all over the place. The boss was playing sweeper, with me and Robert Lee in central midfield. We both called for the ball but he said he didn't need us in there. You wonder who is in this squad and who is the manager. He still thinks he's good enough to play.

Got beaten 4–0 at pool by Anderton. Surely I've got to beat someone soon. Watched Holland beat South Korea 5–0 and they look the best team so far. Shearer and Teddy got hammered because a lot of the lads had Cocu to score the first goal at 14–1. Shearer was not happy.

Sunday 21 June

Kids rang early to wish me happy father's day. Can't wait to take them on holiday and spend some time with them. Rang my dad and wished him all the best for the day.

Tony and I watched a film, *US Marshall*, starring Tommy Lee Jones, which passed a couple of hours before we left the camp at 3.15pm to travel to Toulouse for tomorrow's match against Romania. Also beat Rio 2–1 at pool, but Rio is the worst pool player around.

We trained at the stadium and I really enjoyed it, even beating Owen at finishing again. It is a rule that we don't see any of the papers but I have heard there is a bandwagon back home for Michael to play. I can see what people mean, but Teddy is still playing well and there is no real feeling in the camp yet that Michael should be a starter. The boss seems very pleased with everything. The lads are still buzzing from the Tunisia result and the last few days have flown by.

In the evening we watched USA lose to Iran. Can't believe it.

Monday 22 June
Romania 2 England 1

I was very excited about the game again. Although I wasn't starting, you just never know what might happen and I was ready and fit if called upon. We trained in the morning, just a session to do set pieces. We have taken to calling ourselves the nuggets and lemons on the day of a game because we don't seem to do anything right for the boss on match days. He was in another great mood. Not.

Adams has got a French tape, which he puts into his personal stereo on the way to the stadium. I can't believe it – learning French on top of reading, playing the piano, playing football and sometimes talking in a way I don't understand. We grew up together at the Arsenal and it was 'all right my son' for most of the time. Now he is so softly spoken and polite. There is just such an aura of strength to him these days as well, something that Sol Campbell seems to be picking up. As a striker, you feel that sometimes you just can't get by them.

Romania found a way, though. The game was a nightmare for us as we spent a long period chasing an equalising goal. Finally it came through Michael, to great relief on the bench. Should he have been on from the start? From half-time perhaps. Teddy Sheringham was having a nightmare – along with Alan Shearer – and the crowd were on his back.

Graeme Le Saux also had a nightmare and to his credit held up his hands later after Dan Petrescu had grabbed a winner for Romania. It was a sloppy goal and 2–1 to Romania, a horror result. We never expected to get beaten and perhaps we underestimated them. We should have just taken the point instead of going for the win, but that's the English way I suppose.

The only saving grace was that I got to see Lorraine briefly after the match. We got home at 2.30am tired and deflated. Being positive, everyone is grateful that we can still qualify from a game against Colombia, who are very dodgy, but I think this could prove to be a significant defeat.

Tuesday 23 June

We had a team meeting today and Glenn said that although he wasn't happy with the result, he was pleased with the way we played against Romania. I can't agree with that and nor can many of the lads, but then you can't really speak up because there's a feeling that grudges will be held and you might not get picked.

I don't think I will anyway now. In training – which was just for the reserves, now called the Dunga XI – I had a go at the boss for not moving fast enough for a pass. He wasn't happy about how I spoke to him, but I am not a schoolboy and I will talk my mind. Rio was laughing his head off and trying not to be seen by the boss.

I spoke to Charlie, Ben and Sam today and it's great to hear their voices, though Lorraine is getting fed up with

Charlie being cheeky. It must be because he's missing me. Boys need their dad. I'm getting homesick, too.

Watched Scotland get slaughtered and sent home by Morocco and Brazil unbelievably beaten by Norway. I don't think there is a great team in this tournament. Beaten 16–1 by Owen at pool. Never playing pool again.

Wednesday 24 June

Played pool for most of the day with Michael Owen. He only beat me 10–9, though, probably because something unpleasant is affecting him. Today Michael received an anonymous letter from some loony claiming to be sleeping with his girlfriend. This is just a young lad who is not flash at all, with a lovely girlfriend, who just wants to play football. I just wish people would leave him alone.

I told him about when I was in a pub just before Christmas and some bloke approached me claiming that I owed him £10,000 for cocaine from my mad, bad old days. He said I would be shot if I didn't pay up. He was drunk and just making it up. I told Michael that I am afraid that there are a lot of sick people out there. You do worry.

The redemption to the day for Michael was that it looks from the way we were lining up in training that he is going to play against Colombia. Spain had a great 6–1 win over Bulgaria but it's too late for them.

Thursday 25 June

We weren't training until noon so me, Tony, Bats and Rob Lee watched *Jackie Brown* on the big screen. Not very good, but nothing else to do.

At training, the Dunga XI had to watch the first team go through set pieces and at the end the boss asked Les Ferdinand what the signal for a near post corner was. Les didn't know and nor did Macca or Rio. Teddy Sheringham was trying to whisper the signals to us because he knows, having just been dropped from the team. I wish Glenn had asked me, because I did and would have made him look stupid – just like he was trying to do with the lads. Glenn then had a go at all of us and while the first team went in, made us do set pieces for about 20 minutes. Sometimes with Glenn and his assistant John Gorman, who is a nice bloke, it seems like a good cop–bad cop routine.

Later in the day we flew to Lille for the match in Lens against Colombia tomorrow. All the lads looked very tired. Tony is furious that Gareth was asked to lie about his injury against Romania and he has a point. I mean, the Romanians are not going to wet themselves because Gareth Southgate is in, are they? The boss shouldn't treat us like kids.

The Colombians might wet themselves when they find out about another kid, though. Michael Owen is definitely going to start now against them.

Friday 26 June
England 2 Colombia 0

We watched a video of Colombia this morning. It should be about 3–0 or 4–0 to us. At a team meeting, Dr Rougier warned us about watching television for more than an hour because of the tiring effects it could have on you. It makes me laugh. We qualified for this tournament, and won lots of medals for our clubs, without being told that.

I think you should be able to do what is good for you and television relaxes me.

Another great atmosphere inside the Lens stadium, with three-quarters of the ground English. The win was comfortable enough but they were worse than Tunisia so we shouldn't get carried away for the last 16 match against Argentina on Monday. With Romania getting a draw against Tunisia, it means we are in the tougher half of the draw. I am personally disappointed not to have got on to the pitch with us winning so easily. It does not look as if I will play now.

I felt for Rio because he was going on and then Paul Ince got injured so the boss had to put on David Batty. I was pleased for Darren Anderton, who scored the first goal with a terrific rising drive, because he took a lot of stick at the start of the tournament but has been our best player. I was also delighted for David Beckham because he did sulk for about a week after getting dropped but he has responded brilliantly, scoring a great goal from a free kick and passing the ball well.

Wives and girlfriends are allowed to stay with us tonight at our hotel near Lens, which is great, so no time to write any more now.

Saturday 27 June

Had to get up for training and told Lorraine I would be only about twenty minutes. How wrong I was. The Dunga XI were required for at least an hour. Me, Macca and Les wrote Valderrama, Dunga and Hagi on the back of our training kits with a marker pen. They are the fanny merchants of the tournament and we feel a bit like them, not really central to what is going on. It lightened the mood a bit.

It was a real wrench to say goodbye to Lorraine at 5.30pm when we had to travel back to La Baule, the lads very quiet and tired on the journey. After dinner, I watched some of the Brazil game against Chile before nipping out for a game of pool with Rio – things are getting worse, I could only draw 5–5 – and coming back to watch the highlights. In their 4–1 win, Brazil in general and Ronaldo in particular are looking awesome now.

Do we have a Ronaldo, capable of winning a game on his own? Michael Owen is still maybe too young. Once I would have said Macca, if he is bang on form for Liverpool, but he doesn't even look as if he will get a game.

Sunday 28 June

The boss has named the same team again for the Argentina match, even though Gareth Southgate is fit again. The Dunga XI played the team again at training. We had the rest of the day to ourselves and watched France v Paraguay, feeling very sorry for the South American goalkeeper Chilavert, who was beaten by Laurent Blanc's golden goal. He has been the best goalkeeper of the tournament for me.

Owen and me played Becks and Neville at pool. I can't believe it. This time I've lost and I've got Michael on my team. I then played Michael and lost 10–6. After dinner, went to my room, lay on the bed and watched Denmark hammer Nigeria.

It has been a bad day. I've been with the squad for

almost a month now, trained hard and haven't had a sniff of action. Have I been wasting my time?

Monday 29 June

We watched videos of Argentina this morning and then went and did set pieces, the Dunga XI having to watch and concentrate in case called upon. The boss was getting fed up with Scholesey and Becks finding one free kick routine hard to do and at one point told Becks he wasn't good enough. All the lads felt that was bang out of order.

We flew across to St Etienne and just as we were coming in to land, the pilot took the plane up again, which scared a few of the boys. We never did find out why. I was OK. I was playing cards with Teddy Sheringham and Darren Anderton – them for money, me for interest – and was not too bothered.

The training session at the ground was a light one. I do like this stadium. It is compact and atmospheric, like an English ground. We returned to the hotel to find it had no water. When it did come on, it was like mud.

We watched the two last 16 games and Holland and Germany were very lucky to win. I still think we will have our work cut out if we do get through to play Holland in the quarter-finals.

I'm really missing Lorraine and the boys now and feeling homesick. Lorraine is coming over for the game tomorrow. I've told her that I probably won't get on but she said, 'You never know,' and to keep my head up.

Tuesday 30 June
England 2 Argentina 2
(Argentina win 4–3 on penalties aet)

At last a good sleep. I didn't wake until 10.30am after going to bed at 11.30pm last night. We went for a stretch on the green outside the hotel and then had a meeting just to go over a few tactical points. Glenn spoke mostly about when to drop off and when to push up and squeeze the Argentinians.

After lunch, we went back to our rooms for a sleep but I never can so I watched Eurosport and Sky News. We didn't see the papers and were mostly ignorant of what people were saying back home but Sky News did provide some insight. It was there mostly that the players, led by Alan Shearer, played this game of trying to get song titles into their interview answers. Personally, I didn't find it funny.

I also watched Croatia deservedly beat Romania, with Davor Suker showing plenty of bottle in having to take his penalty twice and scoring twice. I still would have fancied us in that half of the draw that the Romanians beat us to, mind. After that, it was on to the Stade Geoffroy Guichard.

As the coach pulled in, I suddenly got this feeling that this was really World Cup football, this was really a big, big game. Sod the group stuff. Perhaps it was all the English and Argentinian flags around, and all the history of conflict between the two nations. It was daunting and exciting at the same time.

The final may be the ultimate game but we couldn't afford to think like that. This, tonight, was the ultimate game and the feeling grew as we warmed up with the atmosphere building. The night was warm and the pitch was dry. Perfect conditions in which to play. 'Be ready tonight,' Glenn told me in the dressing room. What was he meaning? I suddenly had a feeling that I was going to do something tonight.

After a few minutes, though, it didn't look as if we would. 'Here we go again,' I thought when Dave Seaman brought down Diego Simeone for a penalty and Batistuta scored from the spot. But after a few more minutes, I got the feeling that this Argentina team wasn't that great, certainly not as good as everyone feared.

Michael's run got us back in it almost immediately, though I didn't think it was a penalty. Glenn had told us to play them at their game, to go down if touched just as they would – not to dive but to get your just desserts rather than be too principled and stay on your feet – and it had paid off. Then six minutes later came the goal that no one will ever forget, least of all Michael Owen.

It was so raw and so direct. It was like the kid at school, the captain of the team, who is better than everyone else and just keeps taking people on before scoring. Except that this was the World Cup and Argentina. And they hadn't even conceded a goal up until this point. You just don't do that kind of thing in the World Cup. Perhaps in five years, Michael won't. Perhaps he'll lay the ball off rather than run like the wind with no fear in his soul when the game takes its toll on him a bit more.

For the moment, you just felt privileged to have witnessed it. Goal of the tournament, without a doubt. I turned to Steve McManaman and told him to enjoy playing with Michael at Liverpool while he could. Some Spanish or Italian team would be in with £20 million for him very soon, I said.

The mood was buoyant as the interval approached. When Scholesey was in with a great chance just before half-time, it looked as though it would be our night. Uncharacteristically he missed, though, and the next few minutes of play were sadly decisive.

If he had scored … if we hadn't conceded that free-kick from which Zanetti scored a great goal … if David Beckham hadn't been sent off. Hindsight is a wonderful luxury, but then you just had to get on with the struggle. There was no condemnation of Becks from the players, only sympathy. Of course he shouldn't have kicked out at Simeone, but it was heat-of-the-moment stuff and the game was reaching boiling point.

It was wonderful finally to get a game. I couldn't wait to get on that field when Glenn told me he was sending me on with less than a quarter of an hour to go. Perhaps that enthusiasm was why I kept slipping all over the place. Had the pitch got wetter since the warm-up? Then I literally found my feet.

Even with 10 men we could have won the game, though I always knew Sol Campbell's header was going to be ruled out. I was near the referee and heard the whistle go as Sol was heading home. To be honest, I thought it was a foul and would have been gutted if we had lost to a goal like that. As Sol ran by me in celebration, I wondered where the hell he was going while play was going on.

Not that I thought we would concede a goal. Our defence, with Tony fantastic, was just so good. Penalties always looked favourite. When Glenn came on to the pitch to organise the five takers, I told him I wanted to take one. Those people in the pubs and clubs who saw me miss against Sheffield United in Middlesbrough's promotion run-in must have been wondering why I was volunteering, but I just had this feeling of certainty that I would score. These things are hard to explain but at

Bramall Lane I sensed I would miss. On this huge stage, I was much less nervous.

Then, suddenly and sadly, it was all over. I felt so sorry for Incey and Bats who missed their penalties, but then if it weren't for their contributions, especially in qualifying against Italy, Poland, Moldova and Georgia, England wouldn't have made it here.

There would be some debate later as to whether we should have practised penalties but I wasn't one of those who thought we should. People mess about in training and there's no pressure anyway. It feels too easy to score then. You can't reproduce what it's like in the heat of battle and I think you have to go with those who feel confident on the night. I wish we had realised, which we later found out, that you can change your order of penalty-takers given the situation of the shoot-out. It might have made a difference.

There was a stunned silence to the dressing room but I thought the boss was great, telling us that we had done the country proud and that he was proud of us. It was a very subdued party which flew back to La Baule deep into the night.

At one point I was sitting next to David Beckham and I asked him what he was going to do now we were out. He said he was going to New York to see Victoria in concert with the Spice Girls. I told him that his relationship was more important than anything else, more important than football even.

As I have discovered in trying to recover one day at a time from an addictive illness, there is a life outside the game and it was vital to keep things in perspective. What had happened was the end of the World Cup, but not the end of the world.

JULY

Down to Earth

Wednesday 1 July

Last day at La Baule. I went to the kit room after breakfast to get my England shirts for the lads to sign for my boys. Becks even gave me a signed one of his own for Ben and Sam, who are growing up to love Manchester United, as most kids seem to these days. Michael Owen also signed one of his for Charlie. They will be thrilled.

We left at lunchtime to fly home on Concorde, which was a bonus, though not as impressive as I thought it would be. The cabin is a lot narrower than I imagined, though the feeling of speed on take-off takes your breath away. I'm a nervous flyer but I must say it was an exhilarating experience. As we came in to land, Michael was still having a tour of the cockpit. Teddy Sheringham turned to me as the plane touched down and said: 'Is there anything this boy can't do?' and we all laughed.

I couldn't believe the crowds at Luton airport and the

reception we received brought a tear to my eye. To think that all these people were so proud of us, and to be honest we hadn't really achieved that much. We then went to a nearby hotel to pick up our luggage and I swopped phone numbers with Rio and Michael. They are wonderful young lads with the world at their feet and I would like to stay in touch with them.

I felt most sorry for Glenn Hoddle. I know I have had a bit of a dig at him now and then over the previous five weeks, at the time believing it was justified and in some instances it was, but I can see that all he wanted to do was win the World Cup. He made us all believe in ourselves, that we could win the tournament, and before the penalties against Argentina he gave me the confidence that I would score my kick.

It's a strange feeling coming home. You want to be there but don't. After five weeks, it's a bit unreal being back. It still hasn't sunk in that we're out of the competition. As a person, it is a moment I have been looking forward to for a while, but as a professional I would rather be back in France preparing to play Dennis Bergkamp and the Dutch in Marseille on Saturday.

When I got home, only about 15 miles from Luton airport, the kids were over the moon with their shirts. I was looking forward to a Chinese take-away – no more pasta, chicken and vitamin tablets for a month now. I am free of the rigid regime. On the way to the Chinese, people in their cars who saw me would wave or toot their horns. I felt so proud but at the same time sorry that we haven't achieved more. We did well but, to be honest, not well enough.

Thursday 2 July

I asked my agent Steve Kutner to try and fix me a holiday but he couldn't get a flight anywhere immediately, except America, and I didn't want to go too far having been travelling for the previous six weeks. Steve then rang Bryan Robson to see if I could come back to Middlesbrough a bit later than the rest of the lads, who were due in on the 13th. Robbo asked me to come in for the first three days, and said I could then go away for a fortnight.

Reading all the follow-up articles to our game against Argentina was a bit worrying. Amid all the glory-glory stuff there is a lot of criticism of David Beckham and, alarmingly, the suggestion that he can expect a hard time from fans of teams other than Manchester United when the season starts, as a lot of people are blaming him.

If anybody should be blaming him, it is someone like me. I am 30 years old. I will not play in another World Cup, unlike David. If I can take that without getting on his case, why can't others? The lad was only trying to do his best for his country and he made a mistake. That is human, not disgraceful.

Sunday 12 July

Over the last ten days, I have realised just how big the World Cup is. Out in France, we seemed cut off from everything. Here, just going about the business of normal life, like taking the kids to the park and doing the shopping, you get the buzz of it happening. The papers and the television are full of it and people talk about it all the time. As a fan sometimes, it seems a much richer and more colourful experience than for a player, strange as it may sound. Not that I would ever swap the experience I had.

The final tonight was a big disappointment. In fact, I thought it was shocking and there wasn't much Russ Abbott – not much atmosphere. The performance of the best player in the world was an embarrassment and without Ronaldo firing, Brazil were just a shadow of themselves. France were definitely the better team on the night but they had some luck on the way. Saudi Arabia had chances against them, they could have gone out to Paraguay and in the semi-final they got lucky when they scored within minutes of the Croatians. They were never brilliant.

In fact, I don't think it has been a brilliant World Cup. There hasn't been an outstanding game like, say, Brazil v Italy in Spain in 1982. Though I have watched a lot of the games, I can't remember one that really sticks in my memory.

I know Glenn said he felt that we could have won it, but once we lost to Romania it was always going to be difficult. It was significant that the French came from the easier half of the draw that the Romanians went into after winning our group. Even if we had beaten the Argentinians, then the Dutch, the Brazilians were in wait in the semi-finals. All those heavyweights just drained each other and that was reflected in the final with the French looking the fresher.

Monday 13 July

Caught the train up from Stevenage to the first day back at training with Middlesbrough. It is an easy journey these days, with our excellent new facilities being near Darlington, to where I can get a direct train.

All the lads were wondering what I was doing here. I

looked much fitter than everyone else, especially Gazza, who was breathing out of his arse. In fact, I thought he looked overweight and ill. He wanted all the England gossip and was wondering about the whole experience of France. He sounded envious, naturally, and I felt a bit sad for him again. He was still blaming me for him smashing up Glenn's room. I enjoyed being back among the banter and it was good to see Gary Pallister, who I think will be a quality signing for us.

I have bought a new house up here, next door to Alan Shearer on Sir John Hall's Wynyarde Estate and while it isn't as big as his, I am happy with it. It has cost me £325,000 and another £60,000 for a kitchen and furnishings. It's not quite ready, though, and I was expecting to spend the night at the club house rented in a village called Hutton Rudby which I took over last season after Fabrizio Ravanelli moved to Marseille and which Gazza shared with me – or rather turned into a mad house – in the spring after his move from Rangers.

Then Viv Anderson, Robbo's assistant manager, came up to me after training and told me I was ridiculously fit, way ahead of all the others, so I might as well go home and not bother with the next couple of days. Great. Time to get ready for a holiday with my family and some friends at their villa in the Algarve.

Thursday 30 July

Back from the worst holiday of my life. I should have gone to America after all. I always feel at ease there, always have plenty to do. I'm not really one for sitting round a swimming pool all day. A lot of the time I didn't feel I could be myself, couldn't leave my clothes lying around for example, and I ended up trying to please other people – and failing. I also felt really stressed being around the family all the time and trying to play non-stop with the boys without any of my own space to escape to. Little things began to annoy me, like the fact that I can only drive an automatic and our rented car was manual.

So I escaped into physical activity, running three miles a day and playing a lot of tennis. I felt fitter than I have ever been. I became quite anti-social, though, and sometimes when we went out to restaurants at night, I would just go off with the boys or on my own and sit on the beach.

Lorraine and I spent a lot of time arguing as a result of being under each other's feet all the time and one row on the last day was particularly heavy. We have agreed to separate. She says she wants a divorce and I believe her.

Friday 31 July

Back in training today. Tomorrow, Boro' play against the Italian club Empoli in a four-team tournament at the Riverside in which I was not due to play but I have asked Robbo if I can make an appearance. I really need to get back into action to divert me from a lot of strain I am feeling at the moment.

I can feel something bad coming on. Last night in bed, the panic attacks returned. 'Here we go again,' I thought. I could feel them coming and coming. It was frightening. I couldn't breathe. It was an echo of those dark days when I would gamble for release, to change those feelings that I just couldn't handle.

In those days, as soon as I'd lost enough money, I

would drink for consolation. Then, as soon as I'd had enough to drink, I would take cocaine to try and sober me up, believe it or not. Or maybe it was to get a buzz from another source. And it was much more cocaine than I was ever allowed to acknowledge publicly by the FA or Arsenal back in the days when I first admitted my problems.

Actually, to be honest, the dark days weren't that far behind me. In fact, they had returned earlier this year. Though the worst of my gambling, drinking and drugging had ended back in December 1994 when I went into treatment for addiction at Marchwood Priory near Southampton, I had been gambling all over again in the early months of 1998 when living on my own in Middlesbrough amid all the strain of a promotion challenge.

Before Christmas of the 1997/98 season I hadn't really been living up in Middlesbrough, just travelling up for a few days of training and staying in hotels for those periods. In the New Year, when I wanted to stay up more for the run-in to our promotion campaign, Boro' let me have Fabrizio Ravanelli's old house. It was best that Lorraine and the kids stayed down south until I bought my own house for them all to move into, so my brother Keith came up to keep me company. I was bored without my family, though, and sank into a damaging routine.

I often felt lonely and isolated but the thing that was getting me through was that it was so tight at the top of the First Division and I could concentrate on the promotion campaign. We looked certainties for most of the time but there was still a strain to it. Each day I would go to training, come home, sit myself down in the front room and watch television until it was time to go training the next day. On occasions I would eat out but mostly I was eating microwaved rubbish. I was becoming a groundhog.

I was feeling the pressure and I hoped that a bet might make me feel better. I had come to Middlesbrough – despite what everyone thought – for the challenge rather than the money, though naturally I had got a pretty good pay rise, and I did feel very responsible for the club's fortunes. At first, I really thrived on the buzz of 'get promoted, get promoted' but it had changed from being exciting to being stressful. And I felt that so much was on my shoulders, like it was my fault if we didn't win. That might be too highly developed a sense of responsibility but I noticed that in the programme for one game it said that I was involved in 35 out of 42 goals we had scored.

It really got to me the night I missed a penalty at Sheffield United in early April. We had just lost to West Bromwich Albion, after a terrible March in which we were thrashed 4–0 by Nottingham Forest and 5–0 by Queens Park Rangers and had slipped from top of the table to fourth. It looked like we could be forced into the play-offs rather than the automatic promotion that looked certain for a long time.

I just knew I was going to miss at Bramall Lane, I don't know why. I knew the keeper would go to his right, because I had been putting them that way all season, so I put it the other way and instead of just rolling it, I slammed it and it went over the bar. We missed a couple of good chances after that but it was down to me. You shouldn't miss a penalty. It was the lowest point of a miserable spell.

The gambling had begun again in late February and carried on through March and April. It wasn't fortunes, just £50 or £100 at a time, all on the horses, enough to take the edge off the way I was feeling. I suppose it added up to about £7,000 over the three months, nothing too bad for a bloke earning three times that much a week. But I felt bad about it, guilty and ashamed that I was back in the old secretive, deceitful behaviour.

I don't blame anyone or anything for it, because an addict will use if he is determined to and no-one will start or stop it but him, but it was difficult being around Gazza at that time. He had come to live with me after his move from Rangers. He liked a drink in the house and gradually, without me really realising it, it began to get to me. Most of the time he was fun and great company and I thought I could be good for him with all the problems he had. I lost sight of my own problems, though, and let them creep up on me.

I went to see the gaffer at the end of March and told him I wanted to leave. It was at the end of a week when I had got through about three or four grand and I was feeling done in. Lorraine was down south and wouldn't move up. I told Robbo that the way things were going, I would throw away all my money up in Middlesbrough over four or five years. I'd just as well be skint in London, I said.

Robbo was as good as gold and wondered what he could do to help. He also rang my agent Steve Kutner to ask him for advice. Then I spoke to Lorraine about how we could solve the problem of me feeling so isolated up in the North-East and she agreed she would come up at the start of the next season. She even came up that Spring to sort out a house, the one we bought at Wynyarde.

With that all settled, I felt relieved and pulled out of my depression. Boro' went on a good run to seal the second promotion place with five wins and a draw from the last six games and I was back to my best, I thought. I got myself out of that rut I was in and stopped the gambling. It was just respite, though. To be honest, I never got myself properly right.

Looking back on the World Cup, I found it really hard to handle all the lads betting on all the games. It was like being in the bookies watching matches, which was why I often took myself off to play pool with Michael Owen or someone else. It also felt a bit like sitting in a pub every day. All the lads would ask me for my views on who would win and I would give them. They would also ask me about my gambling addiction and I would talk to them about it. I suppose being around the healthy influence of Tony Adams was the main reason why I never had a bet over the five weeks in France.

Back on my own, though, after the World Cup, I could feel it building up again. I was watching Holland beating Argentina in the quarter-final, for example, and thinking, 'Why didn't I bet on them?' When an alcoholic stops drinking, for a while it looks like everything on the television is to do with drinking. So it was with me and my gambling now. The odds kept coming up and I couldn't seem to get away from them, no matter what I was watching.

Going away on holiday only made it worse. I was just so pre-occupied and unable to enjoy myself. It is that kind of illness where you are just absorbed in yourself. When we all sat down for dinner, I just couldn't make conversation with the adults. I felt much more at home with the children. I lost all self-esteem and didn't feel I was worthy of talking to people because I had nothing to say. There is a passage in the Big Book of Alcoholics

Anonymous where it talks about feeling 'stupid, boring and glum', and that's how I felt. It the end it was frightening and the row kicked off with Lorraine.

Today, this Friday, I am beginning to see that I almost engineered the row with Lorraine so that I would feel angry and justified in coming up to Middlesbrough on my own so that I would be free to gamble alone and in peace. I hurt her by sarcastically thanking her for doing up the house in the North-East that I would now be living in on my own. It was deliberate, again to justify behaving badly.

It's funny – and they say this is a cunning, baffling and powerful illness – how you don't want to live that life but something inside you tells you that you have to because it is all you are fit for. Something bad is coming on, I can feel it. This afternoon I rang my bank up here to get out £10,000 in cash.

Retaking the Gamble

Saturday 1 August

Charlie and his mate Daniel are up for the four-team Middlesbrough tournament but I was more interested in a mate of my own, Justin. I had given him £4,000 of the £10,000 to put on an accumulator on Scottish football, with Ross County, Ayr United and Stranraer all to win at home. Justin was reluctant, but the mood I get in when I am determined to have a bet means I don't take no for an answer. I insisted and he gave in.

We didn't kick off against Empoli until 4pm so in the dressing room before the game I was flicking through the teletext to check on the scores. It was like four years had rewound to the times at Arsenal when I would do the same. My head was in exactly the same place, pre-occupied with gambling rather than football.

Just before kick off for our game, Ross were winning 3–1, Ayr were drawing 1–1 and Stranraer 0–0. Bryan Robson had made me a substitute and from my position on the bench, I called across to Justin, who was in the front row of the stand with Charlie and his mate to find out what the scores were. It was five minutes before half-time in our game. He got on his mobile to his grandmother. Soon he gestured that I had won. He told me that the scores were 3–1, 3–1 and 1–0. I had won £11,000.

Robbo brought me on for the second half and I went out and played like a man possessed, buzzing around thinking I had won a bundle. In fact, I was later made Man of the Match for my hyped-up 45-minute performance even though we lost 1–0.

Justin came into the dressing room at the end of the game. 'Let's go and pick up the money,' I said to him, all cocky. Then he broke the bad news. The other team in the Stranraer game had scored three minutes into added time. They had only drawn.

That gutted me. It was like a message to me, that I just couldn't win. It was frightening. What am I doing getting back into this mess? Did it help having a bet? I thought it would make me feel better. But it hasn't, of course. I just can't get back into all this again. Can I?

Sunday 2 August

The problem is you can't leave it alone once you've lost. You see it all going down the drainhole and you want to get it back. You know you never will but something takes you over. Your head goes. So quickly too.

This afternoon I started for Boro' against Newcastle and played the first 60 minutes. I wasn't even in the ground, though, when it ended goalless. I was well gone, in more ways than one.

I have now moved into the new home and couldn't wait

to get back there. Not because I was looking forward proudly to the new surroundings but because I needed to find out in private how the Dewsbury Rugby League match was going. I had bet on them to win by 20 points. I was ringing them up every 10 minutes to find out what the score was, just as I had been doing with bowls four years earlier. Dewsbury must have been wondering what the hell was going on with my voice on the line all the time. They probably don't get two phone calls a year.

At first it was good news. A woman on the switchboard told me they were winning by 21 points. At half-time it was still 20. Then it got to 12, then went down to 10. I was furious with the poor girl, telling her what a crap team they had there. Eventually I slammed the phone down on her. It is frightening me again. Another loser. And the biggest one is me.

Wednesday 5 August

I haven't had a bet since Sunday. Having Charlie and his mate up for a few days has helped to take my mind off myself and my problems. I also ran out of cash and felt ashamed thinking about getting another bundle out. Yesterday I took the kids back to St Albans, though, and now I am back rattling around my big house in the North-East on my own. Off the leash.

The illness of addiction likes you on your own. It's easier to get at you. In fact, it has often been called the disease of isolation. Because of the guilt and shame an addict feels, he or she often just wants to be alone, often for the best of motives in not wishing to inflict misery on other people, but it is counter-productive. In the end, people around you feel the brunt of it if you relapse.

I think Lorraine can sense that I have had a bet again. Though she chose the house and furnished it, she says she doesn't want to move up here when I am in my current depressed and agitated state. We argued again yesterday when I took Charlie home. We are still separated, theoretically, even if talk of divorce seems to have just been something impulsive.

I was invited to play golf up near Newcastle with Gazza, Chris Waddle and Keith Gillespie's agent but I wasn't sure if I should go. They'll go for a drink later and it's probably not good for me to be around that. I'll just go over for the golf…

I phoned Lorraine on the drive there. We started arguing again. I told her that I felt like a drink again. 'You might as well be drinking, the way you are now,' she said in her anger. I could only agree with her. That very thought filled me with dread and I phoned my agent Steve Kutner to tell him that I thought I needed to go back into treatment. I couldn't get hold of him, though, and I found myself saying the two most dangerous words for a recovering alcoholic – fuck it.

I don't blame Steve for not being there. I was going to have a drink no matter what, I think. My head had gone. At the weekend, I had found out again how bad the gambling was. Now it was as if I needed to be reminded about what the drinking was like.

I caught up with Gazza, Chris and the agent on the ninth hole. I was offered a drink from a bottle of Metz, a Schnapps concoction. I took it without too much hesitation. I was defiant. I was angry. I was off and running.

We finished the golf at about 6pm and I tagged along when the group went to a pub in a nearby village called

Whickham. I ordered a lager shandy and as I drank it, I was convinced that everyone was looking at me. Then I had a pint of lager and went off into a corner to drink it. Then I chased it down with three pints of Guinness. Now I didn't care who was looking at me.

As usual with Gazza, there is some daft game to be played. The latest consists of placing a £20 note on the board and trying to get three darts into it from different distances. It is surprising how many people get the difficult two then lose the money because they miss from the closest mark.

I got talking to a couple of women schoolteachers in their forties and was telling them how I expected to be in the papers for this the next day. By now, though, I didn't really care. They started asking me about drugs and saying that it was a problem at their school. I told them that it was an issue that should be discussed more and dealt with properly at school. It was sound stuff but I felt a bit of a fraud saying it in my current state. Not that I was that drunk. Three and a half years without a drink and Gazza and co. could not believe that I wasn't out of my head inside half an hour.

We went on to a pub in Newcastle City centre and I started drinking vodka and that energy drink, Red Bull. I figured that nobody would know then that I was drinking alcohol. Suddenly I felt relieved and free of all my worry. In Portugal, I hadn't been able to talk to anyone. Now I could talk to all of Gazza's mates. It felt like a big release.

And nothing bad happened. I had left my car at the golf club and now I took a taxi back to the house at about 2.30am. Have I cracked this drinking?

Thursday 6 August

Relief. No hangover. And I didn't feel I needed another drink this morning. Maybe I have cracked it, I thought.

Except that I felt ashamed of myself and my head was all over the place. I went to see Robbo to tell him about the night before. He said he knew all about it. Someone had phoned him and he was ready to come up from Manchester to sort me out at one point. Except that his informant said that Gazza was the one being a pain and I was all right. Give a dog a bad name. I told Robbo that I wanted to go back into treatment. He told me to hold fire, just to see if it was a one-off or something more serious.

The team was going to Holland for a couple of friendlies and Robbo suggested I should come along, though I wasn't due to be going. The thought of playing football did not appeal to me and that just wasn't me. But it seemed like a good idea. It might stop me having another drink. Soon after, I was on a plane and then settled in at a good hotel in a very nice seaside resort near The Hague. I think I've got away with it.

Friday 7 August

The match against Heerenveen tonight was very scary. All day I had had the raving hump probably because I was feeling ashamed of myself and angry that the recovery I had worked so hard for was slipping away. Having relapsed, my emotions are raw again and all over the place.

Somehow I knew early on that I was going to do something stupid and I duly got sent off for catching someone. It wasn't that bad but I knew I had to go. And

I knew it wasn't me. Nor was what happened next and what I felt.

I actually felt like beating up the referee and I don't really know what stopped me hitting him. Then I threw my shirt at the bench, went straight to the dressing room and sat and thought about what I had done.

Later I went out to a bar with the lads but I didn't have a drink. Not many of them did. It is not really a drinking club. A lot of them were actually laughing at me, thinking it was all a bit daft, but I was worried. I am going to be banned for three matches now. What am I going to do in Middlesbrough for a month with no football to play? Drinking and gambling go through my head.

Saturday 8 August

The boss has been good to me again. He has told me that I can go home as I am banned from the game today. I just sat in the sun all day at the hotel waiting until it was time for my plane back home.

Back at the house in St Albans, Lorraine wouldn't let me in, so I went to a nearby hotel, the Noke, and rang my friend Neil to come round for company. The frustration had built up in me again. I was ready for a night out.

I waited for Neil at the bar and ordered a vodka and orange and an orange juice, to make it look like someone was with me. But I drank them both. I thought that people would just think I was drinking the orange. That's how it gets when you're a drinking alcoholic. You think up all sorts of things to cover up because you feel ashamed of what you are doing.

After a while it just became too obvious what I was

doing and I was glad when Neil finally arrived. From there we went to a pub in St Albans called the Peahen and then on to a nightclub at Batchwood Hall. I was wearing jeans and trainers and some lad in the queue told me I wouldn't get in. 'You watch,' I said and when I told the doormen I would make a personal appearance on stage, they let me in. The old arrogance was coming back.

It is embarrassing to recall it. When I got up on the stage I shouted: 'Everybody get pissed.' I was still drinking vodka and orange. The music was blaring and I was getting more and more drunk.

I wasn't that drunk, though. One girl tried to pick me up, saying that she wanted to take me home. 'No thanks,' I said and I began to wonder what the hell I was doing, getting involved in all this. She was only interested in me because I was Paul Merson. That much I could see. It was time to get out of this. What was left of my sanity prevailed and I got Neil to drive me back to the Noke, where I crashed out.

Sunday 9 August

No hangover again, but this time there was no relief. I just feel so guilty and ashamed.

Nothing in the Sunday papers about me but there's bound to be tomorrow, I feel sure. I have been so paranoid the last few days, just like the bad old days, thinking that everybody who drives past me knows that I have been gambling and drinking again and is looking at me in a funny way. Somebody is bound to have rung up the papers and I bet they are following me. I don't think Gazza will have told them, though. He's probably happy to think he's found a drinking partner again.

I know that this has got to stop right here, right now. I am a gambling addict, an alcoholic and a drug addict. Very soon I will be taking cocaine again if this goes on. Maybe I'll even go on from there to something worse.

Lorraine was having a barbecue at the house but I was not invited. I rang Neil and asked him if he would go round and pick up some clothes and my Alcoholics Anonymous book for me. I read some of it lying on the hotel bed, bored. It makes sense, what little I can take in in my current restless state.

In the evening I phoned Lorraine and asked if I could take the boys back to Middlesbrough for a few days with me. She agreed. And it's a good idea. The one thing I am is a good dad and focusing my attention on them will force me to look after their needs and not my wants.

Monday 10 August

Drove up with Charlie, Ben and Sam and saw Robbo again.

I told him that I wanted to go public, to admit what I had done, but he advised me against it. I didn't want to be dishonest, though, and to live in fear of it getting out. It feels rotten when everyone tells you how well you have done and you know that you have relapsed.

Robbo told me to wait and not to rush into print but to think about what I had done. In some AA literature it talks about restraint of tongue and pen. It and he was right. I needed to share this with people who understood about the addiction being a relapsing illness, people who could help me. I didn't need to whip myself again publicly for being a bad boy. It was important that I owned up to myself, first and foremost, and that I understood that I had cheated me more than anyone else.

The fog was beginning to clear, the fear starting to subside. Had I needed this miserable experience just to get me back on track?

Wednesday 12 August

Absolutely knackered. Not the way to be, perhaps, with the start of the Premiership season and our game against Leeds only three days away but at least I have not had a drink or a bet.

On a whim I took the kids to Alton Towers yesterday and today, staying in the hotel there, just to keep them occupied. More accurately to keep me occupied, really. Being with the boys keeps me away from the people I know will put a bet on for me. They think they are doing me a favour, and I don't blame them because it's all down to me, but really they are not helping.

I have given the boys lots of attention over the last couple of days, which they have needed. There is a big difference when I bet or drink – I just have no time or energy for them. Then they are an irritation. It's one of the reasons I know I am suffering from an illness because I love them to bits and I treat them with affection when I am healthy. I know they can't keep me sober, and I know I have to do it for me, not them, but they are the best possible medicine for me.

Thursday 13 August

Robbo really is brilliant with me. He lets me have a couple of days off when I need them, because he knows I am important enough to Boro' and he wants me fit and healthy, mentally and physically. It's not so long ago that he was a player and he understands things. He also lets me bring the boys in to training, like today, and they play on the next pitch while we go through our session. All the lads are really good to them.

Lorraine and I have not been speaking but I rang her today. I needed some help. It is hard for an addict to ask for help because pride gets in the way and he or she always thinks they can cope or do things on their own. Not to be able to manage is a sign of weakness.

But I don't think I will be able to look after the boys properly over the weekend with the game pre-occupying me so I wondered if she would come up with her mum and dad to help me with the boys so that I could concentrate on the match. If not I will have to get up at 6am on Saturday and I will just be too shattered to play well. Luckily she agreed.

Friday 14 August

Lorraine has arrived and loves the new house. I knew she would as soon as she saw it. As a result, when I came home from training, I managed to have a reasonably quiet and relaxing day, which is just what I needed to get myself right, mentally and physically, for the season's opener.

I think we will do well this season. Robbo has undoubtedly learnt the lessons of Boro's last Premiership campaign when they were relegated. We may not have the talents of Juninho and Ravanelli this time around but I think he has bought well, starting at the back this time, which was the weakness before. Gary Pallister, if he stays fit, will be just the experienced defender we need and Dean Gordon at left-back is more than useful.

Then there's Gazza. He has got better in training and he's still got all the old magic in his feet, but I do fear for him because he's still living to excess off the field and his body is going to rebel at some point, I'm sure. Personally, I feel as fit as I have ever done even though I didn't do all that much pre-season, and I am raring to go.

Saturday 15 August
Middlesbrough 0 Leeds United 0

I felt really good today. It is such a relief to be playing football again. No matter what your problems, you really can lose yourself in it for 90 minutes. Nothing gets in the way. All you have to do is react spontaneously to the events going on around you. Your body is straining to give everything, your mind is active the whole time. I love this game.

Actually, not this game because it wasn't one of the greatest, though a goalless draw is not a bad result for us with all the injuries we've got – Steve Vickers, Gary Pallister, Gianluca Festa, Marco Branca, Alun Armstrong. We never looked like winning, mind, but then I think Leeds will be one of the stronger teams this season and we didn't look like conceding either and that is encouraging.

Afterwards, I spoke to George Graham and he said he thought I looked really sharp, which lifted me. He believes Leeds should be beating teams like us if they are going to do anything this season and with the team we had out he is probably right, but then quite a lot are going to underestimate us, I think.

Tuesday 18 August

Lorraine has gone back South with the boys today after three really good days. We have talked long and hard about what happened over the summer and this time we haven't argued but instead have tried to analyse what went wrong in a more rational way.

On the days when I was gambling, the mood swings were frightening. When I'm in them, I can't see what effect they have on those around me but Lorraine certainly knows all about them. Now I haven't had a bet for a little while, I can see it. It is an illness of selfishness and I just get bound up in myself.

I will start playing with the kids in the garden, for example, then be running in to check on my bets all the time. If things aren't going my way, I will then take it out on everybody. Now she says she will move up to the North-East – as long as I don't gamble. I can't ask for fairer than that.

Wednesday 19 August

Lorraine has come back to Wynyarde and I hope we can get on with our lives as a family now. I know I can be a lovely person when I don't drink or gamble but a nightmare when I do. Joe Public may not see it because I put the mask on for them, but Lorraine knows the real me underneath it. I do take it out on her and I feel very sorry about that.

Perhaps in some strange way I needed to have that last drinking bender as a reminder of how bad things can get. Now I am trying to read as much as possible to occupy my time and to get in touch with more positive things.

I am reading a book on obsessive love and looking at

the questionnaire, it seems that I'm co-dependent on Lorraine. I've got every form of addiction, haven't I? Mind you, it wasn't quite as bad as the Gamblers Anonymous questionnaire a few years back. With that, they say that if you say yes to four out of 12 questions, you have a problem. I said yes to all but one. The only thing I didn't do was steal to pay for the habit. I was lucky that I didn't need to with what I earn from football. I probably would have because I still would have been an addict even if I was unemployed. It has nothing to do with money or status.

That much is clear from another book I'm reading, about celebrity addicts and how they stopped drinking. Eric Clapton and Ian McShane are among those telling their stories. It is fascinating stuff and it has helped me a lot.

Thursday 20 August

It's a funny feeling this week. After opening the season last Saturday, we don't play again until Sunday, at Aston Villa. Last season I got used to playing twice a week and enjoyed it. With only 38 games in the Premiership, compared to 46 in the Nationwide First Division, quite often we'll only be playing once a week. A lot of my problems start when I'm not occupied enough. I hope just training will be enough to keep me going.

Saturday 22 August

We trained this morning before travelling down to Birmingham for the game against Aston Villa tomorrow. We have a brand new, state-of-the-art team coach. Trust Gazza to wreck it on its first day with us.

Some of the lads decided to go up to the betting shop in Darlington a couple of miles away before we travelled, so that they could listen to the afternoon's games on the radio on the way down to find out how their wagers were going. They all set off in their cars but Gazza got left behind. It didn't matter to him. He saw that the keys were in the coach so it seemed natural enough for him to take it. Or so he said.

The driveway to the training ground is about a quarter of a mile long down a narrow, bumpy track but he managed to negotiate that all right. The problem came when he went to turn on to the main road. He tried to turn it like he would a car but a coach doesn't behave the same way. It needs a bigger turning arc.

There were two concrete bollards by the side of the road and he scraped the whole of one side of the coach on them. So he tried it again, reversing back into the drive and bringing it out again, but he just made it worse. Eventually he stalled it and just decided to leave it there.

We did manage to get down to Birmingham in it but the kit wouldn't go into the stoved-in compartments on the side and we all had to squeeze up inside to get the kit into the back. It was funny, I have to admit, and we had a good laugh but it was the driver I felt sorry for. He had to explain away £15,000 worth of damage.

Sunday 23 August
Aston Villa 3 Middlesbrough 1

I was having a massage before the game and Doug Ellis, who I know from England as he is on the FA's international committee, poked his head around the door to say hello.

'What are you doing with the Dwight Yorke money, Deadly?' I asked him. He enjoys being called Deadly.

'What do you think I should do?' he asked.

Having just banked £13 million from Manchester United for Dwight, he should get Christian Vieri from Atletico Madrid, I told him. Failing that, Christophe Dugarry of Marseille. He laughed.

He was laughing even more after the match. It is us who need the striker. We were slaughtered. The lads must get fed up of hearing me talking about Arsenal but I keep telling them that they are the best and we have to judge ourselves against them.

We were supposed to play one up and two behind today, like I was used to at Arsenal when Dennis Bergkamp and I played behind Ian Wright, but I ended up on my own up front with the two wide men just following the Villa wing-backs and me becoming isolated.

We were a goal down in a minute and two down before we changed things, with Hamilton Ricard and Mikkel Beck coming on, and me moving back into the hole. It worked well and we got a goal back through Mikkel, punishing them on the counter-attack. I thought we were the better side then, although Villa grabbed a third to confirm they were making a good start to the season.

Robbo took Gazza off because – so he told the press – he was worried he was going to get a red card after being booked. Gazza was off the pace, though. Andy Townsend and I agreed that Gazz is not going to make any real impact until he stops drinking.

Tuesday 25 August

Before training today, Andy told me he had had a phone call from John Gregory, the Villa manager, who is wondering if I have got the hump with him. Apparently it stems from the column in the *News of the World* that I do, where I was putting a player's viewpoint forward in response to him having a go at Dwight Yorke for wanting to leave Aston Villa. I told Andy that it was nothing personal and Andy said: 'That's good, because I think he fancies signing you.' It made me think and I was quiet during training, which is not me.

At the end of training, the boss called us all into his room to watch a video of the Villa game and go through some bad defending. At one point, Robbo paused the tape to talk to us and on to the screen came the Teletubbies. 'I think we're looking a bit static at the back, boss,' Andy Townsend said. 'And our shape's not too hot either.' Even Robbo had to laugh.

I was smiling, too, at being named in the England squad for the European Championship qualifier against Sweden in Stockholm on 5 September. Like the rest of the country, I pick it up when it is announced in London. I check the teletext and there is my name. Official confirmation comes through the post a day or two later.

Wednesday 26 August

I travelled down to London on the train with Middlesbrough's Chief Executive Keith Lamb for a personal hearing at the FA, where I joined up with Bryan Robson, about my sending-off in Holland. The boss didn't think they would give us anything because they took three points off the club the season before last for not turning up at Blackburn and Boro' were relegated. He reckoned I would get a three-match ban. I told him that he'd better let me do the talking then.

I hadn't seen the video of the incident but Andy Townsend had and he told me that it wasn't that bad. So I told the three-man disciplinary committee that it wasn't that bad. Then, after watching it in the hearing, I told them that I was an honest player and that if it had been a bad tackle I wouldn't have wasted their time. Two of them seemed to accept that, though the third one worried me.

We were sent out while they considered their verdict and then called back in to hear that they had reduced the red card to a booking. The boss was chuffed. I put it down to my natural charm and honesty. Outside, I told him that he should let me go back in and they would probably let me have those three points back. Then we'll be top of the table by tomorrow. It made him laugh. I celebrated with lunch at Langan's with Keith Lamb before travelling back to Teesside.

Friday 28 August

There have been more rumours about Aston Villa and the papers have now started to speculate about me moving there. I have to admit that it has been on my mind all week and I have been quiet in training. The boss has noticed because usually I like a laugh and a joke but I've been keeping myself to myself. He has even rung my agent to find out if there was something wrong with me.

I always made it clear to Bryan that I would help get the club promoted but that I didn't want to be part of a team that can't win anything in the top flight. I have come from Arsenal where they were always in contention for something and I don't think I can get used to being an also-ran. So far, we have looked a mediocre side and although we would have a reasonable first team if everyone was fit, we don't look to have the strength in depth to do much.

Steve Kutner has had a call from John Gregory and has even talked figures with him. Villa want an experienced player to help their youngsters develop. They have made a promising start to the season and need to cement it. First things first, though. Tomorrow Boro' need to get something from the game against Derby at the Riverside otherwise we are going to start looking like relegation candidates even at this early stage.

Saturday 29 August
Middlesbrough 1 Derby County 1

I spent the morning reading the papers and speaking to my ghost writer at the *News of the World* for my column. This week I am talking about Ruud Gullit taking over as manager at nearby Newcastle in the wake of the shock sacking of Kenny Dalglish. It will give a boost to the North-East and could well make Newcastle a sexier team again.

Pre-match meal at home was grilled chicken, mashed potato and tinned spaghetti, washed down with a couple of Red Bull energy drinks. Some players can't eat much before a game but I always like a hearty meal. Two, sometimes. I can manage a spaghetti bolognese as well as chicken with pasta on occasions.

Against Derby, I felt out of sorts in the first half and it was nothing to do with the protein, carbohydrate and glucose diet. I was getting the hump with the lads and that is not me. I felt frustrated that we were not playing better football. Derby played quite well, though, and took the lead through Paolo Wanchope after a scramble.

After the break I decided to go and play wide on the right, knowing that Derby have a 19-year-old kid, called Steve Elliott, playing one of his first games. He duly got too tight to me and a ball in behind me by Gianluca Festa gave me room to spin and get in a cross for Hamilton Ricard to head home. I can't say I felt too sorry for Elliott. As a pro, you can't afford that. He is in the big league now and has to learn quickly if he is going to make it.

In the end we did enough for a point and I did enough to win the Man of the Match award from the sponsors. I didn't feel right, though, after everything that had happened through the month, first the gambling and drinking relapses, then the unsettling talk about a move.

As I drove down South to join up with England tomorrow for the game against Sweden in a week's time, I still felt restless. Now Lorraine and the kids were up in the North-East with me, I couldn't really explain why. I also didn't know that I had played my last game for Middlesbrough.

SEPTEMBER

Removal Man

Tuesday 1 September

Yesterday and today were worrying days. I am still trying to put the relapses behind me – to live in the now rather than the past – but always the fear of it happening again seems to be with me at the moment. It is lucky that I am with England. It gives me the chance to see Eileen Drewery regularly.

Yesterday she laid her hands on my head and my shoulders and we talked about my state of mind, but it hasn't worked yet. Today I was unable to train. I told Glenn that my head had gone. I just didn't feel I belonged among the best in England. My self-esteem was really low. It can be daunting, training with the ultimate team. Not many people see that, but even Premiership professionals have human self-doubt. Glenn was very understanding and urged me to see Eileen again.

I told her that I had become a different person with the drink of the previous month. Even though I had stopped again, I wasn't right inside and it scared me. She told me that all my senses had re-opened to bad spirits and I may have some inside me again. It might have happened for a reason, she said – to remind me that I can't drink. Once when I went to see her, she told me it was probably all right for me to have a couple of beers but now I think she understands the illness better.

She put her hands on my shoulders, chest and back but I still didn't feel right. In fact, I was up all night, feeling panicky and wanting to cry and scream alternately. I was twisting and turning. I just couldn't get comfortable. Everything was bugging me. I will need to see her again before we fly out to Sweden.

Wednesday 2 September

Now my back has gone but at least I got out on the training field today. I stretched for a ball and just pulled up. Afterwards, I saw Eileen again not so much for physical help but spiritual and this time I felt some benefit.

It felt as if she had cleared my mind of the negative influences and in the end I felt strong again. I was ready for the help after the low of last night. There was a process to go through, though. She went into all my problems with me really deeply and I felt emotional and very drained. But fresh, too, and my skin was tingling. It is hard to explain. Eileen tries to tell people but a lot just have a laugh at it. The papers have a go but they don't know what happens in her sessions.

Sometimes you get the same effect from AA and GA meetings, though they are very different to what Eileen is about. There is an unexplained force for good in the room. You've got to be there really to understand the things that can happen to people. I had not been going to those meetings and really I should have been. I hadn't developed a network of support up in Middlesbrough. I had not shared much of my pain with many people and it was a bonus being able to communicate with Eileen three days in a row.

I was buzzing and felt like the real me again. The night before, I was getting voices in my head telling me that I was a bad person, that I was finished as a footballer, that I wasn't even going to make it through the night. I was trying to shut them up but I couldn't. Eileen told me that for me, drinking opened my centres up to negative spirits but that they were now gone.

I could pick up negativity just by shaking hands with negative people, Eileen said. And in the days after I had the drink I had been very negative, going into training and finding fault with everything. Instead of not getting involved with the lads, like over their gambling, I had wanted to be in there all the time. When they asked me if I fancied a certain horse or team to win, I would offer an answer instead of making it clear all that wasn't for me.

I had been noticing the gambling a lot more again lately. When I came out of treatment, it seemed to be featured on the television all the time, like in *EastEnders* or other programmes. Now I was noticing when I was watching games on Sky that they would always give the odds, for goalscoring and the like. When you are OK you don't notice it so much. And now I am alright with myself again. I am not at all worried about going to Sweden tomorrow.

Tony Adams is certainly alright with himself. All week his autobiography has been serialised in the *Sun* and there have been critical things said of Glenn. All the lads have found it very entertaining. At a press conference today Tony looked so calm and no-one can understand why. I try telling those who are interested that when you are so properly on a 12-step programme of recovery like Tony, it almost comes naturally.

Thursday 3 September

Good flight to Stockholm. I don't really have a problem with flying now, since someone said to me that it's not the fear of flying, it's the fear of dying that is the problem. Actually, it can be the fear of living that is the real problem in life.

We also had a good hard training session when we got there. Though some of the lads think we train too hard with England, I always enjoy it. I don't think we train hard enough at Middlesbrough and it is good for me. It is difficult for Glenn to strike a balance, because he gets us together so little and he is bubbling with ideas that he wants to work on.

I am feeling positive again and it did not bother me that some of the boys were playing cards after dinner in the hotel, which is very comfortable, on the edge of the city. They were worrying that I thought they were idiots but I never preach to people. There's no problem to me unless they are getting like me and starting to lose £10,000 or £20,000. It's when people start doing more than they can afford that the trouble starts. That used to be my game.

Friday 4 September

Received a phone call in the morning from Bryan Robson. The *Sun* has broken a story that I want to leave

Middlesbrough because of all the gambling and drinking at the club. Gazza is particularly upset, apparently, because he thinks it's all directed at him.

I told Robbo that the story has not come from me. Yes, I've talked to Gazza a million times in the past about his problems, but I'm not going to run to the papers and nor is he. There is no quote from me in the piece, but I think someone close to me has let the cat out of the bag. I do have a problem with some of the things that go on at Boro', culminating in me feeling so negative when I joined up with England.

There is serious drinking at the club sometimes and some gambling, I told him, even if it isn't for mad money. It was nothing for him to worry about but everything for me. The last straw had come the previous Saturday just before the Derby match when Viv Anderson was going round the dressing room at 2.30pm with a pen and paper when I was having some strapping on my ankle.

I thought he was outlining some set plays, but it turned out he was going round sorting out all his bets in this £20 sweep he had going with the lads. There's not too much wrong with that if you don't have a gambling problem, but there is a time and a place and it's not half an hour before a game when we are supposed to be concentrating on the matter in hand. That's what we get paid for, that's what people pay to come and watch. Andy Townsend was also pissed off with it.

I never said to Robbo that I wanted to leave and I had not told anyone else. I simply said to him that I wasn't happy and I asked for a meeting in London on Sunday. He said he preferred Monday, which disappointed me. It sounded a little like he couldn't be that bothered.

After speaking to Robbo, I tried to phone Gazza but

only got Jimmy Gardner, better known as Five Bellies. Jimmy said Gazza wasn't happy. He said he thought Gazza would be ringing me because he had got him the code for my mobile in Sweden. I told him that you don't need an international dialling code for a mobile. I told him to get Gazza to ring me after training.

I went training to exercise my back and all the camera lenses seemed to be on me even though I was just jogging round the pitch and not taking part in the session proper. I will have a fitness test in the morning.

Gazza phoned. He was fine with me. 'You've got to do what's right for you, Merse,' he said to me. 'You've been down that road with your drinking and your gambling and you don't want to slip back there.' He was starting to get honest with his own condition, I thought. 'I'm still there. I can't get out of it yet,' he said. He didn't have many true mates in football, he said, but I was one of them. It was moving stuff.

He has had a lot of problems, Gazza, what with the divorce from Sheryl and the death of a friend of his after a drinking binge he had been involved in recently. They are, though, just excuses to keep drinking. A lot of people go through traumatic times but don't take refuge in a drink, unless they have a problem with it.

When the excuses stop, that's when recovery will start. I love him to bits and he has a heart of gold. He is also the best player I have ever seen in England but it's not happening for him at the moment. If he's playing, he's all right and he will work hard in training. But then, all that just gives him a licence to go out and justify having a drink. I think it will all come to a head when he retires, though I hope it can happen sooner so he can salvage something of his career.

Saturday 5 September
Sweden 2 England 1

Slept well for eight or nine hours and at 10am went for a fitness test with Tony Adams, who also has back trouble, though currently it is his ankle which is giving him more problems. With the boss and John Gorman watching, I went through a couple of shuttles and a bit of long passing for twenty minutes and came through it fine. I will be a substitute tonight.

Match days can be tedious. You can be sitting around for hours, just getting more and more nervous, not knowing what to do with yourself. I'm not an afternoon sleeper, otherwise I wouldn't sleep at night, so I just lay on the bed channel-hopping on television. I also did my column for the *News of the World,* explaining just what was behind all the machinations at Middlesbrough and set the record straight that it was nothing to do with Gazza in particular.

Then I got a call from my agent to say that the Aston Villa manager John Gregory had been on to Bryan Robson on Friday afternoon. A transfer to Villa could be on.

We made a great start to the game with Alan Shearer's goal from a free-kick and I turned to the lads and said that we might as well go home. 'Game over,' I said. That opening spell was terrific and we could have been beating Brazil in that mood. It was the best I have seen England play for a long time and we could have been winning four or five-nil.

It shows how good my judgement is and why I should never bet. Sweden got back in it with a scrambled goal by Andreas Andersson and, as goals always do, it changed the game. If we could have stayed 1–1 for another ten minutes, I think we would have gone on to win it comfortably. They were a Joe Average team, though they had had some good results lately in beating Denmark and Russia and drawing with Italy.

Then came Johann Mjalby's goal and they were buzzing now. We were struggling to cope with their formation of three up front. And after Paul Ince's tackle on Henrik Larsson, for which he deserved to go, we were always struggling. I was surprised that I got on, and thought I did alright wide on the right, but we just couldn't find a way back. We should have had a late penalty when Alan Shearer was brought down but to be honest, we could have been two or three down by that point.

I was gutted that we had lost and the lads did not appreciate me telling them that it was 1 May, against Oxford United, when I last played on a winning team. We heard at half-time that Christian Gross had been sacked as Tottenham manager and wondered, like the public, whether Glenn might now go there. He was asked about it at the press conference but I don't suppose it will take over from our defeat as the real issue. England defeats are big news, and I suppose the time to worry will be when they are not. It was a subdued flight back. Arrived home at about 3am.

Sunday 6 September

Just sat by the phone all day, waiting to hear from Bryan Robson about the meeting tomorrow. When we spoke, we agreed that I should come up for a 9.15am meeting in Middlesbrough tomorrow. The news is out now that Aston Villa are interested in me. Gareth Southgate obviously hasn't yet told John Gregory about that record of mine of not winning a game since 1 May.

The Sunday papers tell of my problems and proposed move and also, I am surprised to read, of one reason for our defeat in Sweden that has not occurred to me. Alan Shearer is citing all the fuss generated during the week leading up to the game by Glenn Hoddle's *World Cup Diary* and Tony Adams's book. Personally, it never bothered me and I don't remember talking about it much with the other players. Actually, nobody really said very much after the diversion early in the week. It was just such a peripheral issue and Alan can only have been talking about himself.

Some of the papers are reporting that I have moved out of my house in the North-East as removal men have been spotted there in recent days. In fact, I had asked a mate of mine who was driving down South to go in and collect some clothes for me ready for the meeting in London on the Monday as all I really had was my England gear.

My agent Steve Kutner rang me to say that the meeting for tomorrow morning is off. It will be too much of a circus up there, apparently. Boro's Chief Executive Keith Lamb wants me to come up but it seems inadvisable, with all the publicity at the moment. I don't want this to develop into a Pierre Van Hooijdonk situation, though. He has done a runner from Nottingham Forest and is at loggerheads with the club. I will certainly be willing to go back up if Middlesbrough want me.

Monday 7 September

Robbo rang in the afternoon to say that now it looks like I am on the market, there have been bids for me from Everton, Tottenham and Aston Villa. I told him that I didn't want to go to Spurs after spending thirteen years at Arsenal.

'The Highbury fans still respect me,' I added. 'Besides, would you want to play for Manchester City?' I asked him and he took my point. Neither do I want to go to Everton. I can't be in a relegation battle at this stage of my career. Villa would be nice.

Kutner later phoned to say that Boro' wanted £8 million for me but that they were willing to accept £4 million plus Chris Armstrong from Spurs. I didn't want that deal and I was worried they were going to price me out of any deal with Villa. I asked him to let the club know that I would come back to Middlesbrough tomorrow and train ready for the game against Leicester on Wednesday. I had spoken to Gazza and Andy Townsend and they thought the lads would be all right with me playing. After all, I hadn't said anything public about my concerns.

Finally, at 11pm, Kutner phoned again to say that Keith Lamb had agreed that I should go to Villa in the morning to discuss terms as the clubs had agreed a deal.

Tuesday 8 September

Up at 5.30am for the journey with my agent to The Belfry Hotel near Birmingham, which has the Ryder Cup golf course and where Villa players and management stay a lot, for breakfast with John Gregory. My first impression is that he is an honest, open sort of bloke, the same as Bryan Robson. And I won't hear a bad word against Robbo. He gave me plenty of leeway, let my kids come to the training ground and play on the next pitch, made me and my family welcome.

It was just that I missed that extra bit of professionalism after my time at Arsenal. When I first left Highbury, it seemed great at Boro', the training slightly less intense. I would get two days off here, two days there, come in a bit late and I enjoyed the novelty. But then it bothered me. I think my discipline got lost. My time-keeping went and my eating habits slipped, the discipline going off the pitch as well as on. I think that's why it became a rollercoaster year for me, with my addictions.

The lads will say I am a bad trainer, though I was always capable of producing on a Saturday. But I love training if it is done properly. In the end at Boro', the boys were all calling me Victor after the crabby old Richard Wilson character in *One Foot in the Grave* because I was always moaning.

After breakfast, it was on to the training ground for a medical, which was A1, then, at 10am, on to Villa Park to finalise the deal. It had to be done by midday if I was to play in the home game against Newcastle the following night.

Boro' were also holding a press conference which was supposed to be at the same time as mine at Villa Park but there was a hitch to the negotiations and I watched Bryan do his live on Sky before mine. Boro' wanted all the £6.75 million fee up front but Villa wanted the usual deal of paying 50 per cent now, and the remainder through the year. Then Boro' wanted half and the interest on the other half through the year. Then they wanted half now, half after 12 months but £200,000 in interest. Villa even asked me to take £100,000 off my wages and my agent to forego his fee to smooth the deal through.

At 12.15pm it was too late for me to play so I just told

everybody that we should call the whole thing off for now and I rang Robbo to ask him where I should meet them for tomorrow's game against Leicester. I just wanted to play football. Now Boro' agreed to the deal and the fee was set, plus another £250,000 after 40 games. I could actually have held out for £1 million as I had never asked for a transfer, but I decided not to be difficult because now I had reconciled myself to the move. After staying with Arsenal so long, I had moved twice in a year for £12 million.

I was asked by the press about my reaction to events in the North-East. They were saying that Keith Lamb was virtually calling me a liar and a cheat but I didn't want to get involved in a slanging match. They also wanted me to slaughter Bryan Robson, who had allegedly said he felt 'disappointed' and 'let down' by my attitude, but I wouldn't.

It was just sad to me that I had gone down in the estimation of the fans, because they really warmed to me and me to them.

After the photocall on the pitch, I went to talk to Doug Ellis in his office when a phone call came through there from Glenn Hoddle. He congratulated me on my move and said that he thought I had conducted myself well. He said he wanted to come up to see me play the next night but I told him that the deal had not been completed in time. It showed that I must be in his thoughts for the Bulgaria match next month and gave me a real lift.

Then I trained with the lads at the ground that night. Walking into a new dressing room, you are always nervous, but I immediately felt wanted and respected. John Gregory told me that Mark Bosnich and Gareth Southgate had been to see him and urged him to sign me and show that the club meant business. After starting the season so badly last year, when they lost their first four games and Brian Little was eventually sacked, this year they had gone top after the first three games. My signing was designed to consolidate their position and perhaps send out a message to the likes of Manchester United, Arsenal and Chelsea that the club was serious.

Seeing all the young faces, it was nice to believe that they might listen to what I had to say as an ex-Arsenal and England campaigner. Sometimes I didn't feel that was the case with Middlesbrough. It felt like I was wasting my breath and there was a lack of ambition there. Ravanelli left, after all, because the training wasn't good enough. He wasn't being stretched.

That night at Villa, it was professional and slick, more like the Arsenal days I had been used to, without too much laughing and joking, though I always need some to make my work enjoyable. They opened the ground up for the fans and the 500 or so who turned up gave me a good reception.

I drove back to the house in St Albans and Lorraine was delighted at the outcome of events. We will now sell the house in the North-East and keep this one on and I will drive up to training – or rather I will employ my good friend John Kennedy to drive – every day. We can do it in an hour and a quarter, which is less than some players around London clubs take to get in.

The move was partly for Lorraine. Up in Middlesbrough, she would always get the flak from me when things were going badly, if the training was crap, or the result was bad. She had enough on her plate anyway, with three kids and moving up a long way from home. She had got comfortable back down South in the week I was away with England and said to blame the move on her, but I didn't want to do that. My family comes first. In five years I will be finished with football and I need to have them around me.

Wednesday 9 September
Aston Villa 1 Newcastle United 0

I was playing tennis with my agent this morning when my mobile rang. It was Bryan Robson to talk about the press coverage that morning.

Robbo said he was sorry about some of the comments that had flown in both directions but that he wanted us to remain friends. He was kind enough to say that I had been brilliant for him and the club. He asked that we let the matter lie now and there should be no more articles or critical comments from either side. I had no problem with him or that, though I did have with statements attributed to Keith Lamb.

He had been quoted as saying that Middlesbrough had rescued my career, which was news to me. The year I left Highbury for the Riverside, I played all but three games for Arsenal and for those I had a hernia. I had been selected for the England squad for the Tournoi de France, though I was injured and missed it. That hardly seems a career off the rails.

I was the one taking the gamble, not Middlesbrough. I left the second biggest club in the country, who went on to win the Double the year I left, and I would have been in the side, no doubt. Arsène Wenger did not want me to leave and he said I was earmarked for the right midfield position now occupied by Ray Parlour. I also jeopardised my chances of going to the World Cup by dropping down

Before the bullet … *Gazza, with Glenn Hoddle at La Manga, his shock exit from the 1998 World Cup squad yet to come.*

Men of La Manga …*The England squad at the pre-World Cup training camp in Spain. The rose between two thorns is fourth from the left, back row.*

Come here you... *There were times when I felt Glenn Hoddle treated us like children.*

The ball boys... *Merson and backing singers in the heat of La Baule.*

Man and boy... *Boredom became a factor during our long build-up to the first game.*

Turning point… *David Beckham's sending off against Argentina was a big moment, no doubt about it, but he didn't deserve the stick he got for it.*

Penalty paid ... *And I always felt confident that I would score mine against Argentina.*

Left: **Come on Eileen ...**
*Personally I found
Eileen Drewery's
influence helpful, but I
couldn't speak for
everyone with England.*

Below: **Bad memories ...**
*During a press
conference to talk about
my friend Paul Gascoigne
going into treatment, all
the old pain came
flooding back and I just
couldn't help crying.*

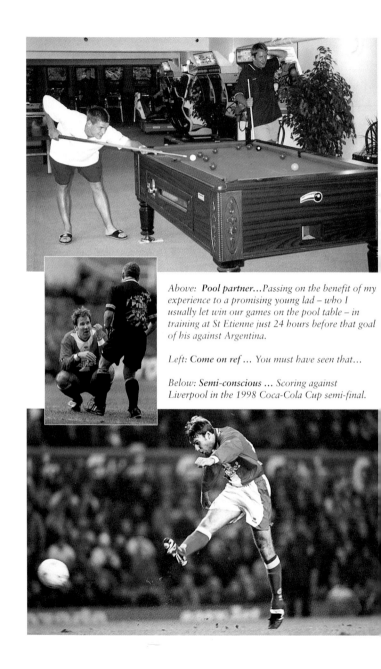

Above: **Pool partner**...*Passing on the benefit of my experience to a promising young lad – who I usually let win our games on the pool table – in training at St Etienne just 24 hours before that goal of his against Argentina.*

Left: **Come on ref** ... *You must have seen that...*

Below: **Semi-conscious** ... *Scoring against Liverpool in the 1998 Coca-Cola Cup semi-final.*

Cellnet mates ... Me and the bloke I shared a house with in Middlesbrough. I told him his life would be a misery if he kept on drinking.

Top man ... The great thing about Bryan Robson is that he treats players as adults and you can also enjoy a laugh in training with him.

The water boys ... Tony Adams and me, both carrying injuries, watch the training before England's game against Sweden in Stockholm in September 1998.

The concerned wife ... Lorraine had to endure plenty along with me during a long and turbulent year.

Not much of a goalkeeper ... Little Sam scoring against me at the Boro training ground

a division. Juninho wouldn't do that for Boro', would he? He went to Atletico Madrid instead.

Neither was it for the money. My wages went up only £2,000 a week from Arsenal, which was not a fortune, and they had offered me a good new contract. It was for the challenge of helping get a promising team promoted and I enjoyed making it a reality. I was also North-East Player of the Year. On top of all that, Boro' made a million quid on me when they sold me and I was another year older, so they shouldn't complain. People have short memories.

Anyway, I travelled up to Villa in the afternoon and was introduced to the fans before the game. It is always a nervy time. You wonder how they are going to take to you, whether they are wondering why the club is buying a player of that age for that amount of money. I am also getting Dwight Yorke's No. 10 shirt, which is quite something to live up to.

I am certain I will produce the goods here, though. This is a perfect stage, a big club with a big pitch, which I will love because I like the space to play. They are top six, at the least, and have a young team, me and Ian Taylor, who is 30, being the oldest. At Boro', we had young vs old in training and players aged 28 made the young team. If it came to a relegation battle, you would fancy Middlesbrough to survive with their experience, but this lot here have the hunger to achieve things at the other end of the table.

Villa made a great start to my time there with the win over Newcastle. At half-time I phoned Lorraine to find out the scores in other games. I was delighted to hear that Gazza had scored for Boro' at Leicester. She also told me that Ian Wright had scored twice for West Ham as they went 3–0 up over Wimbledon. That will make the Dons good and angry for my debut against them on Saturday. Later the press told me about their 4–3 revival and I was amazed. Stayed the night at The Belfry ready for training first thing.

Thursday 10 September

In the morning I was the only first-team squad player in after the night before – though they always have a 40-minute warm-down in the afternoon – and I trained with the youth team. It was actually quite nervy, more so than on a Saturday, as you wonder what all these kids will think of you. Is he really a £6 million player?

Luckily, everything I was doing in an 8 vs 8 game came off and they were going 'Wow', so I immediately relaxed. They even started calling me 'legend'. I enjoyed that respect. It was actually a hard session, which included a series of shuttle runs that I have not done for years, but it was all good for me. Whenever I feel like moaning about fitness work, I've only got to remember the physical state I was in four years ago.

My first impression of the Bodymoor Heath training ground was how bleak and open it was. It's like playing with a beach ball all the time with gale-force winds coming in. But the facilities are excellent and include a great weights room.

I think I'm going to like it here.

Friday 11 September

They're serious on a Friday here. I'm used to a bit of a doss. It was only a 40-minute session but very sharp. We did some work on possession and closing down and then two teams of eight in a square. Two more players come in after 10 passes, then another two come in and it gets competitive. We did some set pieces but nothing like George Graham would do with Arsenal. But then, nothing compares to George for thoroughness. There were times there when a corner to us was like a free-kick now is to David Beckham.

My first impression here is of a good bunch of lads. They have had a great start to the season, having won three and drawn the other of their four games to be second in the table. They are on a high while I felt that latterly Boro' were on a bit of a low. At the Riverside, it looked like it was going to be about survival and if we got in the top half of the table it would be a surprising bonus. Here, there is the real prospect of winning things and that is what I have been used to.

Boro' sometimes seemed to be a collection of stars. When I first arrived, Ravanelli and Emerson were still there, for example, and they had gone down with the club. At Villa, I am impressed by how down-to-earth everyone is. They seem to look up to me, even the boss, as they appreciate what I have achieved in the game, such as the two league titles, FA and League Cups with Arsenal as well as the promotion with Boro'. Gareth Southgate says he has signed a new contract on the strength of me arriving, so it's all encouraging.

Lorraine and I went house-hunting in the Sutton Coldfield area, Gareth Southgate showing me around. By 6pm, I had had enough and wanted to relax, ready for tomorrow's game, while Lorraine kept going with Andy Townsend's wife, who has kept their family home going down here since his transfer from Villa to Boro'.

Saturday 12 September
Aston Villa 2 Wimbledon 0

It could hardly have been a better day. My debut, I score and Villa go top of the table. It was hard-fought though, as it always is with Wimbledon. They have got a great manager in Joe Kinnear and a great spirit. In some ways, you prefer to play them at their place because they are spoilers away from home.

When we were awarded a penalty with the score 0–0, I was wondering if I should take it but John Gregory got a message on that he wanted Alan Thompson to give it a whack, even though Lee Hendrie had scored a penalty against Newcastle in midweek. Mark Bosnich was laughing, wondering what the boss was doing here.

After the game the boss said to the press that he just had a hunch for Alan because he had been phenomenal in training but I don't remember him scoring one the day before. Lee, though, had been putting them in every corner. Anyway, Alan missed and it was back to square one.

When we got another one, I was determined to take it. I was really confident. I scored for England against Argentina, after all. I should have learned from the Sheffield United miss last season – not to mention another one I missed for Arsenal against Sampdoria in a European Cup-Winners' Cup semi-final shoot-out – but again I put it to the goalkeeper's left. Neil Sullivan duly read it like a book and saved it.

I got lucky, though. The ball came out just a few yards, enough for me to touch it home as I carried on my run. I was delirious and the lads mugged me, jumping on top in celebration. It was the turning point of the game. They had a player sent off in the incident and Ian Taylor went on to confirm the result. What a start for me. Any pressure there was has disappeared immediately.

Sunday 13 September

After two hectic weeks, a day to reflect on my move. Everything about Villa seems right at the moment. They are a massive club with massive support and with a real chance of the championship. Having conceded only one goal in five games we must be in with a real shout in the title race.

Preparation for yesterday's match was excellent. The warm-up was very thorough and Steve Harrison, the boss's assistant, is a terrific coach. After the game there are no massages, which I have been used to, but instead a 40-minute warm-down the day after, which the physio Jim Walker says is more important. Since I am still living down south, I am excused at the moment, though, and expected just to loosen up at home.

For the first time in several years, I am playing in a team where everyone speaks English. At Arsenal, Dennis Bergkamp spoke better English than me while Patrick Vieira was picking it up but Nicolas Anelka spoke very little, though I did communicate with him quite well. That was weird. It must be a nightmare at some clubs when three or four can't communicate. At Boro', Gianluca Festa spoke very good English while Hamilton Ricard was learning. At Villa, the ten outfield players are all English while Mark Bosnich as an Australian is as good as, though he acts like a foreigner sometimes. He's got that swagger about him.

This afternoon, I watched Boro's game at Spurs, a good 3–0 win with Beck and Ricard hitting it off up front. Good luck to them. I could hear the fans singing *'Merson is a wanker'*. That hurt. I don't think I deserve that.

Tuesday 15 September
Aston Villa 3 Stromsgodset 2

I haven't been involved with the first team for a couple of days because I was ineligible for tonight's UEFA Cup tie against Stromsgodset of Norway. I wanted to be there, though, and watched the game from the stand with the injured Ugo Ehiogu.

When we went two goals down, it didn't seem like the end of the world for me. It is a tough competition, unlike the Cup-Winners' Cup in which Lazio play this season having spent £40 million on new players. Even in the Champions League you can get away with one dodgy result. In the UEFA, you are playing teams who have come close to winning the league and have usually strengthened themselves ready for another crack.

Then Villa produced an amazing fight-back to win 3–2 with two goals by Darius Vassell and one by Gary Charles. It was amazing stuff, although watching from on high rather than being out there, I can see some cracks developing. There was some sloppy defending but when I went into the dressing room afterwards, all I heard was John Gregory talking about the great fightback.

As an observer, I felt it my duty to point out that if we played like that at Leeds on Saturday we would be thrashed. You don't come back from two goals down against teams in the Premiership. I think we could struggle when we get injuries or suspensions. If one man out of the back three of Ugo, Gareth Southgate and

Gareth Barry is missing, we will be struggling. We were all over the place.

Wednesday 16 September

I trained on my own in the morning again before the first-team players came in for their warm-down in the afternoon. That is, I trained with Steve Harrison, who has a reputation in the game as a very funny man, which I knew first hand from his time as Graham Taylor's assistant with England. By way of re-introduction during my warm-up, he started coughing violently. When I looked at him, he started bringing up … a worm. He must have slipped it into his mouth when I was not looking.

I ended the session with some finishing, 40 minutes to an hour of just making a run and whacking the ball in the net. I like to do it twice a week. Some people might consider it boring, doing it on your own. My response is that if you get bored with putting the ball into the net, then it's time to pack up football.

Recently I saw Tony Adams score a goal and when I was speaking to him a few days later, I told him that I was amazed how calmly he reacted. He said that goalscoring was not what gave him the real pleasure in the game but as a defender, he got more kicks from doing his job at the back well. If it had been me, I would have been running round the pitch like a greyhound.

Friday 18 September

This afternoon we travelled up to our hotel, the Holiday Inn in Leeds, for what was my first away trip with the boys. At first it was a worrying journey. Then it just became funny.

When I signed, John Gregory told me that there was no gambling around the club and no drinking, not even in the lounges. Actually, I didn't really mind about any of that – you're always going to have to endure it around you as a recovering addict. I know that it's me who has to change, not everyone else, and I have to face up to these things.

I was still surprised, though, when I took a seat near the back of the coach next to Gareth Southgate to see Mark Draper, Julian 'Jockey' Joachim, Mark 'Bozzy' Bosnich and Ugo on the back seat in a card school. I had never seen one like it. There were some serious sums being shifted about and at one point I couldn't see the back window for notes, both currency and IOUs. It was frightening.

For a while I thought they were winding me up. After everything that had been in the paper about me and Boro', I thought they would put the cards away any minute now and start laughing at me. But they didn't and in the end it was me who just had to laugh. I suppose it might even have been a sign that I was taken into the fold very quickly.

Ian Taylor asked me if I was all right with it and I was. I'm sure they would have stopped if I'd asked them. That's how much they think of me. But I didn't have to watch or get involved. Mostly I just played a game naming capital cities with some of the other lads.

I don't agree with gambling pre-game amongst the players, mind. It can't be any good for someone going into a match having lost money to team-mates. I've lived through all that, seen it all at Arsenal. The four Villa lads who were playing are normal and seemed all right with it, but if you're a gambling addict and you are having a bad time, you can start arguing with other players and the team's morale can suffer.

Saturday 19 September
Leeds United 0 Aston Villa 0

Rang to wish Lorraine a happy birthday. She seems happy with the boots and handbag I have bought her.

The most entertaining part of the day came in the morning, as it was to turn out. We met in the hotel lobby to go to the game and heard this commotion at the top of a stairway. This figure came rolling down the 20 or so carpeted stairs all of a sudden, past two ladies who were making balloon figures for a wedding, got up, dusted himself down and just walked off. Everyone was shocked. Everyone except the lads, who were laughing loudly. It was Steve Harrison.

It was a poor game but a comfortable 0–0. We're still top and Leeds are up there too but no-one seems to think that either of us will be, come the end of the season. Not even George Graham. Afterwards he was saying that by his reckoning, Leeds will be fourth and we'll be fifth. We'll see.

I had a reasonable chance to score in the first half and Jockey had a better one in the second. When you nick those, you become convinced that you are going to win the league but really there was nothing in it. In fact it was a poor game. Still, we have not conceded in five of our six games now, not conceded in a game I've played in, and we are looking like a very tight unit.

Wednesday 23 September

After a couple of days off, a running day today. At the beginning of the week, John Gregory will give Steve

Harrison his plan for the week and Steve will carry it out. He's the technical coach really, with the boss being more concerned with strategy and the overall picture, such as picking the team. The boss does like to be involved in the training, though – playing at least.

You don't see much of him on the weekly fitness day, though, for some strange reason. It consists of jogging round the pitch for three minutes then sprinting three on and off for three, repeated three times. It is followed by four 20-metre sprints, four 40, four 60 and four 80. It all lasts about an hour and is very punishing.

Friday 25 September

I've had a good, productive week leading up to the game against Derby County at Villa Park tomorrow. I decided to stay at The Belfry all week because I was getting fed up with the journey every day and my driver John has been staying with me. We have played a lot of golf and although he is a better golfer – 12 handicap to my 18 – he cannot beat me. Something to do with the mentality of a professional sportsman, perhaps.

In the evening, I went to see *Something About Mary*, which I thought was a brilliant film, then played a couple of frames of snooker with John. After dinner, I turned in early.

Saturday 26 September
Aston Villa 1 Derby County 0

I seem to be playing against all the teams I played against for Middlesbrough early in the season. And I know by now that if you are going to win the title, you really need to beat Derby at home. Though they're a good side, top-half material, having come a long way with not the biggest of resources, you can't afford to drop points to them.

The boss keeps his team talks very simple. He just likes you to play really, without too much information to clutter you. Just before the bell goes, we will get in a circle, put our arms around each other and Mark Bosnich will talk. He will tell us to go out and be confident. Bozzy's that type himself. Gareth Southgate will also talk. All the players look up to him. It's a change to see him like that when I have been used to him with England. There, very few players will speak up because they don't want to say anything wrong in front of Glenn Hoddle. John Gregory is always asking Gareth for advice.

We started really well and everything I was doing seemed to be coming off. I was dropping off from the attack and passing the ball well, finding my targets. Then, after 14 minutes, I went through one on one with their keeper and I just knew I was going to score. My confidence was really high. My first idea was that I would go round him but a gap appeared and I slotted it in.

It proved to be the winning goal. I thought we were comfortable. The crowd were brilliant and are really coming to understand what we are about, what our game plan is. They know we are patient and like to soak up pressure, then break. And you get the same amount of points for 1–0 as 5–0. In fact it's getting to be like the Arsenal here because we have now won three games 1–0 and conceded only one goal in seven league games.

You can feel the fans' expectation growing though. Until John Gregory came in the second half of last season, they looked certainties to go down and at the beginning of this season would probably have accepted a mid-table position. Now there is more to it than that. Everyone senses something in the air.

Tuesday 29 September
Stromsgodset 0 Aston Villa 3

All in all I'd rather be in Norway as I'm working really hard in training on my own while the boys are away for the second leg of the UEFA Cup tie. It's got to be easier over there and it was, with a hat-trick by Stan Collymore booking us an easy passage into the second round.

I was certain we would win because I thought Stromsgodset were a poor side in the first leg, even if they did go two up. I was less certain that Stan would do the business. He has been suffering from a thigh strain and has hardly done any fitness work at all. In training recently, the physio Jim Walker was trying to make him run but he wouldn't move. It was like watching a stubborn horse.

It is hard to get to know Stan. I change just a couple of pegs away from him but we don't say a lot to each other. It is also hard finding a house to suit me, Lorraine and the boys. We have been looking again today but nothing really appeals. More luck next month, I hope. This one has been pretty lucky, mind.

OCTOBER

The Two Pauls

Thursday 1 October

Gareth Southgate and I were chatting before training. What does the boss do for Saturday's game at Coventry? Does he keep Stan after his hat-trick and drop Julian, who's been on fire early in the season? Or does he drop me? It was a test between me and Gareth to see which one of us is going to make a manager. Gareth said he would pair Julian and me. I disagreed, arguing that he would pair Stan and me. If Stan doesn't play, his confidence will take another nosedive. Maybe the hat-trick is the kick-start he needs.

As usual, Mark Bosnich was the last in to training. He always arrives just before it starts. Bozzy was down to his underpants when Alan Thompson sprayed his water bottle at him. 'I can't have that,' Bozzy said and just got dressed and went home. Everyone was gobsmacked. We had training and not enough goalkeepers for finishing practice.

Then in training, for a joke, I sprayed myself with my

water bottle and said I was going home, which eased the tension. The boss is in a difficult position now. What does he do about it? If he doesn't sort it, someone else might think they can just take off whenever they want. Then again, Bozzy has only got half a season left on his contract and you have to be careful with him. He's a world-class goalkeeper and even if he is going to go at the end of the season, we need him to be performing well now we're top of the league.

Friday 2 October

I had a real go at Bozzy this morning. He was changing with the youth team and I told him he was behaving like a kid, as well as setting a bad example to them. He replied that what Alan Thompson had done yesterday was childish. Two wrongs didn't make a right, I said. Now I know I've done some daft things, and I grant you that taking cocaine wasn't exactly a good example to kids but things, and I, have changed.

Mark was good about it. I thought he would have a go back at me but he just listened. I do think he respects me and I think he appreciated me saying it in private rather than in front of the lads. Sometimes if I am just talking to the lads he will say, 'Just listen to Merse. He knows what he's talking about.' I'm not whiter than white but something needed to be said, because to my knowledge the boss has said nothing, so that we could put the whole silly episode behind us.

No word yet whether Stan will start the game tomorrow. The boss decided not to name the team after training. I stayed at The Belfry again, finding out from the teletext in my room that I am in the England squad for the games against Bulgaria and Luxembourg. In the past, sometimes George Graham or Bryan Robson would tell you, sometimes you just hear from one of the other lads.

In the evening I repeated the winning routine of a week ago – went to see *Something About Mary* again, played the same number of frames of snooker, ate the same dinner and went to bed at the same time.

Saturday 3 October
Coventry City 1 Aston Villa 2

We met at the training ground in the morning for a pre-match meal and I was disappointed that Bozzy hadn't fully integrated himself back among the team. In fact, he sat on his own at a table facing the wall. He has not apologised, nor said anything. Gareth and I were annoyed but we decided to let it go until after the game rather than interfere in a delicate situation beforehand.

Bozzy does have this amazing ability not to let peripheral issues spoil his game, though. He was fine during the team meeting and was just the same for the pre-match huddle in the dressing room. Then during the game he made two world-class saves at crucial times just to prove how valuable to us he is.

I thought we played brilliantly, the typical away team smash-and-grab raid. Normally when I have gone to Coventry, it is them who start well, but today it was the team I am playing for. I should have been awarded a penalty but wasn't so perhaps the goal I set up for Ian Taylor to give us the lead was justice. On television, it did look five yards offside when I got the ball, I admit, but as I made a run, I saw a defender ten yards ahead of me. He was running one way, I was running the other and at pace.

I was playing well that day, Glenn Hoddle was there and things were looking good when Ian scored again to put us 2–0 up. Soon after I found Stan – and I was right about the boss pairing me and him up front – with a nice ball and he crossed to Ian who might have made it three. I patted Stan on the backside and said 'Well done' because I thought he would be substituted any moment. I thought that he must be knackered having played on Tuesday and not trained otherwise.

I could not understand it then when John Gregory pulled me off to put on Jockey to partner Stan. In fact, I was furious.

'What the fuck are you doing?' I said to him when I reached the dug-out. 'I thought the idea of bringing me to the club was for times like this. Two-nil up. Steady the ship.' No-one else in this club, after all, knows what it's like to be top of the league. Paul Barron, our goalkeeping coach who was in the dug-out, told me to calm down, as did a few others. 'I fucking won't,' I said.

I had to let my emotion show and to be honest about the way I saw things. I spent too long in the past bottling it up and look where that got me. And I didn't want to blow my top in front of the lads later in the dressing room. Besides, anyone who is happy about being substituted has got an attitude problem in my opinion and I didn't come to Villa to be subbed.

I am 30 years old and I need to be playing, whether it's at Oldham or Old Trafford. John Gregory didn't have an answer when I asked why he substituted me. I don't think he knew. At the moment he is going with his instincts, doing things off the cuff. Or just because they are different.

At least I was glad it wasn't Alan Thompson. He had been pulled off three games in a row previously and you could see in his face that he thought he was going to be again, no matter how well he was playing. Before the game today I told him just to play his game and not to think about coming off. I think it worked and he had a good game. He is a good player. If only he believed it more.

Anyway, soon Coventry scored and we were under the cosh. I didn't want to say I told you so. Or maybe I did. John Gregory is lucky things are coming off for him. I wonder if they will at another time of the season.

I thought there were signs of my partnership with Stan working. He is so talented but he has just lost confidence. He is still just waiting to happen. He likes me to talk to him all the time, keep geeing him up. I tell him just to give 100 per cent. If you run around and give it all you've got, the fans will appreciate that at least and no-one will ever get on your back.

I think when Stan gets to my age, he'll probably realise he hasn't got many games left and grab his opportunity finally to make the most of his outstanding talent. These days, I take every game as though it's one of my last. No game passes me by now. A few years ago a game could drift on around me, but in the last season or two I don't think there has been a game that I have not had some impact on. Soon I won't have football and it worries me to think like that sometimes. At those moments, I have to get back to living in the day.

I hope Stan gets to that point. At 26, he should be somewhere near his peak. The boss is trying to be good to him, by not bringing him off because it might upset him, but sooner or later he has got to take responsibility for himself.

He's a deep person, Stan. You never quite know where you are with him. Sometimes he'll have a laugh with the lads. Other times he won't. He changes. He never lets anybody get close to him. And that's why I say, where do normal people go and talk? Me, I can go to AA or GA and say how I feel. That's what Stan's crying out for, to get it all off his chest.

Sunday 4 October

Given a day off. Stayed in and watched Liverpool vs Chelsea on television, a 1–1 draw. Even at this early stage you are hoping for a draw and there's only eight games gone. That's two points gained, you think. I've worked out that we are now only five games away from staying up. If we won them all, that is.

Monday 5 October

Met up with England today and I felt as confident as I have done with the national team for a long while. I said to Lorraine this morning before leaving for Burnham Beeches that I really fancy myself to play against Bulgaria next Saturday. I am in some of the best form of my career, and have kept it going for a long period of time now.

When I got there, Glenn Hoddle told me he thought I had played really well on Saturday, which I took as a good sign. I was really buzzing for training, though there were only eight of us taking part, what with injuries and everything.

Tuesday 6 October

Trained again this morning. It is always very hard with Glenn. They are good sessions, very professional, but sometimes there is not enough laughing for my liking. Already I am getting bored with this week as there is not enough to occupy us outside of training and I spent seven hours on the computer playing the Sega football manager game with Ray Parlour. I developed headaches and felt dizzy. This routine is not good for me.

Wednesday 7 October

After training, we were allowed to go to the pictures. It was *Something About Mary* – for the third time. In the last ten minutes, I was telling Ray Parlour word for word what was happening. He was laughing his head off. At least someone is.

Ray always likes to have a laugh. I think he may have gilded the story but he said once when he came back from seeing Eileen Drewery that when she put a hand on his head, he asked for a short back and sides. It may not have gone down too well with Glenn. Anyway, I have known Ray for a long time, with our Arsenal time together, and used to drink together. I think we've both calmed down a bit since then.

Otherwise, this is developing into a very dull week. The pressure is building for a crucial Euro 2000 qualifier but it's not that. It's just that the routine and the regime are so serious and heavy all the time. I don't think one player can put his hand on his heart and say he is enjoying it.

Thursday 8 October

We were training at Wembley in the afternoon so I played on the computer game all morning. Again felt very listless and lethargic and now my back is aching is a bit.

I could hardly move. If there was more to do around here, I'm sure I would be feeling more positive about things, the way I did when I joined up. I haven't needed to see Eileen all week but maybe I should.

Friday 9 October

This morning I could hardly move when I woke up so I didn't train. I wasn't going to play anyway, I knew that. If I had been playing I might have pushed myself a bit more. Instead, it was another of those down days. How did I start the week so well then end up like this? Something is going on that I don't understand.

Saturday 10 October
England 0 Bulgaria 0

I was shocked this morning to read about Gazza. Yesterday, apparently, he was found sobbing and shaking on Stevenage station after coming back from a bender in Dublin, where Middlesbrough had been playing in midweek and has ended up at Sheryl's house. He looked ready to throw himself under a train, someone said. It brought back really frightening memories for me and sent shivers through me. I will try and contact him. He needs help.

At midday, I went to get on the coach to go to Wembley to offer moral support and watch the game but Glenn said not to bother. I would probably only do more damage to my back on the journey and sitting in the stand all afternoon, he said. So I went back to St Albans and watched the game there from the comfort of my sofa. Lorraine then came back to Burnham with me, wives and girlfriends being allowed there for one night before the squad got down to preparing for Luxembourg on Wednesday.

It was a nothing game. Nothing was created, nothing happened and nothing-nothing was the result. Glenn picked the wrong team in my opinion. Take Paul Scholes. He was always going to play ahead of me, it turned out, but he hadn't been a regular for Manchester United and hadn't even played the previous weekend. I know I developed a back injury later in the week and the matter was academic but I was on top of my game. Sometimes when I've been with England I've thought that I was lucky to be here. This time I thought I really deserved to be and to be in the team.

I wondered why we were persisting with three at the back when the Bulgarians offered no attacking threat. Centre-halves aren't going to score. If we'd brought one off, it would have encouraged the opposition to go forward a bit more, thus leaving us with some space to attack and get in behind them.

Why not play 4-4-2? It's almost as if Glenn is being bloody minded because so many people in the press and the stands want us to play that way. And why not bring on Ian Wright and Teddy Sheringham? Wrighty will ruffle them up and Teddy will put the ball through the eye of a needle. Even if he could only do it once, it would have given us the win we needed.

I was back at the hotel by the time the team returned, very tired and dejected. Lorraine and I went out with Rio Ferdinand and his girlfriend Kirsty Gallagher, the Sky Sports presenter, who seemed like a really nice girl, for a meal before returning to the hotel for a drink.

As we got back, Alan Shearer, David Batty, Robert Lee and Gareth Southgate were having a quiet drink when the boss came into the bar. He told them to go to bed. 'It's not like we've won 5–0 or something,' he told them, clearly upset.

Sunday 11 October

The boys trained but I stayed behind in the hotel to have treatment on my back. I was bored witless again. Then, in the evening, Glenn called a meeting of the whole squad and we were subjected to a video of the Bulgaria game before being asked for our views. We were getting fed up with videos, having watched three of them leading up to the game.

Mostly, players do not like speaking up in that situation, worried that their remarks may be used against them in future. Alan Shearer was not at all worried now, though. Glenn had had a go at Paul Scholes for not talking during the game and Alan pointed out that Glenn should know that Paul is not a talker.

Alan added that we had all been bored during the week. We had played only nine holes of golf and trained every day as if we were with our clubs. Why couldn't we train all day Tuesday then maybe have a day off on Wednesday, perhaps shopping in London, he asked. It was why we were so sluggish on the field, Alan suggested and as captain of the team, he did a good job of putting the players' point of view.

Some of it was quite funny. John Gorman, for example, put his foot in it. He complained that Gary Neville, Sol Campbell and Gareth Southgate were not doing any talking. 'Alan Shearer can't do it, he's at the other end of the pitch,' John said. So everyone was left wondering: 'How's he captain then?' It was a prime example of why Tony Adams should be captain, though he was injured for this game. If everyone on the squad had a vote, Tone would be.

Gary Neville said that he thought we should press the opposition, because people didn't seem to be sure whether we should be squeezing or dropping off. At one point the Bulgarians had 12 passes across the back. Alan Shearer wanted Glenn to make his mind up. We never do any work on that, he said. Gary said that Manchester United had got a result against Barcelona in a Champions' League match recently by pressing and that if they had pressed for longer in the second half, they would have won.

Glenn disagreed, saying that United were too tired for the second half and fell away from being 3–1 up to 3–3.

Martin Keown believed that the wing backs should stay forward and shouldn't have to come back. We should have enough defenders to look after the threat. Then Glenn asked Ian Wright if he had anything to say. At first Wrighty said no. Glenn asked him again. 'Yeah, man,' he said. 'You've got to smile more, you never smile. You've got to relax.' Some of the lads were embarrassed, some were amused. You could almost see Glenn thinking: 'What a mistake asking him'.

Afterwards Glenn took me to one side and asked how my back was. I told him that sitting in a two-hour meeting hadn't helped. 'I want you buzzing because I need you against Luxembourg,' he said. I went back to have treatment with Gary Lewin at 10pm that night. Now I was desperate to make it. I told him I would try it on Monday morning.

Back in my room, I received a phone call from David Davies, the FA's director of public affairs, to ask if I would do a press conference tomorrow about Gazza because the press boys are all interested in his latest scrape. David thinks I understand it all and will say nice things about Gazza.

I agreed to do it but I said that I would just tell it how it is. I had spoken to Bryan Robson in the afternoon to ask him how Gazza was. 'Not good,' he said. I told him that if he needed help he should see my counsellor Steve Stephens, who had helped me through my treatment at the Marchwood Priory near Southampton and who now runs his own centre in Nottingham. He is a top man, I said. He doesn't talk any mumbo jumbo and will relate to Gazza in a way that he will understand. 'Ring me if you need any help,' I said.

Monday 12 October

I had told Glenn I would let him know after a meeting with the team doctor this morning whether I would be fit enough, because I didn't want to get all the way over to Luxembourg, find out I wasn't right and have another two days hanging about. I would get back in the early hours of Thursday morning, have to go up to Villa then drive down to London on Friday for the West Ham game on Saturday. My back would never get better.

In the event the decision was made for me. I couldn't move again when I woke up and it took me ten minutes to get out of bed. I told Dr Crane, who said he would go and see Glenn.

In the meantime, I did my press conference and it turned out to be an emotional event. The news was out that Gazza was in the Priory clinic at Roehampton in South-West London and as soon as I was asked about what it had been like for me in treatment, my eyes filled with tears. I just recalled all the pain and panic. I knew what Gazza must be going through.

I was honest and graphic, because people need to know the miserable reality of addiction and how tough the recovery is from it. I told people that they rip you apart and put you back together again. Gazza would know a new and better life if he stuck at it, I said, but it was a rocky road. It all really got to me.

After that, I went round the back to gather my thoughts and Paul McCarthy of the *Daily Express* kindly came to find out if I was alright. David Davies wondered if I would now do television and radio. 'Are you sure?' I said. I really wasn't in the mood for any more.

After lunch I waited in my room expecting to get a phone call from Glenn but instead the England team administrator Michelle Farrar phoned to say that Glenn had told her I wasn't going and that she would get me a taxi home. I was glad to get out. It didn't surprise me that I hadn't heard from Glenn. The more the pressure's got to him, the less interested he is in players who aren't available.

I do believe in fate. When I came back from seeing the doctor in the morning, the phone rang. It was a woman counsellor from the Priory. Gazza was talking about me a lot. 'He obviously thinks a lot of you. He knows you're going to Luxembourg, but do you think you could ring him?' she asked. 'I can do better than that,' I said. 'I'm not going to Luxembourg now, so I will come in and see him.'

Then she asked if I minded whether Eric Clapton also came in. He had rung the Priory when he heard that

Gazza was in and, as a recovering addict himself and a volunteer helper, offered his services. He would also like to meet me, she said. Did I mind?

Did I mind? I was delighted. To me he was a legend whom I admired so much. At the World Cup we were all asked to fill in a questionnaire, for advertising purposes I suppose, about who we would most like a one-to-one phone conversation with. I put down Eric Clapton. I wanted to ask him how he managed to get through without taking drugs when his four-year-old son tragically died. That seemed to me like the ultimate test of a recovery.

From Burnham, I went home to St Albans, dropped off my gear then headed straight for the Priory. Gazza was in shock, but seemed pleased to see me. I was honest with him, just told him my story, but he was in a jumpy mood. One minute he would nod, the next he wanted to get out of there. Then Eric arrived and introduced himself. I just thought, 'Wow, this man has come to see you, he's put himself out for you. Get a hold of it, Gazza.'

I didn't want to frighten him any more and just suggested that he should stay until the weekend. I told him that the *Sun* had already been running a competition in the paper, saying that anyone who saw him in a pub should contact them. His life would be a misery if he kept on drinking, in more ways than one. I said that he should stay here, safe amongst people who understood the illness. Eric asked him if he drank on his own. 'I like half a bottle of wine in front of the telly,' Gazza said with the alcoholic's understatement. 'Well, you'd better get used to that man, because that's all your life will be from now on,' Eric said.

After a while, Eric left me on my own with Gazza and

I stayed for another half an hour, just talking about my experiences and how he could now help himself. I asked him what he would do if Bryan Robson told him that he had to stay until he was right, and that he wouldn't be playing until then. 'I'll leave the club,' he said.

I asked him where he would go. 'America,' he said but I told him that someone from their Major Soccer League had already been in the paper saying they wouldn't want him. I told him that no-one would have him in his current state, but off the booze he could be one of the greats again. He said he would stay one night, which was progress. I gradually got him to agree to think, at least, about staying until Friday.

Then a nurse came around with some medication for him and I left, saying that I would come back if he wanted. I went downstairs and Eric was still in the reception area. 'How is he?' he asked. 'A bit disappointed,' I said. 'He doesn't like your albums much. He was hoping the Spice Girls would be coming to see him.' Eric thought it was funny too. He asked me if I wanted to go for a meal with him, but I said that I had promised Lorraine I would bring in a Chinese takeaway. My driver John couldn't believe I turned down the chance of a meal with Eric Clapton.

Eric had already rung Bryan Robson to tell him that tomorrow we should make it hard for Gazza to leave, that he really needed to be in this place. On my way home, I rang Robbo myself and reinforced the sentiment. 'You've got to be firm with him,' I said. 'If he does leave treatment, at least tell him he can train but that he can't play on Saturday just so that he sees he can't just get back into his old ways.'

Robbo said he would be in tomorrow and would think

about it all. He was worried when I said that it could be a couple of months before he was ready to play again. The head of treatment had asked me to come back the next day, but I got the feeling that Robbo didn't want me there.

Then I rang Steve Kutner to get Keith Lamb, the Boro' Chief Executive, on the line. I said to him that because Robbo is such a tolerant bloke, he might go along with Gazza wanting to leave the Priory but that the club had to get tough. In fact, it is called tough-love. Keith Lamb agreed and said he would talk to Bryan.

I was really tired when I got in with the Chinese but satisfied that I had done my best to help someone who seemed to have reached some kind of rock bottom with this illness. Steve Kutner phoned one last time. Keith Lamb had rung him to say that he was sorry that my transfer to Aston Villa had provoked some bad feeling at the time but he would never hear another bad word about me. He didn't believe I could be so caring about Gazza.

But that is what this illness is all about. It is called Twelfth Step work, which means that to complement the work you do on yourself, you help others recover. It is a paradox that you've got to give it away to keep it. Helping another addict was helping me too and if Middlesbrough benefited as well, all well and good. It felt good. I felt good. And Gazza's state was a good reminder for me of how devastating this illness can be.

Tuesday 13 October

They rang me again from the Priory and asked me to come in. 'The more here, the better,' they said. When I got there, about 11am, Sheryl, Eric Clapton, Robbo and all the doctors were in Gazza's room. It was D-Day. Eric had been there a while and had been talking to him. When he left, he wished me well as I took my turn at persuading Gazza to stay.

He seemed to be ready to leave again. His face dropped when I got there. He was probably watching all his escape routes being closed. He slumped into a chair. We all just asked him to stay for one week. He started crying and so did I. You could see that his illness wanted him to leave but that the part of his soul that was screaming out for recovery knew that he had to stay. I recognised that horrible space he was in – scared to carry on drinking and scared to stop.

'Let's go and meet the other people in here,' I said to him so we did. 'It's like *One Flew Over the Cuckoo's Nest* in here,' he said and we laughed. That was his way of dealing with the pain of it all. When we came back, he talked to Sheryl while Robbo and I went shopping in nearby Putney for some clothes for him.

When we got back, he had calmed down and he agreed to stay for a week. Robbo was as good as gold. A lot of managers would have wanted him out of there. Gazza's mobile went. It was Andy Townsend wishing him well. Gazza was like a little boy, telling Andy that Eric Clapton had been in.

I was delighted to think that my old mate might finally be giving himself a chance of realising the potential he had, not just as a footballer because we had all seen that, but as a human being. I'll say it again. He is a lovely bloke with a heart of gold but alcohol just robs him sometimes of his nature. One day at a time, though. There was a long way to go yet. Now he needed a couple of days of space to get his head into treatment. And I needed to get back to the matter in hand with Aston Villa.

Wednesday 14 October

The back has eased a little and I went up to training to do some light work. I would never have made it for tonight's England game in Luxembourg but with a little more work, I may well be fit for Saturday. I watched us struggle to beat the part-timers on television. I would have fancied myself to get in amongst them. I suppose we have to be grateful for the 3–0 win, though Glenn can expect a bit more flak.

Friday 16 October

We trained this afternoon, in advance of tomorrow's match at West Ham, at Watford's old training ground in Honeypot Lane, Stanmore, North London. It was a strange feeling. I used to play my Sunday football as a ten-year-old for Belmont United here. I got there early as I don't live too far away, so I rang Gazza on my mobile while I waited for the team bus to arrive.

He told me he had agreed to stay in for another week and that he had decided that he had to quit the booze. He had never said that to me before. In fact, it was the best I had ever heard him. He was really positive. Later after training, when we got to our hotel at West Lodge, Cockfosters, I phoned Robbo to tell him. He seemed really pleased.

With us for the first time was Steve Watson, who we have signed for £4.5 million from Newcastle. It shows the boss's ambition and the squad is starting to strengthen. Steve should be a good player. He is quality and very versatile.

Saturday 17 October
West Ham United 0 Aston Villa 0

Woken at 6am by a fire alarm going off. Not the best start to the day. I hadn't slept well anyway because my back is beginning to play up and hotel beds do not help. There was some stuff in the papers this morning about me going in to see Gazza and Gareth Southgate, who is one of the nicest footballers you'll ever meet, was asking me about it all. He was very interested and very understanding.

When I was away with England last week, all the Manchester United and Arsenal players were saying that the game against West Ham would be our first real test, with them playing so well. Well, we dominated the game, which wasn't a great one, and should have won it. Sadly I missed a gilt-edged chance, an open goal really. I didn't meet the shot properly and Shaka Hislop got back to save.

I was sick, but I tried to look at it positively. I did my fair share during the game and I'd been contributing lately. I'd scored and set up one against Coventry in our last game. And I didn't mean to miss. Besides, as a recovering addict, I couldn't afford to get too down. I just had to keep it all in perspective. The point was valuable and perhaps 1–0 in our favour might have made us a bit complacent. A 0–0 draw keeps our feet on the ground.

Sunday 18 October

I was lucky to have the day off because I am not going to Spain for Tuesday's UEFA Cup tie against Celta Vigo. The others have to go in for their usual warm-down.

This morning all the papers are going on about how hard Stan Collymore worked yesterday. Well yes, but as George Graham used to say, that's the least you expect. World-class players work hard, that's the basics and that's what I've told Stan myself. But then it's all about talent. And for £1 million a year, I think fans are entitled to expect talent as much as hard work. To be honest, I'm surprised how far downhill Stan's career has gone.

Gazza phoned me tonight. He seems to be doing alright. 'You're lucky you're in there,' I said to him. 'I missed a sitter yesterday and I'm getting it worse than you are.' He asked me if I was alright. 'Yeah, I've had a Red Bull and a wine gum,' I told him and he laughed.

Tuesday 20 October
Celta Vigo 0 Aston Villa 1

Trained with the reserves, as I had done yesterday. They are good lads and work hard. You can't just go through the motions with them. My back went a bit again, right in the base of the spine. It is just spasms and the muscles tighten up, but it is starting to worry me a bit. Usually it clears up after a hot bath.

Watched the game at home with Charlie, Ben and Sam, letting them stay up a bit as a treat. It was live on Eurosport. It was a great result against a very good side but I think we are papering over cracks. You can't keep defending for 90 minutes and hope to stay goalless then nick it on the break. We are relying on last-ditch tackles and that won't go on happening. It's only a matter of time before we get a good hiding. I just hope it's not in the league. Stan worked hard again but he didn't even have a shot.

Thursday 22 October

The boys were back in for training today and I joined up with them again. I said to Stan that I didn't think he could keep working that hard. 'You're running around and when we get the ball, you're knackered.' He didn't say anything. He just looked at me as if to say: 'Have you finished?'

It's a serious matter though because he could be such a key player for us. I spoke to John Gregory and Steve Harrison about it. It's all very well him working that hard, and everybody praising him for it, I said, but in four games' time it'll be: 'Stan hasn't scored in seven games' and he'll get hammered. Then he'll start thinking, 'Sod it, I'm not running around like this,' and be out of the habit of scoring. It's about getting a happy medium with him, I said.

While we're having a meeting, I said to them, can I clear up a few things? I was not in the best of moods and my back was giving me pain. The boss wondered why I was not my chirpy self in training. 'The lads look up to you,' he said. I had been disappointed with training, I said, and I wanted to do more. He said that they had had a hard week, going to Spain, and he couldn't work us too hard.

It was fair enough, as was his explanation that he pulled me off against Coventry partly because he knew I had an England game coming up and he didn't want to overdo it with me. It was when he said, 'Besides, I don't want to lose Stan. I need to keep his confidence high,' that I got angry. 'I'm not here to keep Stan happy,' I said. 'I'm not coming off every fucking week just so he can stay on.' He took my point, but I don't think anything got resolved.

On my way home, I got a call from Gazza. He was in a state. 'I want to leave,' he said. 'Are you asking me or telling me?' I asked him. 'Because if you're asking me, I would advise you to stay in there. If you're telling me, I will say that it's your decision. You've got to do what you think is right for you. You've made a good start, but you've still got to do it out in the real world.' I don't know which way he will go now.

Friday 23 October

Gazza has left the Priory and I fear for him. I just hope I'm wrong. I had a call from the head of treatment to let me know what was happening. She said that he was going to come back two days a week, which I suppose is better than nothing.

I then rang Gazza to wish him all the best. He said that he believed that training and playing would keep him on the straight and narrow, but I'm not sure that will be enough. He said he was having a press conference today in Middlesbrough. 'Stay strong,' I said.

Having had experience of press conferences like these, I decided to ring Robbo. He was concerned about it all, but I told him I thought it was a good idea to get everything out in the open. I was a bit worried that it was just going to be him and Gazza, without a professional counsellor to explain some of the background to all this, but I told Bryan not to let Gazza hammer the press as he usually does. It's not their fault. They're not the ones who've been out on the benders. They're just doing their job by reporting it. If he sat in like I did, they wouldn't have any stories. Besides, it might be a good idea to get the press on his side for the future – and they would be if he was honest with them and didn't blame them.

I hoped he would say that he was going to take it one day at a time and that all the stories had been true but that now he was trying to change. I hoped he would ask for respect, just to be allowed to live his life without intrusion and that if he did end up in a pub with a drink in his hand, everyone would know about it.

I watched the press conference live on Sky News. I was shocked when I heard him talk about never having another drink again. You're just a hostage to fortune with that kind of stuff. An alcoholic can't look beyond today. Look at me. What he should have said was: 'I'm just not going to have a drink today.'

My own experience made me anxious for him. There I was four years down the line and bang, before I knew it, I was nearly on it more than I was then. This is a serious business. I had got to a point in my recovery different to Gazza, wondering about what goals I had left in my life having just been to the World Cup. But then again, I was just the same as him – trying to stay off booze for just this 24 hours. Every day I did that, I equalled the world record. I hope he's got that simple message at least.

Saturday 24 October
Aston Villa 1 Leicester City 1

I knew this game would be a banana skin for us. Leicester are a better team away than at home, they can play a bit, they're tight and they're hard to beat. We're also expected to win games like this.

They went a goal up and we looked a mess. I felt a lot of the lads didn't want the ball and it frustrated me. The fans were wondering why we weren't winning 3–0 and for the first time we looked vulnerable. Ten minutes before half-time I was running around telling everyone to keep it tight, just to keep it to 1–0 until the interval so that we could get in and sort it all out. We could have lost the game in the first half.

The break did us good. John Gregory had a bit of a go, I had a bit of a go – saying that everyone wanted the ball in training and now we had to want it here – and we got our heads together for the second half. We were positive and Ugo Ehiogu got us an equaliser.

I wasn't happy at being substituted again, though, just as we could have gone on to win the game. I fancied I could be the one to do it. Again it looked like being just to keep Stan happy. He had played 90 minutes in Vigo, looked knackered and was half-fit. My unhappiness was obvious to all inside Villa Park, I should think.

Steve Harrison came up to me and said not to worry but I was in no mood. 'If you're bringing me off, don't put your arm round me. You're either right or wrong to do it,' I said. Paul Barron also said something to me in the shower but I told him that I didn't like being treated like a kid. After getting all that out of my system, I was all right. Being around Tony Adams had taught me that I needed to speak my mind in this game to get out my resentments, then to let it all go.

Before leaving, I asked Steve and the physio Jim Walker what time we were in the following day but they said that it was pointless me travelling up and down just for half an hour of warm-down. My back would stiffen up on the journey home, they said.

I was just leaving the ground with Lorraine when some press men came and asked me about my reaction to being substituted. I said that if you ever saw a professional footballer laughing as he was being taken off – 'given the hook,' as some say in the professional game – then he didn't deserve to get paid. They said that John Gregory had said that he didn't 'give a shit' about my reaction. I was upset by that and then really had my say, telling them that I thought he was wrong to take me off.

Sometimes I think I care too much. I rang Gareth Southgate on the Saturday night, feeling a bit guilty that I had caused a stir in the dressing room after the game. I asked him what the lads were thinking, because I didn't want to rip team spirit due to any disagreement between the boss and me. He told me not to worry, that the lads respected me.

But I do worry. With us top of the table, chances like these only come up so many times in a career. You can play 15 seasons in the game and never have a start like we have had to the season. I keep telling the lads that next season we could have, say, Manchester United, Liverpool, Arsenal and Chelsea as our first four fixtures and not have a prayer of winning the title after that lot. This season, big clubs like Newcastle and Blackburn were out of it after half a dozen games, and then relegation creeps into your mind.

Also, when you're a kid, you think it's going to be like this every season. I did. I couldn't see what all the fuss was about when we won the title at Arsenal in 1989. We'll do this again, I thought. The next year we never had a chance, though, and although we won it again in 1991, I then had four long years of not getting a sniff. The kids need to grasp this. Maybe I was a bit hard on them. Maybe I was a bit hard on John Gregory. Perhaps I should have bitten my tongue.

Sunday 25 October

I should have bitten my tongue. The papers have reported a row between the boss and me.

I was out watching my brother-in-law play football on the Sunday morning when my mobile went. It was John Gregory. 'The lads are training and you should be here,' he said. I told him that Steve and Jim had said I wasn't needed. I'm 30, I said, I'm not like that. I wouldn't just not turn up. He said that no-one had told him and I said to go and ask Steve and Jim. 'OK then, see you tomorrow,' he said.

That struck me as strange. When I spoke to Gareth on the Saturday, I told him that I was just going to be normal on the Monday when I came in, to try and forget about it all. 'We're not in on the Monday,' he said.

When I got back home, I was annoyed to find that John Gregory had phoned Lorraine to find out why I wasn't in training. What's it got to do with her? That just stirred it.

Monday 26 October

I arrived at training to find that I was the only one of the first team there. The boss just said: 'Good morning' to me, and that's all I said back. Then I trained with the reserves. 'You can bet your life you'll get injured again today,' Jim Walker said and sure enough my back went again.

Tuesday 27 October

My back was all right again today and I trained. Afterwards, the team was announced for the Worthington

Cup tie at Chelsea the following night and I was rested, which suited me fine. I was going to go to Stamford Bridge to watch them but John Gregory said that he knew I would be there in spirit but not to sit out in the cold with my bad back. 'Have a rest and a night in with the wife and kids,' he said. He had made his point and got me in to training on the Monday. This was the other side of him. He can be good as gold to you. Good man-management or not? I'll have to think about that one, ready for my days as a manager.

Wednesday 28 October
Chelsea 4 Aston Villa 1

A good result – not because I have always been a Chelsea fan but because the Worthington Cup is a competition we could do without if we are going to be in contention for the Championship.

I watched the game at home and thought it was a prime example of what could happen to us in the league if we are not careful. It was by no means our first team and two of the regular back three were not playing but it shows what could happen if and when we get suspensions and injuries. That's another reason why I say it was a good result – it should wake everybody up at the club and stop complacency setting in. If anyone inside Villa Park thought we were invincible, this will tell them differently.

What did upset me was Dennis Wise's nasty tackle on Darren Byfield, which got him sent off. They were 4–1 up as well with Vialli having given us the runaround. There was nothing left at stake so what was Dennis thinking about? Good for the referee, though, not bottling the decision. Chelsea are starting to look ominous. As well as Vialli in reserve, they've got Tore Andre Flo. As John Gregory said, their reserves were better than ours and they will be up there with us at the end of the season.

It just confirms that you do need a deep squad more than ever these days and ours is not deep enough yet.

Thursday 29 October

I woke up this morning with flu, but there's no way I was going to miss training. You get players who ring up with a headache when you know they've got a hangover but since getting sober, I've always been one who wanted to get in both at Arsenal and Middlesbrough. I don't know if it's paranoia or what but I like to show my face and let them make their mind up.

John Gregory said I shouldn't have come but he sent me home and told me to go to bed. He wanted me ready for training tomorrow at Bisham Abbey, where we will be based before our League game against Chelsea on Saturday. I went straight to bed when I got home and stayed there. The boss phoned me at 10.30pm to see how I was. I've never known a manager do that before. That was nice of him. Mind you, I think I've had a few phoning me up that late just to check if I was in.

Friday 30 October

I still felt ill but made it over to Bisham for the 3pm training. I told John Gregory that I didn't think I would make it for tomorrow and he said to go home, have a night in my own bed and see how I was tomorrow.

I thought that was good management. There's nothing worse than being in a hotel when you're ill.

Saturday 31 October

I felt better and rang the boss, who told me to report to Stamford Bridge for 1.30pm. The traffic was a nightmare and I thought I was going to be late. Then on the M25 I spotted Doug Ellis. I wound down the window and said I would follow him, which was handy. I thought that I could blame it on him if I was late.

In the event I got there before the lads only to find that the game had been called off due to a waterlogged pitch. I thought that was another plus, an example of how the luck was going our way at this point of the season. Speaking to Gareth on Thursday we both agreed that the 4–1 had been damaging to our morale. So if you've got a good hiding off a bloke in a pub, you don't want to go back into the pub three days later, do you? And now we didn't have to. Gareth and I agreed we would have taken a 0–0. We also had a big UEFA Cup game coming up on the Tuesday.

I had given my driver John the afternoon off after he had dropped me at Stamford Bridge because he supports Queens Park Rangers and couldn't bring himself to watch Chelsea. I couldn't get a cab home, though, until a security man hailed one for me, my sister and brother-in-law. I opened the boot, threw in my bags, shut the door down and ... two Chelsea pensioners jumped in the cab. You can't say anything, can you? Not to Chelsea pensioners. So the cab sped off with me chasing it trying to get my bag back. Eventually I did, then waited twenty minutes for another cab.

On the way home I was listening to the radio and when you're up there, you just want the others to lose. I said to the lads, let's watch the others get beaten and they both won – Arsenal 1–0 at Coventry, Manchester United 4–1 at Everton – which wasn't nice.

The main thing is that we're still top, though, and no one expected that going into the fourth month of the season.

NOVEMBER

Backing England

Tuesday 3 November
Aston Villa 1 Celta Vigo 3

These are strange, almost lonely, weeks for me, not being eligible for European competition. The boss gave me a day off on Sunday, which was good of him. That's the other part of him again. One week he's hammering me in the papers, the next he's ringing up to see how I am, then giving me a day off. He's a good manager, but a young manager and he's still learning the job. I respect him so he doesn't have to play games with me.

I trained with the boys on Monday but had a much harder session on my own today. I did plenty of stretching, some good running and lots of finishing, running through ladders or jumping over little hurdles before having a shot. It was a hard session but good.

At Villa Park, I watched the game up in the stand with Mark Bosnich. 'We'll lose this by three,' I said to him. I don't know where I got that from. I just knew that Celta were a good side just from the fact that they were top of the Spanish League and we have been ripe for hammering lately.

Celta duly came out and ripped us. Stan got his usual European goal but their slick movement was too much for us. I was sad to be missing out on Europe, and it is a great saving grace to a season if you make it through to the quarter-finals in March to keep things going, but I thought it was no bad thing again for us to go out. Our priority has to be the league the way we are going. A good hiding is also no bad thing for concentrating minds within a club.

After the game, the players always go to a lounge upstairs for some pasta. Me, Gareth Southgate and Ian Taylor – the three oldest ones – got talking at a table in the corner. I was so into analysing where we were going wrong at the moment that I hardly noticed three people sit down at a table next to us.

'We're not getting tight enough. We're not working hard enough,' I was saying. I was getting very animated, and effing and blinding, as I can. Then the boss came over. 'All right, boys. Talking about football?' he said. We said hello and he moved on to the next table. 'Hello bruv,' he said, and I should have noticed that his brother was the spitting image of him. It was like the Take-Two Brothers.

'That's you sub on Saturday,' Gareth said to me. Now George Graham had also been at the game, scouting us before our home game against Spurs on Saturday, I had had a word with him in the Directors' lounge earlier, and there had been rumours in the papers that he was still interested in signing me. When Gareth made his substitute remark to me, I looked out of the window and shouted: 'George, come back.'

Wednesday 4 November

I went in to see the boss after training. 'I don't want you to think I was saying things about you behind your back last night,' I said. 'I don't know what your brother heard, but I'm happy to discuss them with you here and now.' He said that all his brother had heard from the next table was swearing. 'That will have been me, then,' I said.

'Can we talk about things anyway?' I asked. He said yes, he was always happy to talk about football. It was just that when he joined the lads up in the lounge, they were usually talking about women so he drifted off somewhere else. When he was a player at Queens Park Rangers, he said, he used to suggest things to Terry Venables and enjoyed it when he would come in a day or two later to find that Terry had laid on a training session relating to what they had discussed.

I listed our current flaws, as I saw them, the main one being that not enough people take responsibility, that too many are frightened of making mistakes. 'It's like watching England at Wembley sometimes,' I said. 'No-one was trying to do anything different. The attitude seemed to be, "You do it wrong, as long as I'm all right."' That had been the problem against Leicester, I said. Personally I'd rather be seen giving the ball away and risking the wrath of the fans, trying to make something happen rather than hiding.

I added that I thought we didn't get wide enough, or get round the back of teams, that none of the midfield players overlapped Gary Charles or Alan Wright. We were getting too easy to defend against, I said, because we played through the middle all the time. We had to have better movement to pull teams out of shape. He listened and agreed with a lot of it. I think he appreciated the input.

Then I asked him what the position was with Dion Dublin. There had been a lot of speculation in the papers about him leaving Coventry and I reckoned he would be a great signing for us, not just because he's a mate of mine. 'Well I want him, and I reckon I might get him,' the boss said. He could be just the lift we need with signs of us slipping.

Thursday 5 November

Spoke to Dion today. He has signed, which is fantastic news for us. We do need a 20-goals-a-season striker. I'm not going to score that many, because my game is as much creating goals as scoring them, and I don't think either Stan or Julian is either. Dion is in for training with us tomorrow for the first time and I agreed to meet him at Junction 4 of the M6 to show him where our training ground is.

Friday 6 November

I couldn't find anywhere to stop at Junction 4, so I rang Dion on the mobile to talk him to Bodymoor Heath. He said he was running out of petrol and didn't think he would make it. 'That'll make a great story on your first day,' I said. 'Star striker on £25,000 a week runs out of petrol.'

He just about made it but in training, I was paired up front with Stan for some shadow play. 'You not playing tomorrow?' I asked. 'Well, he told me I was,' Dion said. Then Dion and Stan were paired. 'I want you playing just behind them in a free role,' the boss said. 'Great,' I thought. This will do for me.

Afterwards, I did an interview with Henry Winter of the *Daily Telegraph*, who is a nice bloke and one you also know won't stitch you up. I also did one for Sky TV mainly about the England squad for the forthcoming friendly against the Czech Republic, which will be announced on Monday.

I stayed the night at The Belfry and what a night it was. After watching a film, *Still Crazy*, I turned off the light to go to sleep at about 10.15pm but a group of Norwegians in the next room were having a drink and keeping me awake. They might as well have been sitting on the end of my bed talking, it was that loud.

At about 11.30 I rang reception to get another room but when I got to that one, there was a party going on outside the window. I went back to the original room and just had to wait for the Norwegians to pack in. If there's one thing worse than a party going on and you're not invited, it's a party where you can't understand a word anyone is saying.

Saturday 7 November
Aston Villa 3 Tottenham Hotspur 2

I haven't slept well but at least I ate well, as usual. They're good at The Belfry. They always bring me pasta and chicken, and I also like a yoghurt and apple pie, at 12 noon even though it's not on the menu. The lads laugh at how much I eat. Then it was off to the game with Steve Watson, who is also staying at The Belfry.

It's funny. I had a bad feeling about the Leicester game but I was certain we would win today. Spurs are still trying to absorb George Graham's more disciplined tactics and philosophy and we are just the sort of team to exploit the fact that they are still getting to know his new defensive strategy. With Dion, all fresh and keen, making his debut, we should have been up for this.

I missed a good early chance but Dion scored two in quick succession to make himself an instant hit. There was no way I could play a free role. Spurs played three in midfield and I had to do a lot of tracking back. I couldn't just stay upfield and leave their midfield to attack ours.

After sitting in the dressing room at half-time, my back seized up as I ran out for the second half. I tried to run it off, and Stan scoring with a great finish two minutes into the second half helped take my mind off it, but I was getting knackered with all this running. Spurs got back into it – first 3–1, then 3–2 – to make it look close but it was a false result. They had three chances and scored with two but the game was already won and lost.

By the time I had showered, I could hardly move and when I got home, I just rested up, missing a bonfire party to which Lorraine had taken the boys.

Sunday 8 November

I couldn't touch my knees when I got up this morning. For a 30-year-old footballer it was a frightening moment. You do start thinking about your career when things like that happen.

There seems to have been a bit of a stir created about the Sky interview which was shown yesterday and all the Sunday papers have followed up. I had simply said to them that sooner rather than later I will have to pack up England, because at my age I'm not sure that I can keep going away for a week and not playing.

Quite often when I'm with England I will phone up

Lorraine at six o'clock in the evening and she's been rushed off her feet, picking the boys up from school, giving them dinner and a bath then putting them to bed. She'll ask me what I've done and I'll say: 'I trained, had a jacuzzi and a sauna, then I watched television for six hours and someone cooked the dinner and I helped myself to that. Now I'm going to lay on the bed and watch television until 12.' And I'm not even playing. People may think it's glamorous but you're often on your own in your hotel room for more than twelve hours a day.

John Gorman phoned on Glenn Hoddle's behalf to see what it was all about and I told him that I wasn't looking to retire yet but that I was looking into the next year or two. Glenn will be the first to know, I said. John seemed OK with it and said he would confer with Glenn.

My family is vital to me and it is hard to explain to some football fans who get the game out of proportion that you would rather be with your family than sitting around with an England squad. Money doesn't come into it, either. The prime example is Brian Laudrup, who has quit Chelsea to go home to Copenhagen. Fifty grand a week he's turning down to be with his family and I understand that. People at Middlesbrough complained about me, but I had to put my wife and kids first.

There's also some stuff in one of the Sundays about Gazza back on the booze. It turns out that some counsellor or other thinks he will go back on the booze. The headline was misleading and disgusting. He phones me regularly and he's still on just the Red Bull so to my mind he's doing well.

He scored a wonder goal from a free-kick for Boro' against Southampton yesterday and really seems to be trying hard. I know he loves his football and it is the best medicine for him. It's so much more of a buzz than booze. There is an England squad named on Friday for the Czech Republic game and it might do him good to be around Tony Adams and me. If Glenn has forgiven him for the summer, that is.

Thursday 12 November

I can't see myself making the England game, even if selected, with the way my back is. On Monday I was trying to stretch off the pain at training but it went into spasm again, then on Wednesday it was fine. Today I was sore and it was pointless me turning up. I hardly took any part in training. It is scary stuff for me at the moment.

I worry about being without football, and what it will do to me, both in the short and long term. One day at a time, though. That philosophy works both in recovery from addiction and in life and I have to keep it in mind all the time.

Friday 13 November

Unlucky for some and today is for Gazza. I feel sorry that he hasn't made the England squad and hope that he can cope with it. I'm grateful to be in there and just pray I get a game this time – if my back holds up.

I think Gazza these days could be the one to play just in front of the defence, like Paul Ince does. He's not going to dig in like Incey but he can dictate the pace of the game from back there. He's not got the lung capacity to run 80 yards down the field so he could hold in there, passing the ball long or short. A prime example was in Rome against Italy when he got on the ball and never wasted it. He sees everything, he'll slow the game down or he can quicken it in a heartbeat. And it would be the best use of such a major talent now he's not going to run at defenders in the free role.

I'm worried about my own free role at Villa. It doesn't look like it will be that. Instead, I'm developing into a central midfield player and the way our 3-5-2 system is, you have to do a lot of work in there. I'm doing more defending than I ever have. I think the boss is just accommodating me at the moment and I'm beginning to wonder where I stand. One minute he says I'll be good up front with Stan, the next I'm in a free role. I can see myself being frozen out.

A problem is that the defence plays so deep, so you have to get up and down plenty. I talk a lot to Kevin MacDonald, the youth coach, and he agrees. I think we get ahead then get so concerned about defending the lead that we drop off too far, instead of doing the things that got us into the lead in the first place. We were well ahead against Coventry and Spurs and nearly let them back in it. The boss had to tell Gareth to make sure the defence played higher up in the field.

Today we trained at Chelsea's training ground at Harlington, near Heathrow, before travelling down to Southampton, who we are playing tomorrow, and we had a laugh on the coach going there.

Stan started asking Mark Draper about his possible move to Tottenham, because there has been speculation in the papers. Drapes said he had a press man on to him last night, asking him to comment, so there must be something to it. All he could tell the journalist, he said, was that he was flattered by Spurs' interest. It turned out that it was Stan who had phoned him posing as a reporter. Stan had nailed him big time and the lads really hammered Drapes.

At the Meon Valley hotel where we stayed, they all remembered me from a very drunken trip with Arsenal there once. It was the time Tony Adams, in his drinking days, headbutted a television and also thumped David Hillier. Everybody was well gone. I think we wrecked the place but it's been done up since. I'm sure I could have paid for the refurbishment with what I was handing over to William Hill at that time. The manager recognised me again but this time he said: 'You're quiet these days.'

I asked for a board to put under my bed for my back but they said they didn't do them. So they went to the store room, brought out four shelves for me and I put them under the mattress, which seemed to do the trick.

Saturday 14 November
Southampton 1 Aston Villa 4

The boss gave a good team talk today. 'I've lost against two teams since I've been here,' he said. 'Barnsley and Bolton. I blame myself for them. I didn't take them seriously enough. But now I'm taking these games seriously and if we all don't, we'll get hammered.' It was a timely message because although Southampton are bottom of the table after an atrocious start to the season, they can be dangerous, especially at the Dell which is narrow and tight and claustrophobic. The bigger clubs hate it.

It made a change from sometimes when we seem to have had a dangerous attitude in my opinion of 'we'll hammer them'. It was good for the lads to hear the boss being less gung-ho because a few of us have been worrying about some of the things he has been saying on the telly which have been winding up the opposition. I think we might have lost a bit of sympathy.

Because we are an all-English team, I think a lot of the
Premiership teams and fans have had a soft spot for us.
The boss going on *Match of the Day* and saying 'Well, if
we don't win it now, it's down to me,' suggested that we
were better than maybe we are though. Players at other
clubs, especially the older players, don't like to see any
hint of arrogance from relative newcomers.

We had a great start today, with Dion Dublin scoring
after a few minutes. I was enjoying it, just holding and
passing, keeping everything going. We were really
comfortable. It was beginning to feel a bit like Arsenal,
that if we went a goal up, it was game over.

Then early in the second half, they got a brilliant
equaliser through Matthew Le Tissier. It was one of his
specials as he turned Gareth Southgate and Gareth Barry
before slotting home a low shot. Not many people do
that. I do like to watch him, though I wouldn't like to be
in his team or support it. It might get frustrating. I don't
see many better players than him for skill but when you
watch him not knuckling down sometimes you do think
'if only'.

The thing about Southampton, though, is that they
only have one match-winner and if he's not doing it,
they're going to struggle. The top dogs have five or six
match-winners. Take Arsenal. If Bergkamp doesn't get
you, Anelka, Overmars, Petit or Vieira will. That's what
we have to be working towards.

We were lucky to get a break soon afterwards when
Ugo Ehiogu glanced the ball on to our crossbar but that's
what happens when you're top of the league. When
you're in a bad run, that goes against you.

Dion then restored the lead and this time instead of
defending too deep, we went for it. Gareth played a great

ball out to Stan on the right, he found me coming through the middle and without breaking stride I hit a sweet low shot that made it 3–1. Seven seconds from one end to the other. Great stuff. Dion then completed his hat-trick – five goals in two games. Amazing. He is such a good lad to have in the dressing room as well as an excellent striker. It completed our best performance since I had been at the club.

John Gregory brought me off just before the end with the game won and asked me: 'Is it alright to bring you off with two minutes to go?' I had to laugh. He knew I had a chance with England and my back wasn't the best. Then at the final whistle he said: 'Come on, let's go,' and headed towards the Villa section of the crowd.

I thought it was just to thank the fans but the boss called for our photo to be taken to mark the club record of 12 unbeaten games at the start of the season that had taken us to the top of the Premiership. I had my doubts. It looked a bit flash, not the sort of thing Manchester United or Arsenal would do. I was at the back, out of picture. 'Have we got the Premiership trophy, the FA Cup or both down there at the front?' I shouted. We'll be in a studio recording the Cup Final song this week, I reckon.

Sunday 15 November

The press have been kind to us this morning, not taking the piss about our team photo. They like John Gregory, which is fair enough as he is good for them, being honest and open, even if he can wind up other teams. I hope this doesn't. All he was saying, I think, is that we're not up there with the Arsenals and Manchester Uniteds yet, so we are just enjoying our little moment. If it does all go pear-shaped, God forbid, at least he's got something to look back on.

The game yesterday answered in the affirmative a couple of questions about us. Could we score enough goals and could we step up a gear when we needed to? We are working our nuts off and I think we deserve it. At the moment we are a very drilled team, well organised, though we do have a few who can turn a game on its head by doing something unusual. But we could get better.

I still think we need another striker. If I was the manager I would break the bank and go out and buy Emile Heskey from Leicester. Dion's doing it, but he needs a consistent partner. I'm not sure Stan or Julian will be that and the boss has me earmarked for a free role rather than up front.

Stan is still waiting to take off. Personally I would play him on the right wing. He looked good there when he drifted wide yesterday. He's better running at people than trying to turn a marker. In fact, he could probably rip any full-back.

But we're all right for now. We've got Mark Draper still to come in, and Alan Thompson, who's finding it a struggle at a big club after his summer move. The boss impresses on us not to give the ball away and Alan takes it too literally, I think. He gets frightened to do anything with it. He just needs to imagine he's back at Bolton and play with more freedom. Luckily, Ian Taylor is doing a great job in midfield for us as the holding player. He's like our Patrick Vieira.

One problem the boss has to address is keeping everybody onside. I keep reading that Gary Charles, Drapes and Jockey are all unhappy because they're in and out of the team but if we are going to stay up there with Manchester United, Arsenal and Chelsea, we are going to need a big squad for after Christmas when injuries and suspensions bite. Nobody likes being on the bench but the lads at the big clubs will tolerate that discontent for a while if they are well paid and think they might be part of something successful.

I do worry when we come up against a team with five or six match-winners in it, I have to say, but the great thing is that we seem to be taking advantage against the lower teams. Manchester United drew against Newcastle; we beat them. Arsenal lost at Sheffield Wednesday; we beat them. They also drew with Southampton and we beat them. Everyone says that you've got to win the big games but if we do lose to Manchester United and Arsenal in a few weeks' time, they're only making up ground they've lost to us.

It was looking good as I took stock of our position. We've got 28 points from 12 games and are four points clear. Only 10 more points and we will be safe from relegation. Another 20 and we'll be thinking about Europe.

I joined up with England at Burnham Beeches at 9pm. I wasn't really sure I should be there, with my back playing up so much, but so many people had told me to give it a go, that I thought I would. There were also hints that I could be in the side with a few people having withdrawn, so I just had to make the effort. A chance of a cap at Wembley is real bait.

After a plate of sandwiches, I went to see the physio Gary Lewin, who examined me. He was a bit shocked, I think, by the state of my back. I've got an inflamed disc, like Tony Adams, who is out at the moment, but Gary says mine is worse than his.

I then had a brief word with Glenn. Unknown to me, he

had been at Southampton yesterday and complimented me on how well we were playing. 'Your movement was brilliant,' he said. 'Great goal.' Perhaps everybody is right and I will get a game this week.

Monday 16 November

Didn't train today but had some healing on my back from Eileen Drewery. She laid me out on a bed and rubbed her hands on my back. There was a real feeling of warmth and it did feel better. It also helped having some treatment on it from Gary Lewin.

In the afternoon I had a phone call from Steve Kutner. John Gregory has been on to him asking if I am wanting a move because he's heard from three different people that Tottenham want me and I want to go. It's rubbish and I phoned the boss to say so. I was angry. 'Do you want to sell me then?' I asked. 'If you're not happy, just sell me instead of winding me and my agent up.' He said he was happy but I thought there was no need for all that.

Tuesday 17 November

Glenn pulled me aside before training to ask me how the back was. I said I would push it in training today. He said he wanted me to play tomorrow so to give it a good run-out. I didn't have to do all the warm-up stuff, just enough to get me loose, and then I gave it a real go in a practice match. I felt good, probably buoyant that I had been picked.

I'm going to be playing just behind Dion and Ian Wright, which should be an interesting threesome. We are all experienced players but we're so enthusiastic about this one. Glenn told me I had nothing to prove, just to go out there and play, but none of us is a first choice and this is a rare chance to impress. Glenn was looking for the front three to show plenty of movement, which had been the problem against Bulgaria the month before. In fact, he had sent videos of it to all the players last month. 'All I want you to do is make those runs like you do for Villa,' he said to me.

Glenn also asked me about retirement. I said I thought that Euro 2000 would probably see the end of me. He said he thought I could go on to the 2002 World Cup because I was so fit. 'You give us another dimension,' he said to me and it was nice to hear it all. To be fair to him, every time I have been playing well, Glenn has picked me, which I think is what the England team is about. So often you see players who aren't playing well being pitched in and those in form left out. It is hard for players to understand, just as it is for the public, even if the coach has a strategy in mind.

After training I had more treatment from Eileen and Gary Lewin and it felt alright. Then I phoned Lorraine to ask her to bring the kids to Wembley tomorrow night. I took them once when Terry Venables was the coach and they also went to the Coca-Coca Cup final to see me play for Middlesbrough last season but playing for England is different. I want them to see their dad live in the flesh in a national team shirt. I don't know, after all, how many more times there will be. If any. Once I took going to Wembley for granted. Now I can't afford to.

Wednesday 18 November
England 2 Czech Republic 0

We did some light training this morning, just some set-pieces, and as I got out of the bus, I could hardly move.

Now my ankle hurt as well. I am developing into a hypochondriac. Gary Lewin warmed it up then told me to have a hot bath. I found it hard to relax in the afternoon because I was so worried about it. My back was in spasm giving me pain, but the ankle was worse as I boarded the bus for Wembley.

We were buzzing, ready to go by the time we got to Wembley, though. I think that sometimes it works out better when Glenn doesn't have so much time with players to work on things. You feel freer and you also don't have too much time on your hands at Burnham Beeches. There is pool, table tennis and snooker and a video club but spending so much time in your room on your own makes you lethargic, in my opinion.

I didn't do the warm-up with the other players, which I am used to at Villa and enjoy, because I was taking another hot bath. Now I was also raring to go. I felt a lot better. I decided that with the kids in the stand, I was just going to go out and enjoy playing, not worry too much about anything, to set them an example of how playing should be enjoyable.

At first I was giving away the ball for fun, though. In the past I might have thought 'shit' and gone into my shell, not wanting the ball. It affects so many players who pull on the England shirt. How you overcome that is what makes you an international player. Now my experience told me to play my way through it, just to dig myself out of it and keep trying. That was probably the most pleasing aspect of the night, that I stayed positive and persistent.

Maybe it's good to start badly. Quite often an England team makes a rod for its own back by starting well, then petering out if a goal doesn't come. This time we just got better. Wrighty and I were making runs and I felt myself getting stronger and stronger. The bloke up against me in central midfield eventually had to stop making forward runs of his own just to sit in front of his defence to counter me.

The highlight for me was a goal. Wrighty sent in a cross, Dion flicked it on and I arrived to steer home a low shot. It was satisfying. No, it was fantastic. What a memory for me and, I hope, my boys. With Darren Anderton also scoring, it was a good win.

A lot of the time you make runs and they don't really get noticed or mentioned but tonight they did. Dion also did well. It does make a difference playing with someone from your own club team because I knew what he was going to do. Others might think, 'I'm not going to make the run because he won't see me.' I found myself getting in a lot of space and the lads were finding me as well.

Really, I was just trying to open things up for others even if I didn't get the ball. Often with England, if you blew a whistle and stopped the game, everybody would be in the same positions as when they started but tonight we were pulling the Czechs out of shape. It was one of the best England performances for a long time.

I was also pleased Robbie Fowler got on because I think he is a great player and he's been injured for a long time. This might be the kick-start to his season he needs. I was more pleased for me, to be honest, though. It's nights like this that you're in the game for.

Thursday 19 November

I went over to Sopwell House at St Albans to see the Arsenal physio Gary Lewin for some treatment on my back and a jacuzzi. Arsène Wenger and the Arsenal boys were all very complimentary about last night.

The back is sore but I suppose I'm ignoring it because of the satisfaction of last night. In the last three games, I think I have covered more ground than for years. I may be in a free role but I've had a lot of tracking back to do as well as making a lot of 30 and 40-yard runs forward.

Sometimes you don't think you're going to get through the game but then your second wind kicks in. My stamina and energy levels are high these days, but I still don't think I should be feeling this tired. The satisfaction following three of my best games for a long while, though, should sustain me for a little while yet.

Friday 20 November

The spirit is willing, but the flesh was feeling weak today. The back is really sore and I'm not sure how long I can keep putting my body through this. I hope I can give it another go at home to Liverpool tomorrow, wearing the back brace that I first used at Southampton last week.

Saturday 21 November
Aston Villa 2 Liverpool 4

It was a real shock today. Liverpool haven't been playing well and we didn't expect this. The funny thing is, though, I thought we played quite well and didn't really deserve it.

We were two down in six minutes, the team as stiff as my back felt. I am having to have a hot bath before every game now instead of warming up and you know you are struggling when that happens. We started off really poorly, though they were passing it really well. The first

157

goal was my fault. I should have had Paul Ince at a corner but I let him go. Then they broke away and scored again.

It was end-to-end stuff and we could have been back in it before half-time. I really thought we could still win it from here and, messing about, I said to Incey: 'I'll bet you five grand we win this.' He wasn't having it. 'No. If you score one, you'll go on to win,' he said with a smile.

It was knockabout stuff in the second half. Dion got us a goal back but we couldn't hold it at 1–2 for long enough and the same happened when Dion made it 2–3. At 2–4, he had a chance of a hat-trick from the penalty spot, his second in three games since coming, but he missed and was stuck at a mere seven goals in three games.

By that time, Stan had been sent off and he deserved to go, though not for the offence that did prompt the red card. First he went over the top to Steve Harkness and could have broken his leg. Then when Michael Owen did him back, he pushed the lad. What did everyone expect Stan to do after a two-footed tackle? Get up and shake his hand? You couldn't blame him for his reaction, because it was a nasty challenge, but then he shouldn't have done what he did to Harkness in the first half. At half time, the gaffer told him not to lose his head but the damage had been done.

Apparently it all went back to some racial abuse Stan had taken when he was at Liverpool but it was strange that he had never mentioned anything at the training ground to us all week. Usually, a player says something to his team-mates but not Stan. That's him all over, bottling things up.

It was a strange defeat. Everyone was saying that our bubble had burst and that we had lost to a really good team. I couldn't see it. Liverpool did tear us apart at the back, as we have been ripe for these last few weeks, but they were shocking in defence and I thought we deserved at least a point. I thought the result was just covering over their own cracks and I couldn't see any way they were going to have a successful season. I think they were just relieved to be playing away from Anfield, where the fans have been giving them stick.

The test for us now will be how everybody at the club reacts to our first Premiership defeat of the season.

Tuesday 24 November

I have rested the back for two days but three games last week have taken their toll. I travelled up for training today but couldn't go through it so I just did some pedalling on the exercise bike to keep me ticking over. An hour and half each way in the car has done me no good, though.

Wednesday 25 November

Again I don't think I should be training but the boss has asked me to give it a go. I prefer to train rather than sitting around so I did and it wasn't too bad. He's given me a day off tomorrow because they are only playing indoor cricket, which the boss likes to do once a week just to add variety and fun to the training.

Friday 27 November

After a morning's training, which I took very gently, we made the short journey to our hotel near Nottingham. The bed is atrocious. It is a single bed so there is no room to move and they do not have any bed boards. Sleep is vital to me these days – a far cry from my 'Wild Thing' days when I used to have the old bravado attitude that I would sleep when I was dead – and it's depressing lying awake worrying about my back seeing me through the game tomorrow.

Saturday 28 November
Nottingham Forest 2 Aston Villa 2

We went for a walk first thing and it felt like I was dragging my legs. Once at the City Ground, I missed the warm-up again to have a hot bath. Doug Ellis came in the dressing room for his usual goodwill visit to the team and asked me when I was moving up to the Birmingham area. That was the last thing I needed at this time. He does pick his moments. 'I can't sort that out right now, can I?' I said.

The match was embarrassing for me. Pathetic. I could hardly move as we went 2–0 down by half-time and it could have been worse. At the break I came in and said that I couldn't play on. Everyone could see it. Actually, it probably did us a favour. We reorganised for the second half, with Alan Thompson replacing me and Stan Collymore coming on for Gareth Barry to make it three up front and four at the back.

I watched from the dug-out and saw Jockey grab us a point with two goals. We might even have gone on to win it, with Dion having a late chance but you can't have a go at him because his goals have got us here in the first place.

Afterwards I said to Jim Walker that I wasn't going to train or play again until I had seen a specialist to get the trouble sorted out. I had put it off for too long now, thinking I was doing the team a favour. I'm in no mood to jeopardise what is left of my career and I feel angry that I could have been doing that lately.

Sunday 29 November

I was watching the Liverpool vs Blackburn game on Sky and Andy Gray was going through the film of our game. He seemed to think that Villa might be a better side without Paul Merson. The boss doesn't seem to think so. His quotes in the Sunday papers are about our 3-5-2 system being good enough to have hammered Southampton and get us 3–0 up against Tottenham. 'It's just that Merse is not fully fit,' he said.

It's nice of him but I think he could have the best of both. I do think we look better with 4-3-3, because four should be enough at the back, and the game is all about creating and scoring goals. Stan played wide on the right again and I thought he looked a good winger. He's facing the goal, which is his strength, rather than playing with his back to it. He's two-footed, he can get at people and he can cross in a great ball.

Despite what Andy Gray says, I think I should be part of all that, as one of the front three, but it could be with this back that I may not be again for a while.

DECEMBER

Unhappy Christmas

Tuesday 1 December

I went into training yesterday to see the boss and Jim Walker and it was agreed I would see a specialist so today I went to a hospital in Birmingham for an MRI scan on my back. I hate it, being put through one of those long tubes on a trolley, and I had a real panic attack. To get me through it, they even put a blindfold on me like some horse in the starting stalls.

It goes back to a bad experience I had when I was an apprentice at Arsenal. We were all sent on some pot-holing course in Wales that was supposed to be character-building and I freaked when we got into this narrow space. I was kicking and screaming, desperate to get out but I was trapped in the middle of everyone and it was a scary time until I was back in the open air. Ever since then I have hated enclosed spaces.

From the hospital I went to the house of one of the club doctors. He put my X-rays up and said that I had one inflamed disc and one dehydrated. 'An epidural and rest will clear it up,' he said, but then seemed to reconsider when Jim Walker looked at him. 'I think you can play on for the moment, though.'

I was furious at hearing this. 'I'm in pain and I can't,' I said. 'That's why I'm here.' He said that he thought that now I knew what the trouble was, my mind might be eased and therefore I would feel able to play on. I was still angry. 'I'm not carrying on just to end up in a wheelchair,' I said.

Then I went to see a specialist in something called the McKenzie Back Exercises in Sutton Coldfield, a bloke called Andrew. He had a bed that bent you up like in a *Carry On* film and could do 150 different movements. He was very good and I left feeling better.

Thursday 3 December

Andrew came to the training ground, examined me and pronounced me fit to train. I wasn't so sure because he hadn't worked with that many footballers but I gave it a go. I went out with Jim Walker and did a warm-up, then some twisting and turning followed by some shooting with the goalkeepers. It felt all right.

Perhaps I will try to give it a go on Saturday. It is Manchester United at Villa Park after all, and I feel I want to be part of the next ten days if at all possible. After United, we've got Chelsea at Stamford Bridge next Wednesday, then Arsenal at home the following Sunday. It will be a crucial phase of our season because these three teams will definitely all be up there next May.

Friday 4 December

The back felt fine when I reported for training so I told the boss that I thought I would be fit for tomorrow. 'Are you?' he said, surprised. He had already told Alan Thompson that he was playing in my place and I didn't want to upset that. Alan's just got back into the side and he's a lovely lad. He just needs more self-belief. It's a real shame, though. I was buzzing in training and you hate to miss a game against Manchester United.

Saturday 5 December
Aston Villa 1 Manchester United 1

Not playing turned out to be the right decision. I could hardly move again this morning and I wouldn't have been able to play. It is one thing just kicking a ball around, different altogether trying to run, turn and jump.

I took Charlie, Ben and Sam up to Villa Park. Ben particularly loves United. Their team sheet was unbelievable. They had four internationals on the bench, compared to our four kids who hadn't even started a Premiership game between them this season. Up in the lounge with me they had Solskjaer and Johnsen who didn't even need to get their suits off.

We did all right, though United were playing well within themselves. It was cagey stuff with neither side wanting to lose the game and both of us happy to take a point. Paul Scholes gave them a lead just after half-time but we were well worth the draw that Julian Joachim's goal gave us soon after. I think Dwight Yorke was just pleased to get the game over on his return to Villa Park. His frustration showed with a booking. '*What a waste of money*' our fans sang at him but I think he'll prove anything but that.

Personally, I thought it was a good result for us. We

looked tighter and more solid than we have done at times recently, though strangely I thought we played better against Liverpool, certainly going forward. People seem to be taking us a bit more seriously now, though, as we have matched United in our first game against one of the top dogs.

Tuesday 8 December

Travelled over to Nottingham with Jim Walker to see a back specialist, a Dr Webb, one of the top men in his field. He gave me a bone scan before referring me to a physio at the hospital. She has worked with Nottingham Forest's players, including my old Arsenal team-mate Kevin Campbell, who is now playing in Turkey.

She examined me and told me that one of the discs had dehydrated again, which was causing the stiffness. I asked her how long it would be before I'd be playing again. 'Four to six weeks,' she said. This was getting alarming and I was starting to get worried. That turned to anger after I had been back in to see the specialist.

He wanted me to have another MRI scan but I was reluctant after my experience of the previous week. He then offered me some kind of tranquilliser to get through it. 'Do you know I'm an addict?' I said. 'I can't take tranquillisers.' He apologised to me. He asked me to wait outside with Jim while he spoke to the hospital physio.

When I went back in, the physio said that they had decided against the MRI scan and that they were going to wait ten days to see how the back settled down. He said that I would not make the Arsenal game on Sunday but that I had a chance for Charlton Athletic on Monday week.

Now I lost it. I was annoyed that three different people

were giving me three different answers. A club doctor last week was telling me that I could play on, another was saying four to six weeks and the third prognosis was now ten days. 'Don't try and impress me. Don't try and get me back playing football quickly,' I said. 'Just treat me like any other person. I don't want to keep breaking down. What is the best thing?'

'Backs are dodgy things,' he said. 'I would like to give you an epidural, but I don't like doing that on a first consultation. Just stretch and rest, come back in a fortnight and we'll see what course of action to take then.' I'll go along with it for now, but I am not happy about the advice I am getting.

Wednesday 9 December
Chelsea 2 Aston Villa 1

I wanted to go to Chelsea for our re-arranged game, and John Gregory wanted me to come along because he does like my input, but Jim Walker warned me that the cold, and sitting up in the stands, might not be good for my back so I stayed at home.

Instead, I watched Manchester United play Bayern Munich in the Champions' League on the television with the volume down – the 1–1 draw being predictable with that result suiting both of them to reach the quarter-finals – and listened to our game on the radio.

Chelsea may have deserved to win on the number of chances created, hitting the post and the bar, but it was still a sickener losing to a goal by Tore Andre Flo four minutes into added time. I felt gutted. We had done well to get back in it with a goal by Lee Hendrie 90 seconds after Zola's free-kick, as well.

These are the sort of results you look back on at the end of the season as being significant. I felt so sick that I was in bed by 10pm.

Thursday 10 December

Travelled up for treatment to be told by Jim Walker that there was no need for me to come in today, which annoyed me. All I did was ten press-up exercises designed to strengthen the back then went home.

Friday 11 December

Up again to Bodymoor Heath for my programme of stretching. That's all I can do really, stretch, stretch and stretch. Usually Jim Walker oversees me but if he and his staff are busy, I can do it on my own. Mostly I keep myself to myself because when you are an injured player, you don't really feel you belong and don't have much to contribute.

It can get lonely. And depressing. Sometimes I travel all the way up and back, a three-hour round trip, for just twenty minutes on the exercise bike and think to myself, 'Is this my day?' At times like that, I can get more deeply into myself, and sorry for myself. I'm thinking today, 'What have I done this week?' and can't come up with much of an answer.

Jim gave me Saturday off and said he would see me on Sunday at the Arsenal game.

Saturday 12 December

Lorraine went to the boys' school to help with the Christmas fête so I went round to my mum and dad's. There I watched Sky's *Soccer Saturday* programme and could not believe the results coming in. Both Manchester United and Chelsea had a chance to go clear of us at the top and both blew it.

United were two up in twenty minutes at Tottenham thanks to Ole Gunnar Solskjaer – and what a player he is, coming in now and then so that Yorke or Andy Cole can take a rest – but then they conceded two late goals to Sol Campbell. Chelsea also drew 2–2 and conceded one in the last minute, to Dean Sturridge at Derby. United went above us only on goal difference when it looked as if they would be two points clear, while Chelsea are a point behind us.

A point at home to Arsenal tomorrow will now put us back on top. I reckon today was a big psychological day for us. When you get breaks like that, you have to be thinking in terms of the championship.

Sunday 13 December
Aston Villa 3 Arsenal 2

For me, it's always sad to miss games against Arsenal. I know them so well and want to do well against them, show them what they let go. I thought I did with Middlesbrough when we played them in an FA Cup tie the previous January and I scored in a 2–1 defeat. This time I had to watch the game from the restaurant with a friend and my brother-in-law, along with Mark Bosnich.

On the Friday before the game, I had been asked by the press about the match and I said that I thought it was a must-win game if we were to stay in contention. Big teams win big games and this was a big game. We had been on a wobbly run and defeat would mean that we had only two points from five games.

We would not have been seen as championship contenders – possibly by ourselves, which would have been the worst thing, having failed to record a win against all the top teams as soon as the going got tough. We would also be playing catch-up against the big clubs, as our next game is not until tomorrow week. Then we kick-off after everyone else on Boxing Day. That constant demand to win just to stay in touch can drain you mentally.

Arsenal were without Tony Adams, who's got a similar back injury to me, though they have got Dennis Bergkamp back now after he missed some of their Champions' League games. He and they looked as if they were determined to make up for a bad first half of the season with their first-half performance. Dennis scored two brilliant goals and I thought it was game over. It usually is with Arsenal in that position. In fact, when they're 1–0 up, let alone 2–0. Then something bizarre happened at half-time which changed everything.

Unknown to the players, there was a parachute display going on and one poor lad hit the roof of a stand trying to land on the pitch, breaking a leg, as one of several serious injuries, in the process. At this point, the boss was going to take off Julian Joachim and put on Stan Collymore but as half-time wore on, towards the half-an-hour mark, he decided to wait to see if he needed to bring on a defender because of an injury to Gareth Southgate. Gareth had been involved in a clash of heads and his eye was swelling up. They held off and left things as they were for a while, to see how the second half developed.

Gareth seemed all right when the game did get under way again and instead the boss decided to give Gareth

Barry a rest and go 4-3-3 again, with Julian, Stan and Dion Dublin up front. It was a good move in my book. The system hadn't been working and the only way we looked dangerous was with Julian's pace.

Amazingly, goals by Jockey and Dion got us back to 2–2 and I was delighted to be escaping with a point – despite what one punter up in the restaurant seemed to think as he was watching my reaction to each goal thinking I might be cheering for Arsenal. I said to my mate John and brother-in-law Steve that I would meet them at the car five minutes before the final whistle.

In the event, I ran into them in a lounge watching it on television on the way out to the car park and we were staggered to see Dion's winner go in. That just doesn't happen against Arsenal. They had conceded only seven goals in 15 games. What a bonus. In the first half, it looked to me as if Arsenal would be retaining their title. Now Chelsea and Manchester United meet on Wednesday and we're the ones in pole position.

Monday 14 December

The lads were off today but I went in just to do my exercises. The papers are saying we are now serious Championship contenders so it must be right. That was a big win yesterday because we have now come through a spell against Chelsea, Manchester United and Arsenal with four points, which is not a bad return when it could have been none as we were trailing both United and Arsenal.

Knowing that we can come back from behind should really help us a lot. It is one thing to do it against Nottingham Forest, another against that lot. Some of the lads are saying that Arsenal have gone but I can't see it on the strength of one result and the odd disappointing result in the Champions' League. If we finish above them, we could well be champions. They'll get strong again after Christmas. All they are doing now, like all the big teams, is hanging in there ready for their final push.

The match also confirmed to me that we look better in a 4-3-3 system. I think Gareth Barry deserves a rest now. The lad will be an excellent player, who will play for England I'm sure, as he is probably the best passing centre half I've ever seen. But now is the right time to give him a break so that he's ready for the latter stages of the season. Come February, March and April, every game assumes a huge importance while at the moment, some teams treat them as run of the mill. In the spring, everyone is fighting for something – to stay up, to win a title, to get into Europe. It's a lot to ask a 17-year-old to go through that experience when he's jaded.

I also spoke to Steve Bould today about yesterday's match. He wasn't happy that Lee Hendrie, who can be a confident lad, was going round winding up the Arsenal boys and not showing them enough respect. He was saying '3–2' in their faces and was even taunting Dennis Bergkamp. The only time he should talk to Dennis is if he wants to swap shirts. At one point he even told them to give the ball to Martin Keown so that he could kick it into the stand. He even said 'You won't win it' to Bouldy.

Now you don't want to feel inferior to all these big players and you like to see a bit of arrogance in young players. But that should be an inner strength. Outwardly, doing what Lee did was stupid. We play Arsenal in our last game of the season and we might need to win there to take the title and they might be out of it. They would still be up for the game, though, wanting to teach Lee a lesson. We might also need them to do us a favour by beating someone at some point so you don't want to go upsetting them.

Tuesday 15 December

Went in for more exercises and with Jim not there, one of the other physios, Terry Stams, sent me running on some Astroturf, which was not good for my back. Some days now I'm getting angry and resentful about being out for so long and I get fed up with other people. And myself, come to think of it.

The boys are playing a testimonial at Hereford tonight and John Gregory has sent a full squad down there. He's good like that, the boss. Mind you, he's not going. He's been away in France. Just as well, the lads are having their Christmas party tomorrow night. When the cat's away…

Wednesday 16 December

These parties always start off civilised, then something kicks off due to someone having had a few too many. Then, a few resentments come to the surface, of the sort you are always going to get inside a football club where young people with a lot of energy are working closely in such a volatile environment. So it was with the players' Christmas night out. Mind you, I enjoyed it.

It started off fine with a meal at a restaurant owned by the former Villa goalkeeper Nigel Spink and then we went on to a club, where there was a power cut and they brought out candles. It amused me that the lads had to drink wine because the lager was off due to the electric pumps being out. We went to another club where I watched United and Chelsea draw 1–1, Chelsea hammering them in the second half. It was a good result for us. Not that many of the boys noticed.

Stan Collymore and Mark Draper were winding each other up about something or other. At first it was just handbags stuff, then there was some pushing and shoving and you could see that something might develop. I've seen it hundreds of times before when someone pushes someone accidentally and it all goes off. With Stan and Drapes, the pride things got in the way, where neither of them was going to back down and pretty soon they were wrestling and I found I was the one pulling them apart.

These days it usually ends up with me calming the lads down. Some of them must think 'you prick' because I know I did about five years ago whenever someone would try to calm me down. 'Get a life' I would say to whoever tried. When you're the one not drinking, though, you get more observant and sensitive to the mood of the place. I could see that some people in the nightclub were shaking their heads at Stan and Drapes. There was a time when I would never really have cared but I did now.

Alan Thompson always makes me laugh. The drink gets to him very quickly and he goes daft. We played 'capitals of the world' at one point and he said Milan for Italy. We pointed out that Rome was the capital of Italy but it didn't stop him saying Milan again five minutes later. He's good though, Thommo. He knows when he's had enough and he just gets up and goes home.

Among the surprising ones who had had a bit too much was Ugo Ehiogu and he started waving a drink under my nose. It upset me, all the more coming from Ugo who's a sensitive lad. I knew it was bye-bye time.

Thursday 17 December

I had a party today of a very different sort and it was me who ended up fractious this time.

It was Charlie's eighth birthday and we shared a party at Wembley Stadium with a classmate of his. Me, the other lad's parents, plus my dad and a friend, took virtually his whole class – 35 kids – for that tour of the stadium where they go in the dressing rooms, have a look at the big bath and get pictured holding up a replica of the Cup in the Royal Box. Never again. It was a nightmare. They virtually wrecked Wembley. I expected better behaviour from kids at a private school. But then there were only a few girls in the group so there was no civilising influence, I suppose.

We had a do up in a lounge near the Banqueting Hall that becomes the players' bar on match nights. The kids were throwing those big foam fingers off the balcony, hitting the chandeliers, and nearly poking each other's eyes out with sticks. One kid lost a tooth. The next time it will just be a few people and that will be it.

Saturday 19 December

I was planning to go in today and tomorrow, work really hard then see how the back responded on Monday before making a decision as to whether it needed an epidural or not. I had developed a chest infection, though, and was not well enough to travel to Birmingham.

So I watched all the results coming on television and for the first time since I joined Villa, I watched us slip off the top, with Chelsea beating Tottenham 2–0 and United beating Nottingham Forest 3–0. We can go back there by winning at Charlton on Monday but you never know what the psychological toll of today will be.

Sunday 20 December

I was sick all of Saturday night and couldn't even get out of bed today. My mum and dad came over to play with the boys and I could hear them having games downstairs. Lorraine couldn't hear me when I called down for some help. At one point I was going to phone a friend on the cordless phone so that he could phone the house and give Lorraine the message to come upstairs to bring me something up.

I did get up in the afternoon to watch Arsenal beat Leeds 3–1, which promptly sent me back to bed. They are getting stronger and stronger.

Monday 21 December
Charlton Athletic 0 Aston Villa 1

I was still feeling rough, but a little better. Although I have lost eight pounds over the last three days, I knew I had to struggle up to Nottingham for the epidural. I had decided that I wanted this sorted out soon as possible. The hospital said that I could have it even if I was ill.

When I got into the consulting room at the hospital, Dr Webb asked me to take off my shirt and lie on the bed. The woman physio was there too. Then when Dr Webb asked me if I was all right, I just about managed to say 'yes' when I suddenly felt this needle enter my back at the base of my spine. It was like a scene out of

Tom and Jerry. I nearly hit the ceiling. Tony Adams had a similar injection around this time and he told me he had a general anaesthetic but it wasn't offered to me.

I was gripping the side of the bed as I felt the fluid from the syringe enter my back. It was excruciating and I kept asking, 'Is all the stuff in yet?' Finally he said yes and I felt the syringe withdrawn. I felt really sore. I also felt grateful that he had caught me by surprise and got it over with quickly. He almost seemed to throw it in me, in fact. The fluid is apparently a cocktail of cortisone, anti-inflammatory and steroids. It had everything in it. I'm surprised they didn't put a slice of lemon in it with a cherry on the top.

At the end he told me to take a week's rest, then come and see him again. At first I thought, 'Great, I've got Christmas with the kids' but then I thought how strange it will be, not playing football over the holiday period. It's only happened to me once before in 12 years. I always love playing on Boxing Day and I wondered how I was going to cope this year.

John drove me back home and, with the soreness and the back stiffening up, I had to lie on the sofa to watch our game at the Valley on television. Charlton gifted us an early own goal and after that it was a question of clinging on. Not a great game but three more points to put us back on top for Christmas.

People keep saying Charlton are playing well but just not getting the results. To me, that's dangerous. If you are playing well and still not winning, then it's worrying. Once or twice you can write it off as bad luck. Not eight or nine times.

Thursday 24 December

At home now laid up for three days without having been to Birmingham, even though my chest infection has cleared up. It is a strange feeling just resting. You feel guilty, still earning your money while lots of people are out there getting far less than you for breaking their backs. Still, I have to do what I am told and get well, otherwise I am cheating the thousands of people who come to watch and indirectly pay my wages.

In a way, I'm lucky being injured now. Normally, it is my nightmare, the time when a professional footballer can get really negative about being deprived of his livelihood. For an addict it is doubly bad. Even for those who aren't, I'm sure more footballers drink or gamble when they're injured.

But at least I've got Christmas to keep me occupied. In the bad old days, I never really did drink or gamble in the run-up to the big day. It was the time when all the amateurs came out for their once-a-year binge and I never wanted to be around all that. I lived for Boxing Day, when after a game in the morning, I could let myself go in the afternoon with 1,000 race meetings to choose from and I deserved a drink. Looking forward to that would keep me off it for a few days.

Anyway, at the moment there's not time to mope around with three boys to sort out. It's also not like April or May at the club where you are really needed. We've got a fortunate FA Cup draw, at home to Hull City, so that buys me another week too. The boss has been good and says he won't rush me back but luckily we're not losing. It might be a different story if we were. There might be pressure then to get back playing.

John Gregory is also trying to be nice by saying to the

papers that he'll do his best to keep me involved and that he'll still ask me for my input to the team, but to be honest, watching them train and getting ready to play a game is a bit like sitting in a pub watching people drink. I'd rather just be away on my own and get fit again with my own programme.

Lorraine and me have decided that it is better to stay down in St Albans than move up. If the club put pressure on me, I will rent a flat for me but the boys are happy in their school and Lorraine is happy in our present home. It makes sense to me. If your family are happy and you are happy, then your football's going to be better, isn't it? The club should understand that. If I do move up, I'm not going to do much more than I do now, which is sit indoors a lot of the time. It's not like I go out all the time. Anyway, quite a few of the others live a fair way away.

Friday 25 December

I was more excited than the kids this morning, I think. I was up before them anyway. Eventually Charlie came in at about 7am and woke the other two boys and they all opened their presents downstairs. We had a lovely traditional Christmas lunch and Lorraine's mum and dad came over but I felt really restless afterwards.

I was thinking that I ought to be getting up and joining the lads, as you usually do on a Christmas afternoon, closeting yourself in a hotel before the Boxing Day games. I've only ever had this once before in 12 years and I don't remember it being like this. That time between 3pm and 6pm feels dead. It's like the whole population has been given a sleeping pill with their dinner. I felt strangely gloomy.

Saturday 26 December
Blackburn Rovers 2 Aston Villa 1

I had weird echoes of those Boxing Days when I would finish my game at lunchtime, join up with my family and look at all the other results around the country. Of those Boxing Days when I would gamble. It just shows how powerful this illness of addiction is and how it lies in wait for you. Because today I gambled again.

I can give a million excuses. Lorraine took the boys to see *Dr Dolittle* and I stayed at home, with just her dad Stan for company. I was bored, depressed about my injury. I had had a row with Lorraine. The fact is, I am a gambling addict and quite simply, I wanted to gamble again. My mind was fixed on it. I almost planned it in exactly the way I used to.

I rang a friend and got him to put a bet on for me. One bet; that's a joke. One was never enough so I had three different £500 accumulators going on the afternoon's football. I was watching the scores come up on the teletext and going out of the living room to the kitchen to phone my friend every five minutes, just to discuss what was going on. I don't know what Lorraine's dad was thinking. At the time, I thought this was normal.

No longer was I interested in games because of the bearing they had on Villa. Rather, whether they affected my accumulator. It seemed Arsenal had a million shots against West Ham although they only won 1–0. With Chelsea also winning 2–0 at Southampton and Manchester United beating Nottingham Forest 3–0, we were back to playing catch-up that night against Blackburn.

I couldn't watch our game at Ewood Park, although I kept in touch with the details. I was amazed when we got back into the game with a goal by Ricky Scimeca after Michael Oakes was sent off in what was a questionable decision of handball outside the box and I was thinking that a point would take us back to the top. Then came a final minute goal against us.

People talked about Michael getting sent off as costly but personally, in a strange way, I don't think we would have got back into it if he hadn't got the red card. With ten men we just went for it, having not looked like scoring. Michael didn't really deserve to go but then it's swings and roundabouts. The week before we got an own goal at Charlton and they had a penalty turned down.

Meanwhile, I was just flicking through the Internet on the computer to keep in touch with the American football play-offs that were taking place across the Atlantic. Their gambling potential interested me. With my three accumulators going down, I needed to get some money back.

Sunday 27 December

It's becoming a blur again, as it does when I bet. I know I was going into my shell around the family. I know I only came out of it to gamble and to get ratty with them.

I rang my friend again to get a bet on an American football game. Then I went to watch the game on the Internet. No, not live pictures of it but the NFL website, which has a diagram of the field and marks where the ball is on it after each play. How sad is that, cursing when you read the details of the play and watch a diagram intently? I can't remember how much the bet was or even who it was on. I can remember that it lost.

Monday 28 December
Aston Villa 2 Sheffield Wednesday 1

I told Lorraine I was going up to Villa Park to watch the game. When I left the house I rang our physio Jim Walker to say my back was playing me up and I wouldn't be coming to the match. I was off the leash again. So I went round my mum and dad's and sat in front of the television all afternoon following the football scores on teletext and ringing a friend to get bets on for me.

I can't remember details again. That's how it is when I bet. I just lose all touch with reality and get sucked into this world of worrying just about whether I'm going to win or not. It's not even like at this stage I was putting a lot of money on.

Parts of the game at Villa penetrated my gambling frame of mind. I know Sheffield Wednesday had someone sent off. I know that Wednesday equalised Gareth Southgate's goal with an overhead kick by Benito Carbone within a minute. I know Ugo Ehiogu grabbed a winner and we were back on top, though Chelsea and Manchester United meet tomorrow at Stamford Bridge. Otherwise, rather than winners, I was following losers elsewhere and getting fed up with it.

Tuesday 29 December

The gambling is over for the moment. It has to be. It was beginning to frighten me again, as I was getting sucked back into the old ways. I hope it was just a temporary relapse rather than anything serious long-term. Besides, my mate had reached his credit limit of £10,000 on his betting account. He puts the bets on for me because if it was known it was me it would soon get out. I then pay him back.

I went in to training, to do some work on the weights and the bike, for the first time in a while and called in at the coaches' room to see John Gregory and Steve Harrison. They asked me how I was and I congratulated them on the win last night. They seemed more chuffed that their team had just won at indoor cricket by 12 runs. They asked me what I thought for the Chelsea v Manchester United game tonight. I took Chelsea to win and the boss reckoned a draw would be a good result for us. I thought Chelsea winning would be better. Man United will be the bigger problem, come season's end.

Mind you, watching the game, the longer it went on, the more I wanted a draw. In the end, 0–0 was just about a fair result, despite the fact that Chelsea missed several chances in the first half. It wasn't a great match. It's always the same when you're looking forward to a big game. Usually you feel let down.

The way I look at it now is that if we draw away at Middlesbrough and beat Everton at home in our next two games we are at least joint top and another two games have gone. The longer you stay in it, the more chance you've got. It sounds simple, but it's far from easy.

I look at the Championship like the Grand National. On the first circuit round Aintree, all you want to do is stay on the horse. Then as long as you are there with ten fences to go, you never know who's going to fall when they get tired. We have to make sure we're not fallers.

Wednesday 30 December

I thought I might feel worse, having had a few days of gambling but I'm not feeling as guilty and ashamed as I have done in the past. I don't know why. Probably because the sums weren't too big and I got out of it quickly. Relief.

More weights and cycling today while the lads played cricket, the game undoubtedly strengthened by the inclusion of my driver John to make up the numbers. He ended up sweating while everyone else was cold. Steve Harrison said he must have been fielding near a radiator because he did nothing else. Everyone was in a blinding mood, including the boss, I thought.

Then Gareth Southgate came to me cursing because the boss had given them the day off tomorrow but wanted them all then to stay together in a hotel tomorrow night. New Year's Eve in a hotel. I couldn't stop laughing. Said I'd cheer them all up by ringing at midnight.

I did feel for them. I suppose it's a question of trust. If it had been Manchester United we were playing in the FA Cup on Saturday I could understand, it but it was Hull City and they're bottom of the Third Division. Still, John Gregory likes to be professional so there's no arguing with him. That's the job.

Thursday 31 December

The lads can't point the finger at me because I was training this morning – the only one of the first-team staff in, apart from Jim Walker the physio – and I was in bed by 11.30pm.

Lorraine had gone round to a friend's, there was a load

of rubbish on the television, so I thought I would turn in. I never was one for hell-raising on New Year's Eve. Like Christmas, it was another night for the part-time drinker. We professional boozers preferred less contrived nights.

Neither am I one for looking back on New Year's Eve, really. I can't even remember where I was with Middlesbrough this time last year. I suppose it is to do with trying to live in the day rather than the past, though recently I have been having trouble with that basic concept of recovery from addiction. Footballers also tend to think in seasons rather than years.

But on a quick stock-take, it has been an amazing year. I got promoted with Middlesbrough, played in a League Cup final for them at Wembley, played in a World Cup and scored a penalty against Argentina, also scored for England at Wembley, then moved to Aston Villa and ended up top of the Premiership. Professionally, it was almost as good as it gets.

In fact, if I was 34 this season and we won the Premiership, I think I would retire at the end of this season. There's nowhere left to go but down and I don't want to end up playing in the lower divisions when I know I'm not the player I was. I wouldn't mind managing, though. I support Chelsea and love Arsenal but I have soft spots for Brentford, where I was once on loan, and Queens Park Rangers, and would love to start there.

This year I also relapsed with both gambling and drinking and managed to keep it all out of the public gaze. I can't expect to do that again. Not that I want or expect it to happen again in the future. Hang on, what is it they say about one day at a time?

1999

JANUARY

New York Blues

Friday 1 January

I was in the weights room at Bodymoor Heath, where I seem to have lived over the past week or two, when the boys arrived back from their overnighter at a hotel. The boss said 'Happy New Year' to me but Dion Dublin, just behind him, was not so cheerful.

'He's resting me,' Dion said when I asked him what was wrong. He has spent New Year's Eve in a hotel and he's not even going to play against Hull tomorrow. I was creasing up with laughter, as was Ian Taylor, who was alongside me in the weights room as he is also injured. Ian was lucky. He had a party at home last night.

For the next twenty minutes, I was really winding Dion up. 'And I really fancied you for a hat-trick,' I said. 'That would have taken you clear for the Golden Boot, wouldn't it, Dion?' Eventually he cracked. 'Just shut it,' he shouted.

Saturday 2 January
Aston Villa 3 Hull City 0

I didn't go up for the game but followed the news of it all afternoon on Sky Soccer Saturday. It seemed a comfortable enough win and Stan's two goals, with Julian scoring the other, should give him a big lift.

We had some friends round in the evening and played *Men are from Mars, Women are from Venus*, which is now a boardgame based on the best-selling book all about relationships and the battle of the sexes. Whenever either Lorraine or me got a question that was a bit sensitive, though, we passed. I wonder if she senses something?

Because tonight I have had a bet on an American football match involving the Dallas Cowboys. Mostly I was wandering between the dining room and the television room to check on the game, making excuses to escape all the time, like going to get some drinks or offering to do the washing up. The bet went down.

Sunday 3 January

Watched the FA Cup games all day. Liverpool won comfortably at Port Vale while Manchester United overcame Middlesbrough, the right result in the end though Boro could have nicked it at one point.

In the evening I played World Cup Monopoly, the football variation of the boardgame with countries instead of the London streets, which Charlie got for Christmas, until half past midnight.

At the same time I was watching another American football game on the TV, between San Francisco 49'ers and Green Bay Packers and getting really excited by it, though I hadn't had a bet. That was probably why I was enjoying it so much. It looked as if the Packers had won at one point but then the 49'ers went downfield and scored a winning touchdown with 10 seconds left. Lorraine asked me if I had ever been to a game live. When I said no, she said: 'I can't believe that you've never been, seeing how much you enjoy it.'

It got me thinking…

Monday 4 January

Up early to Nottingham this morning for an examination of my back by the specialist, Dr Webb. It has been two weeks since the injection, two weeks of just rest, weights and bike work – no running – and he seems pleased with my progress. He told me to do some light jogging for a week, then to start playing gently and I should be available again for selection in a fortnight. The live Sky game against Everton on 18 January is marked down for my comeback.

Thank God. It has been five weeks now since I last played and I was beginning to wonder how much more inaction I could take. I have started to get really down lately, just going in, doing my own thing well away from the rest of the lads and then going home and getting back into that routine of just watching the telly. I don't think I could go through another five weeks without playing.

When I got home today, I checked the teletext and saw that the New York Jets were at home to Jacksonville Jaguars in the play-offs next Sunday. It struck me that this might be a good weekend to go away, to recharge the batteries after such a long, lonely battle for fitness.

I was not going to be fit for Saturday's game, and

anyway, it was against Middlesbrough. There was no way I could go to that after everything that was in the papers at the time of my move. Someone may be tempted to give me a smack. I've certainly had a few nasty letters from people up there – although some good ones as well – even if I haven't had a bullet through the post like David Beckham got after the World Cup.

I did get one from a young lad who said that he'd been given a Boro' shirt with my name on it and he couldn't afford another. So I sent him a cheque to buy a new one. I didn't want it coming out in the papers, mind. I'd probably get another 10,000 letters.

Anyway, I rang my agent Steve Kutner and he fancied going to the States as well so we fixed up a trip for this weekend. I can leave after training on Friday, get Concorde, take in an ice hockey game on the Saturday as well as the American football match and be back in for training on Tuesday morning. Now I just have to get tickets.

Thursday 7 January

I've trained really hard for the last couple of days, including today with the first team for the first time, so it seemed like a good time to ask Jim Walker if it would be OK to have the weekend off and go away. When he said yes, I went ahead and booked a hotel and flight for New York.

A contact has also got me tickets for the game through the NFL's press office in London. As long as I do a couple of interviews for the TV over there, on why an English footballer likes American football so much, they will get me good seats at the game. I'm starting to get excited by the prospect.

Gary Charles has left the club to go to Benfica. I suppose it was inevitable when Steve Watson arrived to take his position. He will be missed, though. He did a good job for us and would have been a more than useful squad player. I hope he gets paid out there, what with Benfica's problems these days.

Friday 8 January

The first team weren't doing much today as they were off to Middlesbrough so I did some running with Jim Walker, to get rid of the stiffness after yesterday's session. Then I drove home to be met by my dad, who drove me over to Heathrow for the 7 o'clock Concorde to New York. There were only about 40 people on it. The flight didn't really bother me even though I was travelling on my own, unusually, perhaps because I have something else on my mind and maybe am not in touch with my real feelings.

I had also paid for my brother Gary and my driver John to travel out and they took a normal jet from Heathrow in the afternoon. With the five-hour time difference, it was about 6pm when I arrived at JFK airport in New York. I went over from Terminal 7 to Terminal 4 to meet them and still had to wait for them for 45 minutes.

That's the beauty of Concorde. It cost me £6,000 for the return trip, which is a lot of money, I know, but I had a plan to recover all my costs. That's how I think when I'm in this frame of mind. On arrival at the hotel, the Palace on 54th Street and 5th Avenue, I rang up my mate back in England and placed my bets: £6,000 on the Jets to win by seven points or more at odds of 5–6 and a

£3,000 double on the Jets and Atlanta Falcons to get within three points of San Francisco 49'ers in another play-off.

Then we went on to a TGI Friday's in Manhattan, which seemed appropriate, but jetlag kicked in, especially with the hard training session I had had in the afternoon, and I was ready for bed.

Saturday 9 January

Awake at 6am. Went shopping and bought Lorraine and the kids some stuff. Compulsive or what? Lorraine had asked me to get a certain brand of shampoo not available at home and I bought 25 bottles of it. I also spent US$500 on 15 yo-yos for the boys.

In the evening, we went to see the New Jersey Devils ice hockey team lose 3–2 to the Washington Senators at the Caledonian Air arena near the Lincoln Tunnel. It was a real family occasion with loads of kids there for what was baseball cap night, everyone in the crowd getting one free. Although the Devils were top of their conference, they still got some real stick for losing and people were chucking their caps on to the ice. It was reassuring. I was thinking, 'It's the same the whole world over. You can be top of your league but still get stick.'

Back to the hotel for an early night, ready for the big one tomorrow.

Sunday 10 January

The NFL had sent a limo for me at 10am and I did interviews for them in front of the hotel and at the Meadowlands stadium at pitch side. I was astonished how big the players were in all their gear. It was a fantastic experience to be around top-class sport again and I needed that buzz. It inspired me and I really wanted to be back playing again.

Not this sport though. It was fearsome. And awesome. The temperature was minus 14 degrees Centigrade with the wind chill but it was hot stuff as the Jets beat the Jaguars. I had thermal everything on anyway. I've never been to anything like it. If I lived there I would get a season ticket.

It was a funny feeling, though. I was miked up through the game by the NFL film crew and could not let it show that I desperately didn't want the Jaguars to score a touchdown in the late stages when 10 points down to ruin my bet. No-one else seemed to care. In the end, the Jets held on and with the Falcons causing a real upset by pipping San Francisco, my bets had come in. I had covered my costs for the weekend and some.

After that it was on to the Tamla Motown theme bar near Central Park, which I enjoyed – probably because I was quids in. Or should that be dollars. This time I really am going to quit while I'm ahead.

Monday 11 January

I caught the Concorde at 1.45pm NY time, 6.45pm British, and I was back in the house drinking a Bournvita before bed at 11.30pm. I was a bit worried about not sleeping properly and being fit for training in the morning so I took one of Lorraine's sleeping tablets. No temptation to have a bet today. No opportunity, which is a good thing.

Tuesday 12 January

Felt OK this morning and was off to Bodymoor Heath early. My mood was not improved, though, by a call I got from Lorraine on the way up. There was a news reporter from the *Sun* outside the house claiming that they had information that I had been gambling again.

I rang Steve Kutner, who phoned back to say that they had heard that before Christmas I had put £20,000 on a double in the Champions' League – Arsenal to win in Kiev and Manchester United to beat Brondby. Well, the second one I could understand, as that was obvious, but Arsenal hardly had a side out in Kiev and everyone thought they would lose. I've had some daft bets in my time, but this was not one of them.

Anyway, Lorraine would know if £20,000 had come out of my bank account. It is ironic, though, that I have just had a bet. Someone somewhere seems to know something. Maybe someone is using my name on an account. It could be done, where someone rings up and says 'my mate Paul Merson wants to start betting with you.' Bookmakers will keep quiet as long as they're taking the money off you but if you start winning, or they don't get their money straight away, they will tell the world.

The first person I saw at training was John Gregory and he said: 'Cold out, isn't it?' Having been in New York for the weekend, I said 'No, not really.' I asked if I could train with the reserves on the Astroturf in the gym because I wanted to play for them tomorrow night to try and get some match fitness back ready to return for the first team next week.

It's a bit risky but I really have got to get back playing again now. If it goes again, so be it. At least I now know what the problem is – dehydrated and inflamed discs. Before, I was thinking it was a slipped disc and was worried about it going again. Instead, I trained really well.

Afterwards, I gave a talk to the youth team and the first and second year pros about the illness of addiction, as I had been asked to do. I did feel a bit guilty after my recent relapses but I went ahead anyway because I knew what I was talking about. Also I thought it would be good for me, to remind me about my illness.

They seemed really interested and the people in charge of the youth academy, Gordon Cowans and Kevin MacDonald, asked lots of questions on their behalf. The only thing that disappointed me was that Lee Hendrie and Gareth Barry weren't encouraged to come in on their day off. They are in the first team, where all the others want to be and that's where all the trouble can start, when you get a new circle of friends and a lot of peer pressure.

I was really honest with them, and I think they appreciated that. I also told them to enjoy the game, something you can forget when you become a professional. When I came out of treatment, I said that if I stopped enjoying the game, I would give it up.

I have almost come to that point over the last five weeks. It's been one of the lowest times of my career. Right now I think I will give it another month or so to see if I can get fit again and back to my best. If I can't, I will seriously think about packing it all in.

All the coaching staff seem concerned with is the team but not the people who are not in it. It's understandable in some ways and I have heard tell of some managers, from Bill Shankly to Kenny Dalglish, who almost ignored injured players, saying that they were no use to them and they could not afford to think about them.

If I ever become a manager, I think I will have learned something from this time. The fringe players could well be needed at a crucial time later in the season and they need to be kept happy so that they are ready maybe to score that winning goal or make that saving tackle. They can be key players with key roles to play.

I remember a time at Arsenal in the 1989 season when we won the title. Half way through the season, Perry Groves came on as a sub when we were beating Coventry 3–0 and he could have squared the ball for someone to tap in but instead he ran on and we lost the chance. George Graham was fuming afterwards, saying that the title could come down to goal difference. And it did. Had we scored that goal against Coventry, we would have had to beat Liverpool 1–0, not 2–0 in the last game. Still, looking back I suppose that drama was fate but that's another story.

It's not so bad for me at the moment. The boss was good in letting me have Christmas off. Some of the boys who haven't been playing still had to spend their New Year's Eve in a hotel. They all come and moan to me about it, though, and I have to say it gets me down a bit. Sometimes I feel like a bit of an agony uncle, taking on too much responsibility.

Wednesday 13 January
Aston Villa Reserves 2 Derby County Reserves 3

I felt terrible when I woke up and it was hard work getting out of bed. I took another sleeping pill last night and slept from 11pm to 11am. My mood wasn't improved when I read the boss's comments in the papers. Someone has obviously told him that I went to New York for the weekend and he is upset about it.

I went up to Birmingham for lunch with Mark Bosnich at TGI Friday's and we had a long chat about things. I have got on well with Bozzy since he's also been injured with a bad shoulder and we have spent a lot of time together. He knew how down I was before I went to New York and why I had to get away. He was worried about me. I'll definitely stay in touch with him if he does leave the club in the summer, as looks probable.

I got through the game without any twinges, which was the main thing, but I can't say I enjoyed it. It ended in a big row with Igor Stimac, the Derby defender, who had crunched one of our lads after he himself had been subjected to a bad tackle. He could have broken his leg, in fact.

I had noticed that Stimac's number had been held up on the sideline and as the referee came over to Stimac, I said to him: 'You're going off.' Then I said to the ref: 'Be sensible ref, they're taking him off.' Stimac didn't understand and thought I was trying to get him sent off. He got really angry with me and said he would see me in the tunnel. I gave him a gesture. I shouldn't have but he had wound me up.

After the game I sought him out in a lounge to try and smooth things over but he went into another temper, trying to punch me. We had quite a scuffle before being separated. He said I should be respecting him but what for? What has he done in the game? Everybody, except him it seemed, knew I was trying to save him from getting sent off.

A Sky Sports news crew and a couple of press guys were waiting for me as I left. It started innocently enough and they asked me about my fitness. I told them I was about 50 per cent fit. I hadn't wanted to pull a muscle so I took it easy, I said.

Then they asked me what I thought about John Gregory's remarks about my weekend away. I was feeling a bit down after my episode with Stimac and besides, if someone asks me a straight question, I have to be honest with them. Sometimes I can't stop myself.

I told them that I regretted not telling him that I was going instead of him finding out from someone else but I was in need of a boost. I could have gone shopping in London and spent £50,000 to cheer myself up but I didn't. I went to the States. A lot of people do that for the weekend and I thought that if it worked, if it meant I wasn't going to do something more damaging like go on a drinking bender, then it was good for me. I said the boss needed to understand my problems for us to work together. At the moment, I didn't feel he did. I was very comfortable with what I said.

Thursday 14 January

I felt like an old man, my back and joints aching, when I got up but I had to come up to Bodymoor Heath to warm down and get the back moving. I wish I hadn't. As soon as I walked in there seemed to be a lot of negative vibes around the place and no-one was speaking to me. I never got this at Middlesbrough. Bryan Robson understood everything. Sod this lot here.

Friday 15 January

I am always first in for training because I like to get there and unwind after the drive up by reading the papers and having a cup of tea. As I was getting changed, the goalkeeping coach Paul Barron came in to talk to me and locked the door behind him so it was just the two of us. He asked me how I was and I said: 'Not too good.' Then he asked: 'Do you need a psychiatrist?' I laughed. 'I'm not that mad,' I said, trying to shrug it off but underneath I was hurting.

Then there was a knock at the door. It was Gareth Southgate. He came in and very quietly got changed for training, not even saying anything when we stopped talking. Sometimes I think Gareth's too polite. I think he was embarrassed because of everything that had been in the papers the last couple of days.

What had seemed to set one or two lads against me, it seems, was me being quoted as saying the team couldn't win without me. All I had said was that I created chances and I thought the team needed that. On top of the papers misconstruing what I had said about only being 50 per cent match fit in the reserve game – interpreting it as me half-trying – and also getting some stick over saying that the boss needed to understand my problems, which came out as really self-centred, I was feeling really isolated.

Anyway, I lost it then. 'Everyone's fucking blanking me now,' I said. 'This is getting on my nerves.' I walked out of the dressing room on to the field in just T-shirt, shorts and flip-flops though it was pouring with rain. I just cracked up. I was walking around crying my eyes out. Everything had overwhelmed me.

Steve Harrison followed me out and told me not to worry so much about things, not to take things so much to heart, and I calmed down. I then had a good training session. With us not playing until Monday, against Everton, it was a running day and I really enjoyed it.

There was a release in just losing myself in physical exercise.

Afterwards I went in to see John Gregory and we cleared a few things up. He would have had no problem with me going to America, he said, but he would like to have been told. I could only apologise. I told him that I was going stir crazy just doing light training on my own then going home and resting and I needed to get away. He understood.

I had an interview fixed up with Joe Lovejoy of the *Sunday Times*, which I did and which I enjoyed. I managed to get a lot out and felt better for it. I trusted that the broadsheets would quote me more accurately than the tabloids had. As I was leaving the training ground, I saw who I thought was the *Sun's* Midlands reporter Neil Custis and had a right go at him for some of the stuff he had written.

It turned out, though, that the poor bloke I was giving an earful to was John Curtis of the Press Association and he was baffled. He's a nice bloke, I've since discovered, and he didn't deserve it. I must have apologised 100 times to him when I found out. Gordon Cowans came out and saw it all and was crying with laughter. My mood swings frighten me sometimes.

Saturday 16 January

We trained in the gym, just five-a-side, and I felt really sharp. The boss joined in. He's still a good player and passes the ball well. Afterwards he told me I would be in the squad for Monday but he's already said in the papers that I would definitely not be starting the game. I would like to. I think I'm fit enough.

I watched Sky all afternoon and it was a bad day for us. The big three of Manchester United, Arsenal and Chelsea all won and Liverpool are even looking as if they might get back into it after their 7–1 win over Southampton. We have to win on Monday. Even with 16 games left, we might start to lose touch if we don't. United, who beat Leicester 6–2, are looking brilliant at the moment, Arsenal are picking up and Chelsea are having the luck, coming from a goal down to win in the 94th minute against Coventry.

Mind you, I'm going off Chelsea as champions. Arsenal and United have the experience of it and that will count for a lot later. I still think we'll be thereabouts but the pressure's on. We haven't been electric lately, not as strong as in the autumn, but if we click we're still capable of beating anybody.

Sunday 17 January

We did 8 vs 8 in training again and it felt good again. Afterwards I saw the boss and said that I would prefer to train tomorrow if I wasn't going to play. He asked me if I was fit enough to be involved and I said yes. He said he would put me on as sub. He'd like me to go on and open things up if it was 0–0, or to have a run-out if it's 2–0.

Joe Lovejoy's piece with me in the *Sunday Times* is good, with him reporting just what I'd said, but I was hurt about some of the stuff written about me in the other papers this weekend, especially Andy Gray in the *Mirror*. He seemed to be saying that Villa wouldn't win the title with me in the team. Some journalists I don't mind but you know Andy Gray has a lot of influence with fans. I didn't criticise him for not taking the Everton job. Why is he having a go at me?

Then there was Jimmy Greaves in the *Sun* yesterday talking about my alcoholism. I accept that he knows what he is talking about, not having had a drink for 20 years, and I take his point that there is no escape from the illness and just by changing the geography, you don't change yourself. But I knew that in going to New York I was taking me with me. I just needed to get out of a rut I was in. It's not just about my illness. I had been injured a long time and needed a change of scenery, somewhere I knew I was going to cheer myself up.

You do find out who your friends are in these situations. Terry Byrne, the Chelsea and England masseur, rang me from Tenerife where he was on holiday, to see how I was, which was good of him. Gareth Southgate also came up to me when the squad for Monday was announced and said how much the team needed me back.

He said that if I wanted to stay up around Birmingham and couldn't face a hotel again, I was welcome to stay with him and his wife Alison. He does understand about a lot of things, Gareth, because he spent a lot of time talking with me and Tony Adams, and listening, at the World Cup. It is kind of him but I prefer a night in my own bed if at all possible so I drove back home.

In the evening I watched the two American football conference finals, between Denver and the New York Jets and Atlanta and the Minnesota Vikings and I found myself thinking about the way sports people are treated in this country.

In one of the games, the kicker missed a last-ditch chance to win the game for his team but I don't think that in the States the television or papers gave him a hammering because of how much money he earns. There was also a wide receiver who missed a touchdown, who's probably on several million dollars a year. The money doesn't give him glue fingers. Nor does £20,000 a week mean you're not going to miss a penalty or not be subjected to the same stresses and strains as the rest of the world. People react differently, no matter what they do or how much money they get.

Monday 18 January
Aston Villa 3 Everton 0

Lorraine let me have a lie-in then John Gorman, Glenn Hoddle's assistant, rang to see how I was, which was nice of him. I was looking forward to the game tonight but was wondering if the fans would boo me after what Andy Gray wrote.

As it happened, when I was warming up, they were really nice to me and I was getting comments from the crowd when I was near the touchlines along the lines of 'I hope you get on tonight.'

I thought I was going to when Everton had Alex Cleland sent off. I didn't think we would stick with five across the back against 10 men and when John Gregory asked me to warm up I thought: 'I'm on here.' But Dion got injured and the boss sent on Stan instead. Luckily enough, though, Julian scored twice to make it 2–0 and I was brought on for the last half an hour and got a great reception. I even managed to score only my fourth goal of the season. It was a good night.

On the way home I phoned Lorraine who said that Andy Gray had been saying on Sky before the game that

I needed to let my football do the talking now. Nothing afterwards about me having done well.

Football is a macho world where you're not allowed to show your feelings sometimes amid all the dressing room banter. You've just got to be tough and endure it all and stand up for yourself. But you should also be big enough to apologise as well when you've been wrong. I have been and I have said sorry to the boss. I didn't let my pride get in the way. I wish Andy Gray could have done that as well. I think I've had the last laugh tonight though. Things are looking up, finally.

Tuesday 19 January

Today I went in and trained on my own with the physio, having only had half an hour last night, while the first team had the day off. I said to Steve Harrison that I would come in tomorrow and do my finishing but the boss said to take the day off and come in on Thursday to do that, which was good of him.

I got a call from the *News of the World* saying that they would have paid me more than my regular column fee – £800 – for all the stuff I had said in the *Sunday Times,* but I don't say things for money. If I've got something I need to say, or if I'm asked, I will say it. I don't think, 'Ooh, I could get a few grand for what I've got to say about John Gregory.'

One of the things I said in the *Sunday Times* was that I would not be worried if Juninho came to Villa Park, what with the boss having been trying to sign him from Atletico Madrid recently. In fact, I'm all for signing quality players. It may look as if we play in the same position but who's to say I won't play up front, or be the one playing deeper to give him the ball? The boss has paid good money for me – unlike Stan Collymore, who was bought by Brian Little – so he's going to want to accommodate me in the side if he can.

I've also had a call off Sky to say someone has rung them claiming I had a bet of £14,000 on us to win last night. Where does this stuff come from? I also wonder what people's motives are in saying these things. Is there someone trying to stir something up with me and Lorraine? I think she'd probably tolerate it if I sat down in front of the TV and had a can of lager but if she found out that I had been gambling again, she'd be very upset and I'm certain she'd throw me out.

Wednesday 20 January

I took the opportunity of a day off to go with a friend to an AA meeting in St Albans for the first time in ages. I didn't realise how much I needed to go until afterwards. I had a lot to say for myself, a sure sign that I needed to get things off my chest. I can see, too, that I shouldn't have taken those sleeping pills. They were giving me terrible mood swings. It's amazing what insight an hour of AA can give me. I neglect it really, which is why things get on top of me.

The injury took more out of me than I ever acknowledged. It is frightening really. The most I have ever been out before was four weeks, with a hernia, but even then after two I was able to train. There was the time I was in treatment for four weeks, as part of my three-month ban from the game for drug-taking, but then I was just concentrating on getting well again so I was not too bothered about playing.

It has been very lonely. I've not wanted to go into the dressing room too much because I'm not part of it and I miss that camaraderie. You're also a bit of an outcast. The boss never rang me, though Paul Barron did once, but I know he's got a lot on his plate trying to win the title for Villa. I shouldn't need him to nursemaid me anyway. I did get a call from one manager, my old mate Nigel Pearson at Carlisle, who wanted me to come on loan. I hope he was joking. No word from Gazza. I was going to ring him to find out how he was doing but I have lost my mobile with his number programmed into it.

I have got on well with Mark Bosnich, even though he doesn't stop rabbiting, and that's been some consolation. We've helped each other while we've both been injured, I think. I'm glad I didn't move up and was able to be around my family in my own house while all this was going on. It has been one of the most frustrating times of my career at a time when the team was going well.

If my back starts hurting again, I'm just going to try and play through the pain this time. I can't not play again and get so down again. At least I know it's not a career-threatening injury. It's scar tissue. Due to wear and tear, I developed a canal at the base of my back where the muscle had eroded. Now the muscles are starting to build again and I hope I'm going to be like a new player for the title push.

Whether I get back into the starting line-up is going to be interesting. Dion and Julian are looking good together and Stan has come on as a sub and done well. But before my injury, we had beaten Tottenham, won at Southampton and should have beaten Liverpool so I think I was contributing. And how many defenders do we need anyway? Personally I think we have too many, with five at the back and two holding players in midfield. I just hope the boss isn't influenced by Andy Gray. He's not Villa's assistant manager any more.

In the afternoon I picked Charlie up from school and came home with five packs of stickers of Premiership players for the boys. Mind you, I think I enjoy sticking them in the book more than they do. In the evening I watched France beat Morocco 1–0 on Eurosport. It will be a tough game for England at Wembley against them next month.

Thursday 21 January

An amazing incident driving up to training on the M1 this morning. As we were going up the outside lane, at about 80mph, we suddenly saw a car stopped about 100 yards in front of us. John braked suddenly and veered into the middle lane where, unbelievably, another car was stopped alongside. I was absolutely wetting myself. I really thought we were going to crash.

Then John somehow managed to get on the inside lane, just missing a lorry, and we gave the two cars some angry gestures as we sped by. As we passed I could see the bloke in the outside lane was reading a map and the one inside him was trying to give him directions. Then as we drove on, the car in the middle lane started chasing us up the motorway, sticking his fingers up at us. It was scary.

I saw the boss before training to see where I stood if he signed Juninho. He said we would play together and added that he saw a big future for me at the club, which cheered me up. He saw me as playing in midfield. I don't want to leave Villa. I want to finish my career here if I can.

You've got to be mad to leave a club like this. There are so many good young players here. In my opinion, though, we still need five players and now is the time to strengthen.

Friday 22 January

Foggy and frosty again today but at least I got a lie-in as we weren't training until noon. The M1 was less hairy, too. When I got to Bodymoor Heath, the boss took us to a park just up the road from the training ground for a walk. It seemed a bit of a waste of time for me but then I choose to live down South still so I can't complain.

It's like sometimes I feel I have to be cheerful otherwise they'll blame my mood on all the travelling I do to training. As we were walking and chatting, I heard that Dion may need an operation on a stomach injury. That will be bad news for us. He gives us a lot of options with his style, because you can play through him or hit him in the air. I think also we have to do that more often, getting the ball forward early as a variation.

FA Cup tomorrow. It always excites me. We have got a tough one against Kevin Keegan's Fulham, who are top of the Second Division, but it's still one we should win. They did lose 3–0 to Manchester City last Saturday.

Saturday 23 January
Aston Villa 0 Fulham 2

I thought we could have been a Cup team this year, strong at the back, capable of nicking a goal on the counter-attack, even if we may not yet be good enough to go away from home and take the game to another team. Now we won't get the opportunity to find out.

We played quite well in the first half but it was one of

those games where you could play well all day and not score. Fulham were destined to go through. At half-time at 2–0 down we were coming down the steps and I said to Kevin Keegan: 'You're playing well.' He just smiled. 'This isn't the team that played Man City,' I added and he laughed. In the end, they deserved to go through. They did play well and they'll get promotion for sure.

It was still a major disappointment. We are out of the FA Cup and that's hard to take before the end of January. You just have to hope that going for the league, it's a blessing in disguise.

I played the whole game for the first time since my injury, mainly because Stan Collymore, who was to be Dion's replacement, is ill, according to the physio Jim Walker. Jim told me that it was Stan's 28th birthday yesterday – and it surprised me how old he was – and he only got seven cards, which is sad. On the radio, on the way home, they were saying that Stan simply hadn't turned up. Sometimes as a player you are the last to know. John Gregory is supposed to be saying that he has had enough of Stan, that he has really tried to help him.

What cheered me up on the way home was a phone call from Andy Townsend in Israel where Middlesbrough are on tour. He had just played Gazza at tennis and won £250. Andy is not a betting man but he says with it raining so much, he has been so bored that he has been going £50 blind at three-card brag. I was crying with laughter. There's always someone worse off than yourself.

Sunday 24 January

My back felt really sore and stiff after my first 90 minutes in two months. I spent the morning trying to absorb all the stuff about me in the *People*. They were printing responses from readers to an article the previous Sunday, which had criticised me for going to New York. One in particular did move me, from a man whose son had Multiple Sclerosis and said how lucky I was. Well, I know that but it doesn't stop me having bad days, I'm afraid. It hurt that some people thought I don't care about the game or my club. I most certainly do.

In the afternoon I watched Manchester United and Arsenal win their FA Cup games over Liverpool and Wolves respectively. Arsenal's win was so typical. They win their away games when they need to and we have got to aspire to that. Sometimes I think that we feel we've had a good day if we've got a draw away from home. That's the difference and why Arsenal will be so tough in the Premiership, come April.

Monday 25 January

Had a good game between first team and reserves, the first team winning 4–3, which was a good exercise to get everyone involved.

Afterwards I had a word with the boss about Stan, who is to go into the Priory clinic in London for treatment for his depression. I urged the boss to be patient with him and that he may well emerge as a better player and, more important, a better person. I'm not sure the Priory is the best place for him, though. It's become a refuge for celebrities and he might be better off going somewhere lower profile.

He's a hard lad to get to know, Stan. He's very quiet and doesn't mingle much with the lads, spending a lot of time on the Internet, but then everyone's different. He can't take a laugh, I know that, and gets very upset at being ribbed. He could even punch someone, I reckon. Martin Keown used to be like that at Arsenal but he's mellowed out now by all accounts.

In the evening I watched Chelsea scramble a lucky draw at Oxford with a late penalty. It cheered up Ben, who's become a Chelsea fan. He was crying when Oxford went a goal up.

Tuesday 26 January

A day off but I felt like getting up early, letting Lorraine have a lie-in while I got the boys up, made their packed lunches and got them off to school. I have these brainstorms every few months and it knocked me out for the rest of the day. I would much rather be a footballer than a housewife. That's the hardest game in the world, that is.

I recovered enough to sprawl on the sofa in the evening and watch Leicester beat Sunderland 2–1 in the first leg of their Worthington Cup semi-final. It just shows the difference in the two leagues. Sunderland will need to spend at least £10 million if they are to compete.

Wednesday 27 January

Routine day. Five-a-side then running in training, which was quite hard with the ground so heavy. When I got home, I played touch American football with the kids in the garden. Watched Spurs v Wimbledon, which was very boring. I know at Middlesbrough we would have gone out last year to Liverpool if Worthington Cup semis had been one leg, but I do prefer them. This was boring and if Wimbledon aren't careful the same thing will happen to them as against Leicester two seasons ago when they lost at home in the second leg after a goalless draw away.

Thursday 28 January

Very stiff after the running day and I played cricket with the boys in the gym for the first time. My driver John was co-opted to play and I ran him out, though he had his revenge by bowling me in the second innings.

Friday 29 January

I still feel very stiff and very tired, not helped by the trip up to Newcastle for tomorrow's game. I left St Albans at 7am to get the coach from our training ground and we arrived at the hotel at 1.30pm. After lunch we trained at Durham University.

I spent the rest of the time in my room at the Gosforth Park hotel, having dinner on my own and doing my *News of the World* column, about Stan. I'm beginning to think this is his last chance. He was worth £7 million eighteen months ago, now I don't think anybody would take a chance at £2 million. That's how bad his problem is and I hope he can take a good hard look at himself in the Priory.

Saturday 30 January
Newcastle United 2 Aston Villa 1

Had tea, toast and yoghurt in my room and read the papers. They are full of some stuff about Glenn Hoddle and the disabled. He is being interpreted as saying in an interview that disabled people are paying the price for sins in a previous life. His views seem strange to me but he is entitled to them. I can't see what all the fuss is about.

Went for a walk in the hotel grounds and Gareth Southgate was talking about Glenn. As the interview was in *The Times*, it's got to be taken seriously, he says. We watched *Football Focus* on the BBC at lunchtime and Glenn was on. He wasn't denying that he'd said it, it seemed to me, just that his remarks have been taken too literally. I think it will blow over. There was a disabled woman on who says she was not offended.

In the dressing room before the game, we were talking about the need to keep Newcastle scoreless for the first 20 minutes because the crowd will then get on their backs and we could go on to win. They're having a bad time anyway and Alan Shearer is in a drought. Within three minutes, we had conceded, within 20 it was 2–0 and Shearer was back on the scoresheet. The crowd were going potty. It was always going to be one of those days after that.

We improved in the second half and I scored one of the best goals I have managed in ages. I was about 25 yards out, leaning back, hit the ball and hoped and it flew into the top corner. It was a sweet strike but I was just trying to get it on target rather than aiming for the top corner. It was pot luck and the better goals are where someone beats three players and chips it in. It gave me pleasure, though, because it meant I had now scored against every team in the Premiership.

It was not enough to get us anything from the game though and John Gregory went mad in the dressing room at the end. Julian Joachim was told he hadn't tried hard enough. The boss said that sometimes we needed to lump it with the pitches being so heavy and Gareth Barry was told not to overplay so often. As a forward, I had to agree. Mostly you want your defenders to defend. Job done. Ugo Ehiogu usually does but we lost him to a nasty injury, when he accidentally got a boot in the face from Alan Shearer, and he could be out for a while.

One of our problems is still that not enough players will take responsibility when things are going badly. They don't want the ball badly enough. I say to them that we shouldn't be afraid to make mistakes. Show me a player who hasn't made a mistake and I'll show you a skint bookmaker. There isn't one. As someone once said, the worst mistake in life is being frightened to make one.

Steve Harrison took us for a warm-down out on the pitch and I told him that I thought we needed to change our routine. Running should be on Tuesday and not Wednesday so that we can then do more physical work on the Thursday and Friday. At the moment we are not sharp on the Saturday. He said the routine had got us to the top but I pointed out that we were 30 games in and the pitches now were heavier.

Sunday 31 January

Charlie went to see Arsenal beat Chelsea 1–0, watching from our friends' hospitality box at Highbury, and with Manchester United also winning, we have slipped to third place for the first time this season. Blackburn next Saturday now becomes a huge game for us.

The Glenn Hoddle thing seems to be gathering momentum in the press but I was more concerned with the Superbowl – though I didn't have a bet on it – in which Denver smashed Atlanta. Glenn will survive. You can't sack a man for his beliefs, can you?

FEBRUARY

Losing It

February

I remember Glenn Hoddle getting sacked that first Tuesday of the month. I remember most of that first week of the month. But from Saturday the 6th, it became a blur. I was gambling again. Big time. And when I gamble, I lose track of time and days and weeks. I lose me.

I get sucked back into feeling a bad person again. A lot of the things I do and say I feel ashamed of. I'm not like that when I'm healthy. I'm a nice bloke, I know I am. And everybody around me says that. I should know that I suffer from an illness, that I'm sick. But for most of the month I just felt bad. And the knock-on effect of that on family, friends and work colleagues was frightening.

I can only recall how it all panned out by looking back at the dates of the games that Aston Villa played. The fixture list tells me it was Blackburn on the 6th, Leeds United on the 17th, Wimbledon on the 21st and Coventry City on the 27th. It was a bad dream for the club as we failed to win any of the four, lost three of them in fact. And it was a nightmare for me.

It was all right to start with. On the Monday after the Newcastle defeat, there was only a few of us in. Dion was injured and Lee Hendrie had gone for a break to the Canary Islands because he was suspended. Training was nice and light, just a 7 vs 7 game, with trophies and Mars bars for the winners, just to lighten things up. It was a good idea after two defeats on the trot. We knew we had two home games coming up, though, so it would surely get better.

When I went up the next day, I was pleased that the boss and Steve Harrison had listened to my suggestion and brought forward the running day. It was a lot more realistic, too. The week before Newcastle, we went through a punishing routine of jogging for three minutes, striding out for three minutes, jogging, striding, and jogging again before two 50-yard sprints, two 40, two 30, two 20 then back up through them to 50. Finally we finished with six 10-yard sprints. It all takes about an hour and is a slog. But this week it was more shuttle-run work, designed for sharpness and getting the heaviness out of the legs.

It was a good job. Normally when John drives me up, I drink three cans of Red Bull to get fluid inside me but he had taken Lorraine into London to do some shopping so I drove myself and omitted to take in any liquid.

Nobody really spoke much that day about Glenn and the England job. We were unaware that down in London there was a feeding frenzy going on amongst the press. They got his blood all right later in the day. I was following it on the teletext and got quite angry when I saw the announcement that he had been sacked.

It really was a storm in a teacup. I'm convinced that the papers whipped it all up because Glenn had never been particularly helpful to them. They wanted him out for the wrong reasons. He wouldn't let them travel on the team plane any more, for example. His press conferences were never very revealing and the access to the team was very limited. I think people would find it very childish if they knew. Mind you, he didn't get much support from the FA.

I saw it all happen with George Graham. When all the stuff happened at Arsenal, he had very few friends in the press because he didn't cosy up to them. I think he learned a lot from that. It was the build-them-up and knock-them-down syndrome. In a year, everyone will be saying that Glenn was the right man for the job.

Glenn phoned me on the Wednesday, which was good of him what with the way he must have been feeling. He wished me well for the future and thanked me for being a valued member of his squad. 'Keep going and don't retire,' he said. He had talked me out of it three months ago and I had had one of my best games for England.

I was sorry to see him go. I didn't agree with some of the things he did. Sometimes I think there should have been more flexibility in our formation, for example, and the way he dealt with players now and then left a bit to be desired. But he recalled me and took me to a World Cup so I will always be grateful to him.

Almost before his departure, there were names in the frame, starting with Howard Wilkinson, the technical director, who is to become caretaker manager. If it was Terry Venables, I would definitely quit. He may well be a great coach, and technically the right man for the job, but I wouldn't fit into his plans. He told me the day after

I played for him against Greece in 1994 that I wasn't his cup of tea.

Another name being mentioned was Kevin Keegan, which makes me glad that I was complimentary to him about his Fulham team when we played them in the FA Cup last month. Personally, I think three pressmen should be given the job. Then we can look into their private lives, dig up all of the dirt and see how well they bear up to scrutiny. From what I've seen, quite a few of them would have stories they couldn't give a 'no comment' to. The problem is they might do all right. With all the good young players coming through, I reckon I could do it and win the World Cup in 2002.

I remember that Wednesday night watching Spurs beat Wimbledon 1–0 to reach the Worthington Cup final, and I remember being named in Howard Wilkinson's England squad the next day. After that, though, a lot of things merge into one. Because that Friday I started gambling again.

Again there were a million reasons. I was still not getting on as well as I would have liked with Lorraine. Villa were on a losing streak and I felt the weight of the club on my shoulders with an over-developed sense of responsibility for everyone and everything. I was feeling down with it all.

To be honest, they were excuses. I wanted to feel better, or at least different. This flat period was at best boring, at worst depressing and I needed a buzz, I thought. Gambling has always done it for me – temporarily at least – and I convinced myself that I had got away with the few days of it last month. I thought I had some control back.

It began how it always does, with just a little bet. The

same as for an alcoholic who sips a half of lager but eventually crashes into a bottle of vodka. You tell yourself that this time it will be different. I phoned up a mate and asked him to put a few hundred quid on a horse for me. I can't remember the exact amount, or the name of the horse, because what was to come erased all that.

Even on the Saturday, when we were playing Blackburn Rovers at home, it wasn't too bad. My mind was definitely on the game. It wasn't one of those days where I was distracted or preoccupied with the bets I had put on. They were a series of home wins at football matches in an accumulator. And they went the same way as the horse on the Friday.

As I remember, we were dominating the game against Blackburn when Gareth Southgate put one into his own net. We lost some heart once again, then the game, by 3–1. We were 3–0 down before we started playing, Julian Joachim pulling one back. The problem to me was that we had stopped going 1–0 up against teams. We are a counter-attacking team who defend a lead well but frustration sets in when we're a goal down. It was sloppy. 'Here we go again,' kept going through my mind during the match.

Here we go again in more senses than one.

My back was very sore that night and what with the defeat and all my bets going down, I was in a foul mood. Lorraine had come up to the game and when we got home, we had a terrible argument. I can't recall what it was about but I know it was mainly due to my mood. I swore at her in front of her mum and dad, which is not me.

I knew immediately I reported for England duty on the Sunday night for the game against France that they would see I wouldn't be fit in time. Dr Crane and Gary Lewin both had a look at me and sent me home, telling me I needed rest. To be honest, I wasn't that upset. If I got picked for England in my current form, I would be embarrassed.

I hate not playing and Villa didn't have another game for ten days. In my opinion, it was a time when we could have gone away together as a squad for a week, to do some warm weather training and get closer as a group. Somewhere like La Manga, where they have good training pitches and golf courses, would have been good. It might have recharged the batteries and changed things for us.

Anyway, being inactive was another thing that got me down and on the Monday morning I went into my bank in St Albans and took out £10,000 in cash. It was for my mate who was doing all the telephone bets for me so that he could pay off his credit account and I could bet again.

I felt strangely relieved, and also full of anticipation. The buzz was starting. Sometimes an alcoholic can get as much from just buying the bottle as from drinking it. There is the knowledge that those feelings of restlessness and edginess are about to be ended.

I already knew what my bet for the day was going to be. It was the Benson and Hedges snooker tournament at Wembley Arena and I decided to have £1,000 on John Higgins to beat Alain Robidoux 6–0 and another £1,000 to beat him 6–1. The odds on the two results were 10–1 and 8–1. I knew Higgins would win easily.

By the time I got home, I changed my mind. Two grand was a lot to lose first time out, I thought. Just be sensible. So I decided to make it £300 and £300. Higgins won 6–1. Instead of seeing that as £2,400 won, I looked upon it as £8,000 lost. I was well pissed off.

Within two days I had lost control. I had £4,000 on Ronnie O'Sullivan to beat Ken Doherty and all of a sudden O'Sullivan decided to play left-handed, which he can do quite well. But not well enough to win. I was furious. Imagine if all the Villa players decided to play a match using only their left feet. There would be an outcry.

I did see a couple of snooker bets come in on the Wednesday as part of an accumulator and had £8,000 riding on England to beat France at Wembley at 6–4. When you're a gambler, you know deep down that this kind of bet is going to go down. Your £500 bet will win for you. Not your eight grand.

England missed a few good chances in the first few minutes. What were Michael Owen and Tony Adams doing? They're supposed to be my mates. Even so, at this point, I thought I couldn't lose. In the first half, England were all over them. By now, I wasn't looking at it as a game any more, with a critical professional's eye, I was just hoping England scored.

They must have got mugged in the tunnel at half-time though, or swopped shirts with France, because they were two different teams in the second half. I could have thumped Nicolas Anelka, who I'd found a nice lad when I was at Arsenal and was one of the few he talked to, for scoring twice. Looking back, I should have known it would go down. If I hadn't had a bet on them, I know England would have won.

Then, some day after that, I was betting on Tony Drago to win. He was 5–4 up and lost 6–5. I stood to win £20,000 on that. My brother was in the auditorium watching and because it wasn't live on television, I phoned him on his mobile for a progress report. He had to come out and watch it on the closed-circuit feed inside the building to give me a running commentary. 'He's made a long pot,' or 'he's cut one into the middle pocket,' he was whispering down the line.

Then I was watching ice hockey on television and betting on Manchester Storm to beat Bracknell Bees by one goal. The Storm were 2–1 up until late in the game when they scored twice. What do I know? I know more about American ice hockey. At night, I would be in bed checking teletext on the TV in the bedroom and seeing what the odds were for all the various sports fixtures the next day.

On the Friday I only had about £3,000 left so I went back to my bank and took out another £6,000. By now I couldn't go a day without a bet, such was the state I was in. It was slowly taking me over again. All the old feelings were coming back from the old days. I was getting paranoid in case anyone found out. I was worrying that someone would see me going in and out of the bank. I was even scared that the bank staff would tell the papers.

That night I had a bet of £500 on Rochdale to beat Hull City 2–0 in a Third Division match at odds of 9–1. It was only because it was live on Sky. I don't even know what colour Rochdale play in. What happened next is a story familiar to any miserable gambler.

Rochdale were duly winning 2–0 as the game went into added time. I turned the channel over because I could hardly bear to watch, I was so agitated. But I knew for some reason that when I turned back, another goal would have been scored. Where did that feeling come from? When I turned back, Rochdale were winning 3–0. The amazing thing was, I know that if I had had 3–0, they would never have scored.

When you have a gambling problem you do just know. You just know sometimes that when your team is winning, the other team is going to score with five minutes to go. You know that when you're drawing, your team is not going to score. Somebody explain it to me, please.

The next day, Lorraine took Charlie and Ben for a week's skiing trip she had planned to Lech in Austria. I had the youngest, Sam, with me at home. It was lovely a lot of the time but for some of it I could not pay him the attention I wanted because my gambling was pre-occupying me. When I was playing or training, my mum and dad would have him. And with Lorraine away, I was off the leash when it came to gambling.

Because we were out of the FA Cup we did not have a game that Saturday, the 13th, and the emptiness was excuse enough to have a bet with the state I was in. I had an accumulator on five home wins over the weekend – Rangers at 1–5 against Hamilton, Motherwell 1–5 against Stirling, Celtic 1–4 against Dunfermline, Arsenal 1–4 against Sheffield United and Manchester United to beat Fulham at 2–9. I also had £3,000 on John Higgins to beat Ken Doherty at 5–6 in the semi-final of the snooker.

On the Sunday, I had another bet on Higgins to win the final at 1–2, then Leeds to beat Wigan by four points in the Rugby League at 1–2, Manchester United to be ahead at half-time and full-time at 1–2 and Rangers to do likewise at 4–11. They all came in again. I was winning. I was out of jail. Looking back, I wish I had lost, though. It might have stopped me sooner.

It wasn't as if I didn't know deep down how it would all end but by now I was out of control. That first week

Lorraine was away was just a daze, a routine of travelling up for training, getting through, travelling back, then sitting around all afternoon. I would put bets on in the car going up to Birmingham, put them on from my sofa.

Was it the week Kevin Keegan got the England job, initially for four games? I remember thinking that he would be a good man to get the country going again but otherwise it didn't penetrate my consciousness as much as it would normally. And I could remember more about losing bets than I could about the game I played in that week, a 2–1 home defeat by Leeds. Wigan let in a goal in the 90th minute one night that cost me seven grand. That was etched in my memory.

It was like someone or something was telling me: 'There, you've lost. I'm doing you a favour, telling you to stop it now. How many losers do you want before you wise up?' A few more at least.

We were a goal down in five minutes – again – against Leeds and although we dominated the second half, and scored through Ricky Scimeca, the damage had been done by the interval, when we trailed by two. After conceding, we thought we had to get back into it in the next five minutes and as a result of pushing forward too hurriedly, we let in another one. Afterwards I remember talking in the dressing room about not being able to remember a good goal we had conceded lately. Every one seemed to be sloppy.

We weren't playing Wimbledon until the Sunday but met up on the Saturday. I had about £2,500 left of the original £16,000 I had taken out of the bank and I put it on five football teams in an accumulator. They looked sure things and would have added up to about the £16,000. I would have got my money back.

Post-traumatic stress ... Training and a break from the boredom of a rigid routine before England's game against Bulgaria in October 1998.

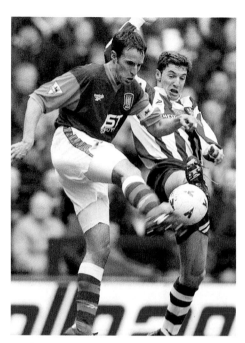

*Left: **Mr Dependable** ...*
Gareth Southgate was a
calming influence at Villa.

*Right: **Back with a bang** ...*
Scoring as a substitute
against Everton in January
1999 on my return after a
miserable period out with a
back injury.

It happened like this... *Explaining my move from Middlesbrough to Aston Villa in*
September 1998 to television and press.

Turning a trick ... Against Wimbledon's Ben Thatcher.

Stan the troubled man ... I found Stan Collymore a difficult character to get to know and I have to confess that sympathy for him turned into indifference.

Midfield rock ... Ian Taylor had a great 1998/99 season in Villa's midfield.

The Deadly Duo … *Chairman Doug Ellis eclipsing manager John Gregory.*

Missing a sitter … *Somehow Shaka Hislop got to what should have been a tap-in against West Ham at Upton Park in October 1998.*

Celebration time ... my goal against Wimbledon on my debut for Aston Villa.

Moving on ... *Mark Bosnich was out of action for most of the season before his well-publicised move to Old Trafford in the summer of 1999.*

On the run ... *In full flow against Derby County.*

Above: **Highlight from Wembley ...** *Scoring against the Czech Republic in November 1998 was one of the peaks of my year.*

Left: **On the ball ...** *Sharp and buzzing for England.*

Below: **The only way is down ...** *What proved to be premature celebrations at The Dell after our record winning streak at the start of the season.*

Bloodied but unbowed ... A memorable 3–2 win against Leeds in the FA Cup Fifth Round, January 2000, but a nasty facial wound after laying on the winner.

Bossing the game ... A rare headed goal in a good season for me personally, against Leicester at Villa Park in April 2000.

When it's not your day ... Dennis Wise takes no pity on me in Villa's disappointing end to the season on Wembley FA Cup Final day.

But that wasn't good enough for me. I got greedy. I always compare it to what I earn a week and decided it wasn't worth having that £16,000. I wanted more than I earned, a couple of weeks, £40,000 or £50,000. So I had it all riding on Ken Doherty to win his snooker semi-final against the little-known Graham Dott and England to beat Scotland in the rugby union by 12 points. Doherty lost and England only won by three. The England result also cost me £200 a point – £1,800 on the spread-betting system. Greed is only one reason why I can never win.

It was taking over the football, I have to admit, and I didn't play well against Wimbledon, although we ended our bad run of four defeats in a row with a 0–0 draw, mainly due to changing the formation to 4-3-3, and we looked a better side. We were now fourth, 10 points behind Manchester United, mind.

Lorraine, Charlie and Ben were due back on the Saturday but there had been an avalanche warning where they were staying. In the next valley, there had actually been one and some people had been killed. It was a worrying time. They were snowed in and nobody could say when they would be home.

That anxiety, coupled with the gambling, made me an argument waiting to happen if anyone crossed my path. In the week following the Wimbledon game, I was angry with everybody at the club and they were all getting the sharp edge of my tongue. In reality, it was because I was hurting inside and crying out for help. Due to the misguided pride of an addict, though, I was just unable to ask for help.

One day, over the school half term, we had to sign autographs for an hour at some do the club had laid on for about 1,000 kids. I was annoyed as I wanted to be home with one of my own, Sam. It showed what mood I was in, because normally I love being around the young fans and signing for them, having a chat with them. I also had a cold sore developing on my lip, which showed that my physical state was beginning to mirror my mental and emotional one.

I was swearing at everybody all the time and wondering why I was putting myself and them through it. But I was trapped inside it, inside me, inside the illness. My driver John refused to put my bets on for me. He also told me that I had been OK for the first couple of weeks but now I was panicking. At the time, it wasn't what I wanted to hear, though deep down I knew he was right both to say it and to refuse to put the bets on for me. He had touched a nerve and that was why I snapped at him.

I wanted to go in to see John Gregory just to tell him what was going on with me. But after all that had happened between us and with everything that had gone on with Stan Collymore, the last thing I wanted – and I think he wanted – was to be in his office saying that I was in the shit. Especially with the slump we were in. I would have been the rat deserting a sinking ship if I'd asked for a week to go back into a treatment centre, I thought. It might have been different if we were eight points clear.

I was in touch with Lorraine several times a day and it was to be the Friday before they could get a flight out. The hotel was running out of food but the boys seemed to think it was a big adventure. By now Lorraine was bored with it all. I should have been more happy to see them when they got back than I was but I had my mind on other things.

That day I had a complicated £2,500 bet of a treble going on a matchplay golf tournament in America –

Andrew Magee, John Huston and Tiger Woods all to win in the morning matches. They all came in and I was flying.

But I let it ride into the afternoon matches, betting on Huston, Bill Glasson and Woods. The first two won but Tiger Woods lost. I couldn't believe it. The sure one of the three went down. He must have gone out on to the course and thought, 'Paul Merson's had a bet on me. That means I've got to lose today.' If FA rules allowed it, I would bet on Arsenal and Manchester United for the title. Then we might have a chance.

I was going mental watching it unfold on the teletext and my mood worsened with the Watford v Swindon game on the television that night. I told everybody at training that morning that Swindon would beat Watford. By the time I got home I had changed my mind. I had £200 on Watford to win 3–0, even though they had a history of losing televised matches. Swindon won 1–0. They were 5–1 to do that. Why didn't I bet on that, what my gut feeling told me, rather than golfers who get the yips?

Lorraine, meanwhile, was upstairs unpacking. At this point she couldn't have known about the money. With it being a Friday night, she couldn't check up on the accounts. But I'm sure she suspected from my crabby, preoccupied mood that I was gambling. She certainly wasn't best pleased when she opened the fridge. There was not an item of food in it. I had eaten out all the time and hadn't even thought about it.

On the Saturday, we were beaten 4–1 by Coventry City at Villa Park. When you looked at it, it should have been the likeliest game for us to get our first win for weeks but instead we folded. I hadn't had a bet that morning because Lorraine was back and I had done so much money the day before. But it had all got to me. I was feeling panicky. The doors were starting to shut.

Personally, I didn't play well. It was one game where I had to hold my hands up and say I was not at the races. It embarrassed me. I even contemplated giving my wages away to charity that week – rather than the bookies – but afterwards I thought that if anyone found out about it, like the papers, then the other players would think badly of me and think they had to do the same. But that's how guilty I get.

With all this, I lost it in the dressing room afterwards. I told people that I didn't have many more chances like this and everyone was ruining it. I was just ranting, coming out with the first angry remark that came into my head. Looking back, it was not very constructive. The physio Jim Walker clearly got fed up with it and told me to shut up, calling me a Big-Time Charlie. He did say sorry to me when we came out of the shower, though.

Going home that night, I phoned through another bet from my mobile in the car – £500 on Barcelona to beat Valencia 2–0 and £500 on Barca to beat them 3–0 in that night's live Spanish League game on Sky. I got in, the game kicked off and Valencia took the lead within seconds. I'm sure Lorraine suspected that I had had a bet on the game. She sits there saying, 'Great goal' when somebody scores to check my reaction. I just have to bite my lip. I don't think I got away with it this time.

John Gregory called a meeting at the training ground for the Sunday to discuss our bad run and just before it I was watching an Under-12 match between Villa and Everton. I was so touchy that when I thought one of the young Everton subs was taking the mickey out of me, making a noise at me, I got hold of the ball he was playing with and kicked it as far as I could. It caught the wind and flew for miles like a Woolworth's ball on the beach. I really had lost it now.

The meeting was good for me and everyone else. Though the boss was upset with everything, he was calm about it and by now I had calmed down too. Some of the excuses were pathetic – like we're not eating enough pasta – but at least we were talking. We talked about tactics, selection, training routines and people's attitude to things and it served to clear the air.

I began to see things more clearly. What was I doing sorting out a 12-year-old kid like that? I felt ashamed of myself. I wanted to go and say sorry but the game was long over and everyone had left. God knows what that kid will think of me and tell everyone he knows in the future. It wasn't me, all that. But then everything that had happened wasn't me. They were the actions of a man suffering from an illness.

Lorraine has trouble seeing it like that. I mean, I don't understand it either sometimes, so how can she? She just looks at me as if I am doing it all on purpose. As if I'm frittering away our money – her money – deliberately. It's easy to say that you shouldn't do it, harder to know how not to. It's like her smoking. She only smokes three a day and I tell her to stop but she doesn't want to, she says. When I'm in the sickness, that's my answer to her with the gambling, though I know deep down I do want to stop.

The first week seemed fine. I had it under control. It was just a few hundred quid here and there. It didn't affect me too much. It was like having a couple of pints with the lads and managing. But it got mad. When I relapsed with drink last August, I managed to stop quickly. With this it is harder once I have started. It showed me – once again – that my primary addiction was gambling.

The bloke who was putting my bets on for me said that he thought it was fun at the beginning, when the sums involved were sensible. Then he got frightened at the end when I was betting £5,000 a time. One day I couldn't get hold of him and was going mad trying to reach him on his mobile. I finally got him as he was coming out of a cinema. He had been taking his kids to the pictures. I was screaming blue murder down the phone at him. Talk about biting the hand that feeds you.

By the end of the month I had done about £35,000. And by the end of the month, Lorraine had got to know all about it. She confronted me with her suspicions and I just couldn't lie, though I couldn't bring myself to tell her the sums involved yet.

It may well be the final straw for her now. She doesn't seem to mind if I have the odd drink now and then. It is the gambling that gets to her. But not nearly as much as it gets to me. My marriage may well be over now. I have got to stop betting. Not to save the marriage but to save me.

MARCH

Dropped

Monday 1 March

A day off but I am trying to keep busy, so as not to think about gambling. I wasn't missing it today. I was just glad that the madness had stopped. I played 'Football Manager' on the computer at home, then went to the pictures on my own to see *This Year's Love*, with Kathy Burke, which was quite good. It had one great line: 'Sorry mate, you woke up with a fat ugly bird,' she said. There were only about six of us in the cinema.

In the evening I watched the Leicester vs Leeds game hoping Leicester would win so that we would not drop out of fourth place, which is the UEFA Cup spot this year. There is talk about us entering the InterToto Cup if we finish fifth as a backdoor way of getting into Europe but none of us really wants that, having to play competitive games in the summer. Leeds won 2–1. We're still sinking.

I am worried about yet another period of ten days without a game – which is our own fault, due to us being out of the cups – not just because we could slip further behind. I also need to be occupied and focused to keep the gambling out of my head.

Wednesday 3 March

Did some running in training, followed by a shooting contest between me, Julian Joachim, Lee Hendrie and young Fabio Ferraresi, who's a good lad but is not the best finisher in the world. Jockey beat me by one goal, the best strike I think I've ever seen.

In the evening I watched the Manchester United v Inter Milan European Cup quarter-final tie. If I was still betting, this is the match I would have bet on, with United to win. Inter have been in a bad way and are missing Ronaldo. It always seems to work out that when you're gambling, though, these bets don't come along. Duly, 2–0 it was.

Last night I had to avoid watching Eurosport with all the UEFA matches on, because I fancy I know a bit about European football and the temptation to gamble would have been there. It spoils your enjoyment of the football when you bet, as well. I wanted United to win tonight for football reasons but if I had bet on them I would just be agitated all the time, wanting the ref to blow the final whistle.

But I'm making some progress again. In the afternoon I took the boys to the golf driving range. There have been times when I've been with them there and been on the mobile placing bets or listening to the racing commentaries while they were hitting their shots. Tonight I gave them lots of attention.

Thursday 4 March

We had to play Stevenage Borough in a friendly behind closed doors at Villa Park tonight, which some of the lads were not happy about. Personally, I always prefer playing a match to training if there is an option. I travelled up at lunchtime and went to watch a film in the afternoon, *You've Got Mail*, with Tom Hanks and Meg Ryan, which I enjoyed. Soon I'll be getting back my old nickname of 'Barry Norman', which the lads at Middlesbrough gave me. Steve Watson's also a film buff and he'll run me close, mind.

I was amazed how fresh I felt in the game, which we won 5–0. I thought I played well, and I finally scored a goal after twice missing good chances by trying to lob the goalkeeper. I was full of running and felt that I could have gone on all night. It just shows what a few days off the gambling has done.

In the last few weeks, I have felt so weighed down by problems and questions like: 'When am I going to get a bet on?' and 'What if anyone finds out?' Guilt was eating away at me and the whole process was just draining me. It is such hard work being an active addict. Maybe now my game will return.

Saturday 6 March

It has been a hard day today with so much sport going on that last month I would have gambled on.

We trained in the snow and I came home to watch the Ireland v England and France v Wales rugby matches. The second one was fantastic, with the Welsh causing an upset by beating the French. I was watching them upstairs in the bedroom, which made Lorraine think I was betting but I wasn't. That hurt me. For a while I got the feeling that if that was what people were thinking, then I might as well have a bet.

We had been getting on better, at least being more civilised with each other, probably because there is some kind of acceptance in me that the marriage is breaking up. It really is a love-hate relationship sometimes. She knows I am a different person when I don't gamble but it looks like I have gone too far this time and Lorraine seems adamant that we are splitting up.

Sunday 7 March

I let Lorraine have a lie-in while I washed and dressed the boys then took them to the golf driving range. At 2pm, I then settled down to watch the Manchester United v Chelsea FA Cup quarter-final on the telly. She asked me if I would pick up Charlie from a party later but I said that it depended on the game being finished.

It sparked an argument between us, which ended with me losing my temper and throwing a set of car keys at her, which hit her on the back. Though I had been provoked, I knew I shouldn't have done it. Immediately I was ashamed, and worried that this had happened in front of the kids. I hate them to see this kind of stuff and fear for the effect on them. I told them straightaway that I was wrong and that it was my fault.

It is the baffling thing about this illness and recovering from it. One day you think you're OK with things, the next something crops up that winds you up. At the moment my moods are all over the place and feelings that I had tried to bury with the buzz of gambling, fearful feelings about my relationship with Lorraine and the state of my football, are starting to surface again.

Monday 8 March

Sam's birthday. He's excited of course, but I am a bit bound up in myself. My mobile rang at 9am on the way to training. It was Tony Adams wondering how I was. I told him I was not good, that I felt like a bad person again with what I had done yesterday. The guilt really was eating at me. He told me that having apologised to Lorraine, I should now apologise to myself and give myself a break. It helped. I can't live in yesterday.

Wednesday 10 March
Derby County 2 Aston Villa 1

At last a game. Just what I needed.

John Gregory's team selection surprised me tonight. Stan Collymore replaced Julian Joachim just a few days after the boss had talked about terminating Stan's contract with him being at the Priory so much these days. Dion Dublin was in central defence, which I think was done just to accommodate people. Maybe to keep me happy and in the side.

I had played OK in the game at Wimbledon but I haven't been playing that well otherwise. Why didn't Dion play at the back against Wimbledon? That would have made more sense. Wimbledon like to lump it, and Dion is good in the air, but Derby are sharp on the ground and I reckoned a more experienced defender was needed.

The good news was that my room-mate Mark Bosnich was back after five months out with a shoulder injury.

We spent the afternoon watching a film, *The Negotiator* with Samuel L Jackson and Kevin Spacey. Not bad.

We had another nightmare start, 2–0 down in 20 minutes with Baiano and Burton scoring, and Bozzy had to make two great stops to keep it down to that. Then again, we were back in it before half-time with Alan Thompson scoring. I also missed a good chance. Steve Harrison went mad at us at the break and the boss wondered what we were waiting for before we started playing.

We did in the second half, passing it around pretty well and we might even have prised a point out of it. In the first half of the season, I think we would have done. It was typical of the way we were now that we got too little, too late.

Our confidence is low and we are missing Ugo Ehiogu at the back. I didn't think we would because he's one of those players you hardly notice. You miss his contribution when it's gone, though. He's solid and puts himself about. He has a presence we need. Gareth Southgate will read the game and Gareth Barry will distribute the ball well, if too much at times, but Ugo is the one who puts his weight about and who is dangerous at the other end with set pieces.

The boss did his best to lift us, saying that this could be a turning point because we had finished the game so strongly. I wish I could believe him. At the moment, I don't share his faith in the team, nor do I have much in my own game. I stayed the night at Bozzy's and we sat up talking till about 1.30am. We will miss him because he's such a great keeper and I will miss him because he's become such a good mate. It does look as if he will be going now.

Thursday 11 March

The boss called a meeting today to discuss remedies for our bad run. He wondered why we were starting so slowly. I reckoned that if we could just get that early goal that we used to, instead of conceding one, we could turn it all around. Mostly, I kept myself to myself, though. He turned to me at one point and said: 'You're quiet, Merse,' but I didn't really have anything to say. Couldn't really. I'm not playing well enough to give my opinion. I don't think the lads would respect it at the moment.

Anyway, how am I supposed to know what we should be doing in this position? I'm used to being on winning runs, not losing ones, at Arsenal and Middlesbrough. He never asked my opinion much when we were winning all the time, did he? I know much more about being at the top. I just hope we're all paying attention to what is happening to us, especially the kids, so we will learn from it for next season.

I do feel sorry for the boss. He's done well in his first full season but has had injuries at a key time and we haven't had the first-choice team out for ages. It shows what depth of squad is needed now. Also, United and Arsenal seem to get their players fit when it counts, which we need to study. When players were out, they stayed in the race, which is the name of the game.

I am beginning to wonder where we are going to get the next win from. We go to Tottenham on Saturday and they are in good form. We couldn't have picked a harder game right now. That's the way it always seems when you're struggling. I asked the boss if I could join them tomorrow at the Royal Lancaster Hotel, by Hyde Park, where we are staying the night, but he said he wanted me up for training in the morning.

As I was leaving, Steve Stone was arriving to sign from Nottingham Forest in a £5 million transfer. Maybe he will give us a lift. He is a good player and will be a good acquisition, but he is an out-and-out right winger rather than a wing-back, so we will have to modify our system for him. John Gregory also spent a lot of money on Steve Watson so we are strong down the right side.

I would like us to match it down the left, where we have Alan Wright and nothing much else. I also think we need to spend money on an experienced midfield player who can tackle then put his foot on the ball and get the young players around him playing. I suggested Emerson to the boss. I know the Brazilian had his critics while he was at Middlesbrough but I reckon he would do a good job for us and we could probably get him back to this country from Tenerife, who are struggling in the Spanish League. We are crying out for someone like him.

My driver John noticed that Steve Stone, Alan Wright and Mark Draper all have a shaved haircut, which makes them look similar, though they're all different sizes. He says he's going to start calling them the Russian dolls.

Friday 12 March

With Steve Stone having signed, I thought we would be doing some team play in training this morning but all we did was a warm-up, which I wasn't happy about. The boss had got me up here for nothing, I felt.

After travelling down to London, we were allowed out in the afternoon and I went into the West End to buy a couple of the Lladro figurines that Lorraine collects for Mother's Day on Sunday. We had dinner at the Royal Lancaster at 7pm, after which me, Bozzy, Gareth

Southgate and Alan Thompson sat talking until 11.30pm about where we thought the team was going wrong. Some things were petty, some important. It was four blokes at least who cared about things.

I said I was upset with the morning's training. We should be doing more work on set-pieces, I said. A free-kick or corner routine that produces a goal could change our whole run, our whole season around. I think we've done one session on dead-ball kicks since I've been at Villa, a complicated free-kick routine that might just work if you are on top of your game. Nothing on flick-ons from corners or back-post headers or anything like that.

I kept talking about Arsenal and I'm sure, like at Middlesbrough, the lads get fed up with me. But they are still doing corner routines that work and produce goals. And to me they have set standards and these days are doing interesting things that we should be aspiring to.

Take Creatine, the vitamin supplement which is designed to aid recovery for muscles and improve physical condition. To my knowledge, Arsenal start taking it in November and it is funny how for two seasons in a row they have set off on amazing unbeaten runs a month later. Our physio says it is all in the mind. In which case, why not try it? What harm can it do? Arsenal's run is not in the mind, is it? The four of us agreed the team needed a lift.

Saturday 13 March
Tottenham Hotspur 1 Aston Villa 0

I had a complete nightmare today. I just could not do anything right and I began to feel the Villa fans in the crowd starting to turn on me. It was no surprise, I suppose, when I was pulled off after 66 minutes.

It's strange. Even when you are having a bad day at the office, you still don't want to come off. Or shouldn't. There is always the chance that you might grab a goal out of nothing, or do something special that surprises you and which will turn your season around. The game did open up late on, which would have suited me better, but in truth I couldn't moan to the boss about it, even if there were others playing worse than me.

It wasn't much of a game. We didn't look like scoring if we had played all weekend but then nor did Spurs, who weren't as good as I thought they would be. Bozzy made a save in the last minute but Tim Sherwood – who himself had been having a poor game – scored from the rebound and it was game over. It just showed what happens when the luck is with you or against you. How the season has turned around both for them and us from when we beat them in November.

Five weeks ago we were above Manchester United. Now we're 16 points behind them, having lost seven of our last eight games. And it's not as if we've lost to United, Arsenal or Chelsea. If we had just won two of those games, we would still be above Leeds in that Euro spot. Now it's starting to look as if they will get it. We've just got to stay positive. If we won four on a roll, we'd be back in it. And we've still got the big boys to play. The trouble is, no-one seems to feel positive.

Our dressing room was gutted. Here we go again. The sad thing was that we had played worse than that in the first half of the season and got a result then. In the shower afterwards I was telling the boss that I had never known my confidence to be so low. He told me just to keep my head up and to work hard in training and it will come back.

What happened soon after the game didn't do much for it, though. I had decided to go for a night out in the West End with Bozzy and on the way into town in the car we had on Radio 5 Live's *606* programme. One Villa fan was on saying that Merson didn't look as if he cared. That hurt. It was unfair. If there's an argument at the club, I'm in it. I want to get things right. I don't just pick up my money. The fan said I had only had one good game, against Southampton. What with the injury and everything, I admit I haven't set the world on fire, but I've had more than one good game.

Me and Bozzy went into the Met Bar just off Park Lane, where Jerry Springer was in. I reckon I could easily be on his show sometimes, what with all the problems I have been through. Then we had a meal at the nearby Titanic Bar before going on to the Atlantic Bar. I was drinking orange juice and lemonade, just keeping myself to myself.

One girl came up and announced herself as an Arsenal season ticket holder. She just wanted to talk about football. Then her mate came up to say that she had overheard a couple of girls saying that if they could get Paul Merson into bed tonight they could make a packet from the newspapers. That was it for me. I didn't want to be there any more. I went home pretty soon afterwards.

Sunday 14 March

Mother's Day and Lorraine was delighted with the figurines, cards and flowers I got her on behalf of the boys.

There is talk in the papers that I will be going to West Ham in part-exchange for Frank Lampard. I've heard nothing about it. It's just paper talk. Unless the Villa fans want me out, then I will see this through. I just want to enjoy it, which is the message I gave to Charlie when I took him to his football this morning at a nearby village, Park Street.

He is only eight but playing for an Under-12s team. He came on as a sub and did some nice things. I am very proud of him. He might make a player, but I'll be proud of him even if he doesn't. Ben looks really promising and little Sam is getting into it.

They are always asking: 'What do you do at work, daddy?' so I lay on little training sessions for them, showing them skills and drills, like on volleying and control. I don't force them into doing anything. I'm not a dad who wants to push his sons into what he does. But they do love football. I suppose that does have a lot to do with me being in the game, but I think they would want to play anyway. I really enjoy having a kick-about with them. When I'm gambling, I just don't feel I have any time or energy for them. When I'm OK, I'll spend every minute of the day out there with them.

Monday 15 March

We trained in the gym and got a good sweat on. Except for Stan. I came in that morning and as we were changing, he was talking across me to Lee Hendrie. Stan was talking about having been out drinking on Saturday night. To me, for someone who's supposed to be in treatment for depression, that's not on.

In the beginning, I have had a lot of sympathy for Stan,

and did have last Saturday when the Spurs fans starting singing: 'You're mad and you know you are.' But being out on the piss when you're not at the club half the time is just taking the mickey. In my book, if you want to be treated with respect, you've got to treat people with respect and I don't think the fans or the other players will respect Stan when he behaves like that.

Tuesday 16 March

The lads all went to Cheltenham races today but it was best I didn't. Instead I got into an indecisive mood and ended up sitting around the house doing nothing. That can be dangerous for me. I need to have a structure to my day.

Bozzy rang me from Cheltenham to see how I was. I told him to put his house on a horse called Istabraq and in truth you didn't have to be a genius or compulsive gambler to tip it because he was odds on. The horse won and I phoned Bozzy to ask if the lads had backed it. 'To be honest, Merse,' he said, 'you're not the best judge, are you? You've not got the best of records, have you?' Me tipping even a hot favourite had put them off. He made he laugh and cheered me up.

Wednesday 17 March

Finally they seem to have run out of grey paint in Birmingham and everything looked better with the sun out. In fact the training was the best I have known at the club as we had an all-day session, playing in the morning and running in the afternoon.

I asked to see the boss at lunchtime because I wanted to tell him that with Lorraine and me splitting up, and with my confidence at a low, I would appreciate a few days off. I knew I was unlikely to make the England squad, to be announced tomorrow, for the match against Poland next week and it seemed like a chance for a break.

The boss had gone when I got there, though, and for a moment I was annoyed. I had to remember again that the world does not revolve around Paul Merson and his problems. Paul Barron said to ring him but this is not for the phone. And after my New York excursion, I had better play things by the book.

Thursday 18 March

Day off. After golf at Aldwickbury in Hertfordshire with John, who beat me on the last hole, I heard Kevin Keegan's first England squad announced on the news. As I suspected, I wasn't in it but then I didn't deserve to be. I would have been embarrassed.

I know class is permanent and form temporary but I do think that players who have been doing well should be rewarded. I am surprised that Dennis Wise keeps getting omitted. He's as good as anyone in midfield. People talk about his discipline but Tim Sherwood is just as likely to get sent off.

There's not too much change yet. There never is really, first time out. And whoever England field should be good enough for this one. Kevin couldn't have wished for a nicer game to come in. When do Poland ever win away?

I went to see Charlie perform at a concert as part of the elocution lessons we send him to and was very proud to see him standing up there speaking out so confidently. I am fortunate to be able to afford his lessons and give him the best. When I am feeling at ease with myself I am grateful for things like that.

Often I am not at ease in this situation with Lorraine where we are living under the same roof but almost as strangers at the moment. The residue of my gambling spree last month is still fresh and there is a lot of suspicion and resentment around.

I have been talking to Tony Adams, who has ended his well-publicised relationship with the model Caprice, and I envy his ability to make decisions and stick to them. It seems with me that when I am fully occupied, I am well but when I am idle I spent too much time thinking about the relationship. I have told Lorraine that it is probably best now that we separate and get on with our own lives.

Friday 19 March

I was nervous about going to see the boss today to ask him for some time off. I want to take the kids to Florida next week. They've had it rough lately too, especially Charlie who lived with my addiction for his first four years and has seen it again recently.

I wondered why I was so nervous. It was what I needed to do and besides, although this week had been good, I had to remember how bad last month was and take steps not to get back into that. I needn't have been that worried with John Gregory, though. He was as good as gold to me.

He told me that the coaches had just had a meeting and agreed that training had been really sharp and bubbly this week. They said it was because I was sharp and bubbly and the attitude rubbed off on the other players. It's true I have worked hard. Recently I have been taking my problems on to the training ground, going through the motions and expecting to perform well on a Saturday. You can't do that, turning it on and off. Saturday is a reflection of what you've done during the week.

I told the boss that I was planning to go away next week. He said, fine, no problem, and that after Sunday's game at home to Chelsea, he didn't need to see me until the Monday eight days later. I felt relieved and straight away was looking forward to this Monday.

Stan said to me after training that he had been to the Titanic bar on Tuesday. They had obviously let him out of the Priory for the evening. It annoyed me. There's me getting ripped off after 66 minutes, while he stays on the field, then him going out living it up while I went back to training. He just comes and goes, never says anything. Least of all sorry. The lads don't know what's going on.

Saturday 20 March

I'm 31 today and it used to be that players would get worried that their career was coming to an end when they got to that age. I can't say it bothers me too much, though, not the way I feel physically. You're as old as you want to feel. I certainly felt a lot older sometimes when I was playing with the drinking I was doing five years ago. And I find it hard to think that I'm that much older than some players I see who are 26 or 27.

The diet and training methods, coupled with the less damaging way I have lived my life in the last few years, means that I have probably played some of the best football of my career as I've got older. I think I've got shrewder as a player and have a few years left in me yet.

Lorraine had bought me some nice clothes – she's good at choosing presents – and I opened them all before travelling up to training. We trained at the ground today in advance of tomorrow's game at home to Chelsea and it was strange. We did some shadow play and I was up front but the boss seemed a bit distant towards me.

I went to see him afterwards to tell him that I was going to America next week. I thought I had better tell him my destination after what happened last time. He still said there was no problem. Perhaps I was imagining him being a bit off with me.

In the afternoon I went round to Bozzy's to watch the England v France rugby match, England winning again, and for something to eat before we joined up at the hotel at 6.30pm. There, we sat up with the youngsters Lee Hendrie, Gareth Barry, Darius Vassell and Darren Byfield, who were interested to hear about my drinking and drugging days and the pitfalls that a young pro faces. The gaffer came over and told us not to be late to bed. He didn't need to do that. Am I being paranoid or has he got a downer on me now?

Sunday 21 March
Aston Villa 0 Chelsea 3

Everybody else always looks at you when the manager names the team and you're not in it. It feels humiliating. There were two reasons why I was upset as John Gregory read out the list in the dressing room.

First, I was in the boss's office for half an hour on Friday and ten minutes again yesterday and he never said a word, even if I did have an instinct that something was wrong. George Graham, for all his reputation about being a hard man, always told me the day before and gave me a reason when he was leaving me out.

Second, the lads had the hump, not necessarily because I was dropped, though several of them came up to me and said they were shocked, but because Stan was in. He hadn't been at the club for weeks, except for yesterday, and now he had got in ahead of not only me but also Jockey, who's done nothing wrong, who's top scorer, in fact.

Alan Thompson came up and commiserated with me, saying that I was the best player at the club. That was the worst thing about it. I agreed with him. I wasn't going to kick up a stink, though. I was going away tomorrow so I decided just to keep my head down and watch the game quietly from the subs' bench.

I could feel we were going to get hammered. Even if two of their goals came in the last five minutes, Chelsea were very impressive, right on the top of their game and passing it around for fun. Their goals through Flo, Goldbaek and Flo again were well deserved. I got on for the last 13 minutes but could make little impact.

Afterwards the boss turned to me and asked what I thought was going wrong. I was a bit wary about saying anything in my present mood and knew what the consequences could be of becoming the team's spokesman. At Arsenal, Brian Marwood had been the team's PFA rep and at one point was going to lead us out on strike over bonus payments, which not surprisingly upset George. Brian's career at Arsenal was limited after that.

I felt like saying to the boss that you should ask one of the other players what it was like to be in such a bad run because I had no experience of it. Instead, I tried to keep it constructive. I just said that the confidence was low and when that happens, sometimes you can try to play too much football. At those times, you just have to get the ball forward early for a 20-minute spell and get the crowd going. At the moment we are not giving them any excitement and we are flat.

If you start playing the percentage game for just a while – as all championship teams do at some stage of the season – at least you feel you are getting somewhere for a while. When you get a result to lift the confidence, then you can start passing teams to death again. If you are a few degrees off, you don't feel you are getting anywhere.

You can see why Chelsea might not win the title. If they have an off day, they will get ripped. Manchester United and Arsenal have more variety to their game and can get the ball wide quickly and whip it in. Chelsea can't.

Afterwards, the boss said that he wanted everyone in tomorrow. I was shocked. My flight to Florida was at noon. I asked to have a quiet word with him and he looked worried. I said it was nothing to do with being dropped and instead told him about my flight. He said it was all right – but not to tell the others. At least I had got one result today.

Monday 22 March–Sunday 28 March

It was a great week, taking the boys – plus Charlie's friend Daniel, who is 12 – to Orlando, but very hard work. I was constantly on the go with four healthy young boys to take care of. They wanted to play crazy golf every day, and go to Sea World and the Magic Kingdom. I couldn't sit down some days. It was much more exhausting than playing football. The only saving grace was that they were so tired in the evenings that they were in bed by 9pm. Mind you, so was I.

We went to a basketball game one night to see Orlando Magic play Cleveland Cavaliers, which was fantastic, but the two youngest, Ben and Sam, were asleep within fifteen minutes. They could sleep on a clothes line those two.

The next day we went to see baseball, with the Atlanta Braves playing Montreal Expos in one of the Spring training camp exhibition matches – like our pre-season friendlies – that they put on at Disney at this time of the year. I didn't think the boys would enjoy it because baseball can be slow but they loved it.

I ate well and felt good in the sun and I thought I would benefit from the break and play better when I got back. I had a fax through from my agent saying that Stan had gone into the Priory full-time so I thought that the boss had to play me now.

It was a downer coming back, though. Lorraine and I had another argument almost as soon as I returned. I was expecting her to take over looking after the boys but she was busy with other things. I was expecting too much, even though I was shattered. I read all about England's 3–1 win over Poland the day before. Pretty much as expected really, though Paul Scholes's hat-trick was rare. He should savour that. You don't get many days like that in your career.

I needed the week away and I enjoyed it, but I have to admit it was extravagant. We travelled first class and stayed in a suite at a top hotel inside Disney World because they were the only things available at such late notice. It all cost around £17,000, in fact. I do worry that

I can lose the value of money sometimes. It may not seem too much now, considering what I earn, but in a few years when I pack up, I know it will seem like a fortune.

Still, it's my money, which I have earned, and I can do with it what I choose. And at least I am not gambling it away, although I can never get complacent about that these days.

Monday 29 March

It was a hard training day back. Steve Harrison sent me to train with the reserves in the gym and some fitness work did me good after a week away. It was only later that I heard no-one else had been in last week either, apart from one day. I am in the reserves for tomorrow's game at Derby. I don't mind. I want to play again.

Tuesday 30 March
Derby County Reserves 1 Aston Villa Reserves 3

Really enjoyed playing with the reserves tonight. We had Michael Oakes in goal and Gareth Barry in defence and we played well. I was the oldest one by a long shot. I was getting the buzz for playing back again and being on a winning team for the first time in a while helps. I set up one goal with a nice pass and I thought I did pretty well. What pleased me most was that I was really motivated for the game and got myself going.

Wednesday 31 March

I heard we would be signing Colin Calderwood from Spurs before the transfer deadline. He will do well for us. We need someone experienced at the back to ease the burden on Gareth Southgate. I played golf with John and he beat me by one hole. That's the second time in a row and that's worrying. What is wrong with me?

APRIL

The Cruellest Month

Thursday 1 April

The team sheet went up for Good Friday's home game against West Ham. My name was in the 'subs from' list. Subs from? Someone tell me this is an April Fool's joke. Nobody did. Because it wasn't.

I was seeing the physio Jim Walker after training and I told him that I felt like packing the game in. It's getting like that now. I am 31 years old and I feel I'm being treated like a kid by a manager who will be lucky to win as much as I have in the game. Jim said he used to get that feeling twice a year during his playing days. The reserve team manager Malcolm Beard told me just to keep going, not to give anyone an argument at the moment.

It all hurt because John Gregory had said nothing to me, though he had been talking to the papers. The press had obviously noticed I was in the reserves and had asked him about it. He had said that I had problems at home and that the club would look after me but that I had to look after them and keep working hard. It sounded to me a bit like he was getting ready to sell me so I had phoned my agent to see if he had heard anything. He had told me just to keep my head down.

Then I was having a cup of tea in the canteen and the boss called me in. He wanted to talk about the stuff that was in the papers. 'They're trying to split us up and ruin our relationship,' he said. The quotes attributed to him had all been embellished by a local freelance journalist, he said. He added that they got more money for a back page lead and thus spiced up the quotes.

He was as nice as pie. I said to him that I accepted that I needed a kick up the arse and that being dropped was justified. It was just that I wished he could have told me. He accepted that he was wrong not to have done and told me again just to keep working hard. We parted on good terms. This was the other side of him again, reasonable and understanding.

Friday 2 April
Aston Villa 0 West Ham 0

We have started to train on the day of night matches, ever since this bad run began, just some light work to get us in the groove. No one can say we are not working to turn things around. I felt a bit stiff and just did some weights. The boss asked me if I would be OK for the game. 'Definitely,' I said.

At half-time he came in and said he was delighted with a brilliant performance. Now I know I am going to be biased because he had dropped me, but I wondered if I was watching the same game. It was a start, I suppose, not conceding for the first 45 minutes for a change but we hadn't created any chances.

I thought I was sure to get on but it got to 70 minutes, then 80, and I knew I wouldn't. All of a sudden, I was on for the last four minutes. 'Is he taking the piss here?' I thought. I took the opportunity to run around and I enjoyed it. I think I touched the ball more than some of the lads had in the previous 86 minutes. The result meant that at least we had stopped the rot but we've now only scored five goals in nine games of this miserable run.

The boss said to me afterwards in the dressing room that I had done well. He told me to be ready and to keep my chin up. I was getting fed up of hearing it.

Saturday 3 April

I had to leave the house again at 8am, having got in at 1am, as we were called in for training this morning. Then I was back home at 1pm and watched Sky's *Soccer Saturday* all afternoon with Lorraine having taken the boys to a point-to-point meeting. It was the day Robbie Fowler snorted the touchline. What was all the fuss about?

Rodney Marsh on the television was screaming that the incident after Robbie had scored for Liverpool against Everton would be discussed and replayed for months. I thought Robbie must have dropped his shorts and exposed himself or something. When I actually saw it, it looked very tame and I think 85 per cent of pub-goers between the ages of 17 and 25 would just find it funny. Nothing more. People have got to start living in reality.

As someone who has taken cocaine, I can tell you that is not funny. But Robbie wasn't taking it, was he? He was just having a laugh about all the rumours. Let's loosen up.

The boys were going to spend the night at their

auntie's so I took them there, only to find when I got back home a message from Lorraine saying that she had gone out for the evening and would be staying with a friend for the night. My imagination started to run riot. Where would she be? Who would she be with? I was devastated. I have never had a feeling like it. My stomach felt as if it had been ripped out.

I actually felt like doing myself in. Once again I found myself uttering the two most dangerous words for an alcoholic – 'Fuck it'.

I went back round the auntie's house in Kingsbury, near Wembley to see my cousin. He was there with a mate and, more important, a bottle of vodka. The three of us drank it between us, me mixing Red Bull with it. My two youngest boys were sitting there watching me. As the drink was going down, I felt ashamed of myself.

'What are you doing?' I was thinking, but it was too late to stop now. I was determined to go through with it. I was angry with Lorraine and this was my way of dealing with it.

After finishing the bottle, we went on to the Titanic bar. This time I felt a different person to the quiet, withdrawn bloke who had been there a few weeks before. I was buzzing, talking to everybody. I was really outgoing. People who had been in there the last time were coming up to me and saying as much.

One bloke came up to me and said he hoped I wasn't drinking. I said no. 'Taste my drink if you don't believe me,' I added. I knew that he wouldn't be able to make out the vodka with all the orange juice I mixed it with, even though I was drinking double vodkas. Anyway, people have usually been drinking themselves and have the taste of what they're on in their mouth.

Teddy Sheringham happened to be in there, celebrating his 33rd birthday, and he was also worried for me. He knew the seriousness of what I was doing, that this was not right for a recovering alcoholic. He kept asking me if I was all right and offered to take me home but I was too far gone now. I had to see this through. It did dawn on me how many people care, though, and I felt quite humble all of a sudden.

I got talking to a girl called Jodi and started pouring my heart out to her about my problems. She seemed an understanding type and didn't seem to know much about football or who I was, which was reassuring.

We went on to a nightclub, The Emporium, and then back to the girl's flat. I know I had had a lot to drink but I could remember what happened. We talked until eventually I fell asleep on her bed – fully clothed. When I woke at about 8am, I called a taxi and went to get the boys.

Sunday 4 April

I felt really rough this morning. It is Ben's birthday and I took the boys ten-pin bowling, then to the pictures, where I was falling asleep. When Lorraine came back in late afternoon, neither of us spoke about last night. I went out and got us an Indian take-away which was probably not the best idea with the acid stomach I had that was the legacy of last night. I was too pre-occupied with feeling physically bad to feel anything else.

Monday 5 April

We didn't do much at training today. With it being Easter, there is a holiday feeling around even though we've got a game at Leicester tomorrow night, for which I will be sub again. It disappointed me that we didn't have much on. I said to John on the drive up that I hoped we did plenty.

I wanted to sweat the alcohol out of my system. It took me back to my bad days at Arsenal. I could remember being away with them in Spain and trying to get rid of the booze by sweating it out in the sun, or running round a pitch wearing a bin liner under my kit to make me sweat more. I managed to get some sweat on, though, and the old feelings came back, of guilt and remorse about drinking again. My voice was also croaky again.

It didn't stop me thinking about next Saturday, though, and where I would be going for my next night out. With Lorraine taking the boys away tomorrow for a week's holiday in Tenerife, I would be off the leash.

It was going through my head that if I could just keep it to once a week, maybe I would be able to control it and not get back into my old ways. I felt bad, but maybe not bad enough and, to be honest, I had felt some respite from all the anxiety I have had both in my personal and professional lives.

Tuesday 6 April
Leicester City 2 Aston Villa 2

The chairman came up to me in the dressing room before the game. 'Are you going back to your house in North London tonight?' he asked. I knew what he was really asking. The boss overheard and said it was time for him to leave. I pointed out to Mr Ellis that I was out of the team when I thought I should be playing but that I wasn't kicking up a stink in the papers. 'No, you have been very professional,' he said. 'In which case, just let me live where I am happiest at the moment, please,' I replied. He accepted the logic of my argument. We get on pretty well. He has his off days and I have mine.

In the game, we started off like our old selves. Lee Hendrie gave us a lead in the first minute – the early lead we have desperately needed – and we started defending solidly again. It was like early season once more. The boss was delighted at half-time and when Jockey grabbed a second early in the second half against his old club, it looked like our winless run was coming to an end.

Then we went. All of sudden we looked wobbly, seemed to get nervous, not having been in this position for a while and we let them back in it to score twice. Emile Heskey was brilliant. He will be a top player one day soon. He was quick and strong, bang on his game. He was chesting down balls that I would be looking to flick on.

I was disappointed not to get on, with us struggling to hold on for a point in the end. I thought I could have brought a bit of calming experience to the job. Afterwards, I thought the boss would go mad but instead Steve Harrison was telling everybody how well they had done. Not many teams get a result against Leicester, he said. Well, plenty do at Filbert Street. Manchester United won 6–2 here. Leicester are much more comfortable away from home where the onus is not on them to attack.

We haven't had that balance lately between defence and attack. One day the defence will be on its game, like against West Ham, but the attack won't be. Tonight it was vice-versa. We are two units as opposed to a team at the moment. And there is never a Quincy, never an inquest. If Arsenal had conceded two late goals, there would be hell to pay in the dressing room.

Not having got on, I was worried that I would have to play for the reserves at Leeds tomorrow night. Everyone was saying no, though; no first-teamer plays twice in a row for the reserves. Even Michael Oakes was excused. Then Steve Harrison came and told me that I was required at training at 11.30am and would then travel with the reserves. I told him that when I played for the second team, the manager Malcolm Beard said I did not have to train on those days.

Bozzy phoned me in the car on the way home. Before the game he had asked me to watch his performance and to give him any advice. I told him that his shot-stopping was brilliant but he still had work to do on his kicking. I also didn't like to see him waving the ball away when it was going wide. It just fires up the opposition's forwards.

He listened and took the criticism on board. He is world class already but wants to get better and that attitude will take him a long way. I would love him to stay at Villa, and he'll probably get as much money here as anywhere else, but I think he feels he could win more somewhere else. With Peter Schmeichel moving on, Manchester United is surely the best bet.

Wednesday 7 April
Leeds United Reserves 3 Aston Villa Reserves 4

I reported for the reserves at 1.30pm, which Malcolm was happy with. He said he would rather be taking a happy Paul Merson to Leeds than one who had been forced to come in early. To me that is good management. Certain managers know how to treat players individually to get the best out of the talented ones. Why is it, for example, that David Ginola is playing some of the best football of his life when everyone thought he would be a casualty of George Graham's regime at Tottenham?

Paul Barron was at the training ground asking me the best directions to get to Chelsea. He is going to scout the Real Mallorca goalkeeper Carlos Roa, the Argentinian whom I had scored past in the penalty shoot-out in the World Cup, at the Cup-Winners' Cup semi-final first leg as Bozzy's possible replacement.

My attitude was spot on at Leeds. In fact I scored after 45 seconds, curling a shot into the top corner from the edge of the box, and everything seemed enjoyable after that. It was nice to have a good battle with David Batty, who was making his way back after injury.

Afterwards our goalkeeper Peter Enckelman, a young Finnish lad who is going to be a really good keeper, said to me that he couldn't believe how much I enjoy my football, be it playing or training. And I do. He said he was amazed how mad I went whenever the team scores a goal.

I just love the game to bits and especially my team, no matter who I'm playing for, scoring goals. In the first team, only one or two come to congratulate the scorer. I think everybody should, no matter who he is – whether you like him as a bloke or not – and no matter how far you have to run to do it.

I felt satisfied driving back down the M1 with John. I wasn't thinking at all about the drink of last weekend, though next weekend crossed my mind.

Thursday 8 April

A day off but I couldn't relax. I was pre-occupied, almost obsessed now, with thoughts of planning my drink this coming Saturday night. Pre-occupied, too, with the knowledge that for me it wasn't right. It may be for others but not me.

Something inside me told me to ask for help, so I rang a friend from AA, who came over to see me. I told him about the drinking and about looking forward to the next one. He said that he thought I probably could control it for a while and get away with it. How long before I started gambling again, though? How long before I went on to cocaine? Or something worse?

It frightened me. I knew he was right. Who was I kidding? There is not only my profession to consider, because if I got drug-tested again having taken cocaine that would be it this time. I hadn't been tested with Villa all season – although I was every time I linked up with England – but sod's law says that I would be this time. It is more how bad I feel about myself when I drink, drug or gamble. Everything crumbles, both around me and inside me and I cannot function properly.

I decided I had to get active again and rang John for a game of golf. I lost 6 and 4. Then I went to a restaurant with him where a waitress spilt a plate of food over me. With Chelsea only drawing 1–1 with Mallorca, it was not my day. But I hadn't had a drink and I knew I didn't dare have one, so maybe it was not so bad after all. I know it is a fragile feeling, mind, and can change from day to day. I have to be on my guard.

Friday 9 April

I found out again that I was not playing tomorrow against Southampton so I asked the boss if I could train with the reserves, because they do more on a Friday. He said OK and asked me how I was. I told him that I was struggling and that I had had a drink last Saturday night.

He said he had been asked about me and my domestic problems by the press and said that he had not had a problem with me here, that I had been brilliant. 'Why aren't I playing then?' I asked but he didn't answer. I told him not to keep telling me to keep my chin up because I will do that anyway. I reckon I'm always a trier. I have decided now that when I feel bad, I should not bring it to the training ground and tell all and sundry about my worries but speak to AA people instead. They know what this illness is about and how to respond to it.

I got talking to Paul Barron about Roa. Paul thinks he is brilliant, the best in the world, but I thought he flapped at some crosses and made a meal of others. David Seaman and Peter Schmeichel are still the best in the world. I told him that the club had to break the bank to keep Bozzy, though I don't think he will stay. It's not all about money anyway. I've told Bozzy that the grass is not always greener somewhere else. Maybe I'll have to tell him again.

As I was leaving, a journalist from the *Sun* approached me with pictures of me leaving a nightclub with that girl last Saturday night. I told him there was nothing in it. Later I phoned my agent Steve Kutner and he got on to the *Sun*. I think they believe me and will drop it but I'm worried that the photographer will offer it to another paper.

In fact, Kutner thinks that the girl, whose name is Jodi Morris, might have gone to the *News of the World* with an account of that night. I know nothing happened between us, but I suppose they're interested in the fact that I have fallen off the wagon. It worried me and my first thought was that I could do with a drink. That's an alcoholic thinking.

In the evening, Andy Townsend phoned me and I could hear Gazza on the other end. 'Come and live with me, you bore,' he said. I told him that I had been out last Saturday night and that I was drinking. He went quiet. They said to come up to the North-East for a couple of days and they would cheer me up. I don't think that's what I need, though. I heard from Charlie Miller, his old Rangers colleague now at Leicester, that Gazza's back on the drink, having been spotted at a Rangers function drinking booze out of a teacup.

After he got over the shock of me drinking again, Gazza was in good humour on the phone. He said he was looking forward to playing against me, but it looked as if it would be in the reserves now. He had played at Burnley the other day and there were two dogs and a man there.

He has been going to bingo a lot with Jimmy Five Bellies to keep himself out of mischief, he said. And had I seen all this stuff in the *Sun* about Bryan Robson and Clare Tomlinson, who used to be an FA press officer and is now a Sky Sports presenter? When he saw it, he said to Robbo at training: 'Two for bingo tomorrow, boss?'

Saturday 10 April
Aston Villa 3 Southampton 0

I was right. Steve Kutner told me that the *News of the World* have the story. Even though I'm one of their columnists, there's no way they will keep this out of the paper as a favour to me. I was thinking that I would have to think up some story for Lorraine ready for when she came back from Tenerife next Tuesday, like the girl working in the nightclub and coming out to order a taxi for me when the flashbulbs went off.

I can't take much more of this. I was sitting there on the substitutes' bench before the game really depressed and thinking, 'Right, I'm going back into treatment after this game.' I told some of the senior players before the game that they could expect to read something about me in the papers tomorrow morning.

I was surprised to get on, in place of Mark Draper, only five minutes into the second half as we were only one up at the time and he had scored it. I was determined to seize the chance and enjoy the game. It was going to be my last game before going into treatment for I didn't know how long. I thought I did well and was really pleased with a chipped through ball for Jockey to score. At the end I felt really emotional and could not stop myself crying as I applauded the supporters.

I was crying too when I went to see the boss in his office after the game. He was pleased with my performance and said that perhaps I needed to have a drink every Saturday night. It was meant as a joke but he doesn't understand the seriousness for me of what he is saying.

I told him what I was planning about treatment and he said that he would go along with whatever I thought was best but that he would like to have me available at Liverpool next Saturday. I said that I would take it one day at a time and if I felt bad I would go into treatment but would try and see it through to next week.

That night, I went with John and an AA friend to an Italian restaurant then went home to watch *Match of the Day*. I need to be around people like that. It kept me out of a bar.

Sunday 11 April

The *News of the World* have not run the story. What a relief. I could enjoy without worrying a day going back up to Villa Park to see the FA Cup semi-final between Arsenal and Manchester United with some mates from the hospitality box that Mark Bosnich and I have rented for the day. Though it was goalless I still enjoyed it, but I had a nervy desire for a drink at one point with the stuff being available in the box.

Monday 12 April

I had made an appointment for the afternoon to meet my old counsellor from treatment, Steve Stephens, at a hotel near Nottingham, where he now lives.

On the way there after training, my mobile went. It was the girl from the Titanic Bar, Jodi Morris. She said there were hordes of press outside her door and what should she do? I told her not to worry about it because nothing had happened between us, had it? At that point the phone went dead. I suspected straight away that she had someone with her and that it was probably a set-up to see if I knew her. I knew then that it would be going in the paper the following Sunday.

I was in bits when I saw Steve and I was crying as we sat and talked in the lobby of the hotel. He always speaks in a very clear and simple way that helps me a lot. He was just what I needed. He said that the article may be going into the paper in the future, but that the drinking relapse happened in the past and I couldn't change that now. All I could do was accept it and learn from it so that I didn't repeat it. He did me a power of good.

Tuesday 13 April

Lorraine came back with the boys today and I told her about the events of that Saturday night and that it would be going in the paper. I decided that I had to start getting honest again instead of trying to make up excuses.

I'm not sure if she believes me that nothing went on between me and the girl. She said she had been thinking about our relationship while she was away and had already made up her mind that she wanted a separation anyway. As soon as I could make arrangements, she wanted me out of the house. I think I knew it would come to this but it still hurts to hear it and the reality of what it means frightens me.

I was supposed to play for the reserves in a big game against Birmingham City tonight but was pulled out because I had done well against Southampton, which could mean that I'm going to start the game at Liverpool on Saturday.

Wednesday 14 April

There was a club golf day at The Belfry, which helped take my mind off things, as I enjoyed playing with a group from Reebok, who were a good laugh. From there I went to Villa Park for the Arsenal vs Manchester United replay, which was a sensational game. I was gutted for my old team when Dennis Bergkamp had a penalty saved in the last minute of normal time by Peter Schmeichel and amazed that Ryan Giggs found his way through their defence for the amazing solo goal that took them to Wembley. Bozzy told me that Alex Ferguson had phoned him last night to check which end was best for penalties. That is some research.

On the way home, I was stopped for speeding, doing 97 mph. I can expect a ban now, I suppose.

Thursday 15 April

The boss named the team for the Liverpool game and I wasn't in it. I was furious and stormed in to see him. 'I put off going into treatment because you said you needed me,' I said. He said he had never said that I would start the game – and to be fair I suppose he hadn't – but that was what I read into it.

We talked for ages. I said that the lads were amazed I wasn't in the team and I hated being patronised like that, lesser players telling me how sorry they were for me. I told him that if he was trying to get me to put in a transfer request so that the club didn't have to pay me a cut of any fee or the next instalment of my signing-on fee I was due, then I would do what he wanted. This wasn't about money, I said. I'd rather be on a lot less and be playing at Bury or somewhere. I need to be playing. If I am training every day and playing regularly, then I am all right.

He told me that he didn't want to sell me and that I was a big part of his plans. He said that at the moment, he had a home team in his head and an away team, and I didn't figure in the away starting line-up just now. He felt the team he had named would get a result. Of course I disagreed, but in the end we had to agree to disagree.

Friday 16 April

My agent has been in touch with the *News of the World* and they agreed to show him what they are planning to print from the girl. He duly faxed me the interview with her, for which I was told she was getting £20,000. Apparently she had also done a photo session with them.

The account was a travesty of what happened. She is recorded as having said that I was going to the toilet all the time. The account was trying to suggest, it seemed to me, that I was using drugs there, which was not true. It also made out that I had told her I loved her, that I knew Lorraine was having an affair and that I was feeling like killing myself. I didn't recall saying any of those things. I didn't mind admitting that I had poured my heart out to her about how unhappy I had been lately.

None of what she said sounded good from my point of view and I rang the reporter who was writing the story. I wanted to get my side of it across. I held my hands up and said that I had been drinking and had gone back to her flat but I swore that I did not sleep with her. I was crying on the phone to him and I talked to him for a couple of hours so I think he could see that I was telling the truth.

Now I will just have to hope that they quote me properly alongside her story. I rang Lorraine to tell her that it would all be going into the *News of the World*. She's just fed up with it all and I don't suppose I can blame her really.

Dinner cheered me up tonight. As we were all eating, on a raised part of the dining room four steps up from the main dining area, Steve Harrison came through all the business people eating and fell up the stairs. He had the whole room in stitches. It was a variation on his celebrated Norman Wisdom walk.

He is also adept at sitting down at the table, knocking everything over deliberately as he reaches for something and making a real racket. 'Ian Wright does that,' I said to him the first time I saw it. 'Where do you think he got that from?' he said.

Saturday 17 April
Liverpool 0 Aston Villa 1

A fax arrived from the *News of the World* in the morning. I was relieved that they had gone with my story rather than her interview. They must have accepted that I did not sleep with her and must have seen the story of me falling off the wagon as more significant than her saying she had been with me in a nightclub.

It was a balanced and fair account, I have to admit. I could only accept without whingeing that they had got me. If you are in the public eye and you do something wrong, that's the only attitude you can have really. I've never been in the papers for sitting at home watching the telly.

The only thing I took issue with was a statement about the drinking not being the real problem for me. It certainly was, and is. I tried to phone the reporter but couldn't reach him. Then I phoned Lorraine to tell her what was going in the paper and to apologise if it caused her embarrassment. She was not in much of a mood to listen.

My problems were put in perspective by what date it was – the 10th anniversary week of Hillsborough, and we were going to Anfield to play Liverpool. Bozzy and me decided to buy 96 red roses, one for each of the dead, to lay in front of the Kop as a mark of respect. There was also to be a wreath from the team.

I wanted to do it when we arrived at 1.30pm before the crowd arrived, because it was a private gesture, but the boss decided we should all pay our respects together when we went out before kick-off. We received a very touching reception, which embarrassed me a bit. I didn't mean for it to be a public gesture.

It was the worst Liverpool side I could remember, though we had to take some credit for not letting them play. Some confidence was coming back in the lads after the Southampton win and we passed it round well, Ian Taylor's goal being fair reward. I got on for the last 20 minutes and enjoyed it.

As the lads were warming down after the game, I said to the boss in the dressing room that he had got the tactics right and I couldn't complain about not being included. He seemed surprised. He replied that I was one of the most honest players he had come across. He has also admitted when he has made some dodgy decisions so we must have a reasonable basis for a working relationship.

I got back home at 9pm and Lorraine went straight out. She did not want to discuss what would be in the *News of the World* in the morning.

Sunday 18 April

The doorbell rang a couple of times first thing – reporters wondering if I had anything to say. I didn't and to their credit they accepted it and went away. I was relieved that what was in the paper wasn't worse. They still have her interview, though, and maybe they will use that next week. It was still bad enough. Charlie saw the paper and asked who the girl was in the picture with me. I couldn't lie. I told him that Daddy had had a drink again and he had done wrong.

I wanted to get out with the boys and I decided to take them to Thorpe Park. I thought people might be staring at me having read the paper, but mostly they were too busy with their own families to bother about me. That is just the paranoia and the self-obsession of this illness. I don't think many people are in a position to judge me anyway. There must be quite a few blokes who have had an argument with their wife and gone out and got drunk.

Monday 19 April

Lorraine was back late last night and we didn't have a chance to talk. This morning she told me she wanted me out of the house. She said she was worried about me living in a hotel, so suggested that I stayed with Debbie and Marco, two friends of ours in Cheshunt over the other side of Hertfordshire. I packed some gear and drove over there.

My head was spinning as I drove. Sometimes I want to be with Lorraine, other times I don't and I think she probably feels the same about me. At the moment, we are just winding each other up and probably need to be apart. I know that she isn't the reason I had a drink, and she certainly didn't pour it down my throat, but our relationship and the way I react to it is part and parcel of what is still wrong with my recovery.

My phone went in the car. It was the *Daily Express* to say that Max Clifford was now handling Jodi Morris's story and it could be going to the highest bidder this week. I was distraught. How much more of this was there going to be? I drove back to St Albans to see an AA friend of mine and cried my eyes out with him, trying to get out all the pain inside me.

It helped a lot. So, to take my mind off things, did going to Highbury that night to see Arsenal beat Wimbledon 5–1 from the box that Debbie and Marco share with Tony Adams and his family. I needed to get out. I then stayed the night with my AA friend and began to calm down, feeling a bit less scared of how things might be turning out.

Tuesday 20 April

I really gave it everything in training today, probably more than I should have at this stage of the season. At Arsenal, Arsène Wenger likes to keep sessions very short, to about 45 minutes, and would probably think we do too much. There is the danger of burning out and not looking sharp but I needed to be active. I was doing weights, press-ups and I was the last one to get changed at the end. I wanted to get that feeling back of trying to be the best again.

Afterwards John drove me to the hotel near St Albans where he is leaving his car each morning now, me driving over from Cheshunt to link up with him. Debbie and Marco have a wonderful place, with swimming pool and gym, and they make me very welcome. Soon I am going to have to find a place of my own where I can have the boys to stay, though, because they need to get some stability amid all this turmoil.

Wednesday 21 April

I woke up very early but I couldn't get up and go downstairs because I was worried about activating the alarm system in Debbie and Marco's house. I was still up at 6.15am and leaving for training at 6.45am. I now have an extra half hour on my journey every day. It's OK. I need to be occupied. I have to change now, I can't get back into the old vegetating routine and at least driving will keep me active.

Thursday 22 April

Another good day in training. I think people at the club would probably say that my training has been the best it has been since I came from Middlesbrough. The cricket and running have disappeared from our training schedule now. Something had to change with the bad run we were in.

I like to get stuck in to all the drills and games. It has been my release from all the cares and worries of these difficult and dangerous times for me. Instead of whining and sulking, I have got more involved. This game really can kick you in the bollocks. When you cost £6.75 million, you almost take it for granted that you are going to play.

When you get dropped, it concentrates your mind. I took football for granted, like I did with my recovery and both backfired. Now I want to be the best again and on my day I am. I have to get back in the team again. I actually think I'm not the only one who deserved to get dropped. There is some complacency within the club. But I have to take responsibility for myself now, not worry about anyone else's performance or feel I am responsible for keeping the rest of the team happy.

Friday 23 April

I spoke to Tony Adams on the phone on my way to training. He was ringing to see how I was doing. I told him I was managing. He asked me if I had been to any AA meetings and I said no. He said that maybe I needed to. I knew he was right.

After training, I rang the AA Birmingham number and they told me of a meeting that night in Tamworth, about 15 minutes away from The Belfry where I was staying. I was determined to get there and was glad I did. There were only about eight of us there but it was instructive and inspirational. Two in the room were drunk and it did me good to see what awaited me if I went back on to the bottle.

Saturday 24 April
Aston Villa 2 Nottingham Forest 0

Often I check into The Belfry on a Friday afternoon and don't leave my room until it is time to go to Villa Park at 1pm on the Saturday. I just have room service meals delivered. Today, as part of trying to do things differently, I got up and went down for breakfast at 8am, then for a walk with Colin Calderwood, who is also staying in the hotel.

An AA friend has suggested that I have to do things differently this time. He's right. Look where doing things my way, in the old ways, got me. I feel things have been getting better gradually all week. I have got to a meeting, been reading books and got into the day quicker rather than slopping around.

It's just doing the basics of a recovery programme really, like with football when you're coming back after a bad patch. You practise five-yard passes and it looks easy but how many times in a game do you see players mess them up? You can never afford to take anything for granted, in football or in life.

The fact that I feel better is shown in my reaction to

Jodi Morris's story appearing in the *Daily Mirror* today. It really doesn't bother me any more. She has been reasonably honest but the worry about people thinking badly of me has gone now. It just goes to show, as an AA friend of mine says, that it is not what happens to me in life that is important, but my attitude to it.

With Lee Hendrie having a bad ankle I was back in the team in his place and it felt good. It was pretty easy too, with Forest being relegated as a result of their defeat and not looking as if they believed they could stay up. They were the worst Premiership side I've seen for quite a while. We could have had loads more goals than those by Mark Draper and Gareth Barry.

I had been invited to a party at Dion's house in Stratford-on-Avon and we drove back to John's house in North London to pick up his girlfriend before travelling back to the Midlands. It was a good party and it was nice to see Ian Wright and Paul Ince, who had travelled from their games.

On the way home, at about 1am, the car got a puncture on the M1. The spare was also punctured so we had to go and ring for a recovery vehicle and wait for him to come. It was 4am when we got to the Noke hotel, where John's car was, so I just booked in there.

Sunday 25 April

Up at 9am to go over to Kwik Fit in St Albans to get two new tyres. From there I went over to Cheshunt to get showered, shaved and changed. Then back to St Albans to pick up the boys and take them to play golf. After that, I took them back home and played football in the garden. I was shattered.

I felt well, though, but Lorraine brought me back down to earth by saying that she still wanted to end the marriage and that we needed to make some arrangements. I didn't want to speak about it at that time and left with some more of my clothes. The boys were crying.

When I got to Cheshunt, Lorraine rang and put Ben on the phone. He was upset and wondered when I was coming home so I drove back over to St Albans to get him off to sleep. Lorraine was annoyed with me, saying that I would come for the boys but wouldn't come to speak to her. I felt I couldn't win whatever I did.

It was another day when I had to just say that at least I had stayed sober, although things are getting a bit frantic.

Monday 26 April–Thursday 29 April

These are up-and-down days, and even within those days I can be up and down.

The relationship between Lorraine and me occupies nearly all my attention. Some days I think we have to just make a clean break, on others I think we should be trying again for our own sakes and the boys'. Some days I feel well and cope, on others I am upset with it all. It seems that we are both affected by each other's moods and we take them on board. I think this is what they call a co-dependent relationship.

It helped to go to an AA meeting at London Colney on the Monday. Strange to think that I used to train with Arsenal less than a mile away from here. I heard a lot of sense and got a charge from the meeting.

I was still trying to keep active. On Tuesday, I went to

the pictures on my own after training to see *Civil Action* with John Travolta, which I enjoyed. I also went on the Thursday, with Colin Calderwood and Steve Stone, to see *Waking Ned*, which I thought was rubbish.

I was commuting between the training ground, The Belfry, Cheshunt and St Albans, trying to give as much time as possible to the boys and to my football. I seemed to be in the car a lot of the time, though, up and down the M6 and M1 and round the M25. My back was feeling fine. I had just developed a blood clot behind my shin bone, though, after a kick in training, which was painful and being in the car didn't help.

I tried to balance it with some time for myself and on the Wednesday I played golf with a friend. Always the stuff between Lorraine and me, with us being hurt at what looked like the ending of a marriage, would intrude, though. Charlie phoned to see if I was coming round in the evening and I said yes.

But when I got there, Lorraine was angry at me appearing the hero who came round and did all the nice things with them. She had to cope with Charlie not doing his homework and his moods at being affected by all this, she said. I offered to take Charlie back to Cheshunt with me that night so that I could talk to him and I wondered if Lorraine wanted to have dinner one night so that we could discuss formal arrangements both for the boys and money matters. She said she didn't want to be pressured.

Then on other days she says she wants it all sorted out. Like me, I suppose this illness, with its inconsistency of reaction and behaviour, has got to her and she is also in pain.

Friday 30 April

I was driving in to the training ground this morning just as Mark Bosnich was leaving. I asked him what the problem was and he said that John Gregory had refused to give him another 24 hours to prove his fitness for the game against Manchester United tomorrow. The boss apparently said that he needed to know now.

Bozzy was particularly angry because the boss had given Dion Dublin and Gareth Southgate, who are also injured, the extra time. It is probably something to do with Bozzy wanting to leave the club and the fact that United could well be in for him.

I was angry myself. 'Who am I going to share with now? Isn't the boss thinking of me? Now I have got to be on my own.' It was another lesson about the selfishness of the illness and realising that the world doesn't revolve around Paul Merson.

At our hotel, Mottram Hall in Cheshire, I sat watching golf on television on the terrace in the afternoon and got chatting to one of the staff at the hotel. She turned out to be separated from her husband and it was interesting to compare experiences. Of course the lads made a few wolf-whistle noises as they walked by but it was just nice to have a civilised conversation with someone.

I felt human again and able to communicate without a drink, as I had been unable to do in the Titanic Bar those times. To me, that experience now showed just how alcohol changed my personality for the worse. On the first visit, I got out as soon as things got uncomfortable. On the second, I just got into trouble.

Lorraine phoned to tell me what she was doing over the weekend. The boys were going to stay with my mum and dad, she said. She was going into London to the

Prada shop and I asked her to buy me some clothes. She was then going on to the Titanic Bar. It was where I was planning to go too, with some friends, so that was out of the question now.

Later Bozzy rang me to say that he had heard that the boss was going to cane him in the papers, saying that he had refused to play. He wanted me to tell the boys that he had wanted to play and would never let them down. I told him not to worry. The boss can be over-talkative with the press sometimes, but who am I to judge?

Recently, John Gregory told the press that I had been crying in his office and I was a bit upset with that but he said he had simply told a friend and it had somehow got out. He apologised to me. Sometimes you get emotional and say too much in the heat of the moment and I think he can be like that. Also, I think he does get misquoted now and then. The next day it all blows over. That's how it should be. You shouldn't hold grudges.

I was more concerned about my own performance. I had been named in the side for the game tomorrow and was looking forward to it. It was the first time I had been in the starting line-up for a match against one of the top three this season and it also represented a healthy respite from all the strain I was feeling. Pressure in football? There's a lot more outside it.

MAY

The Best at Last

Saturday 1 May
Manchester United 2 Aston Villa 1

We could, and probably should, have done some serious damage to United's title chances today. For the first 20 minutes we seemed a bit overawed by Old Trafford – which is one of the things we need to learn for next season, that we belong up here with these teams – but after that we should have got something out of the game.

They took the lead with Steve Watson's own goal but we deserved to be level at half-time thanks to Jockey's goal. Then David Beckham scored with a world-class free kick. People criticised us for not having a wall but brilliant as he is with a dead ball, he shouldn't have scored from there really.

They had a penalty soon after, which Michael saved. Then we should have had one, when Blomqvist brought down Mark Draper. You don't get penalties at Old Trafford these days, though, do you? It is like Anfield used to be. Afterwards, people were saying that the last time the opposition got a penalty there was five and a half years ago, Ruel Fox for Norwich.

When we got back south, I went with John and a couple of mates to a bar near Heathrow called Morleys and drank orange juice. After a while, I wondered what I was doing there. I'm frightened to be on my own on a Saturday night, I suppose. Frightened in case I missed something. I didn't want a drink, just company, but it's a dangerous place for me to be keeping company.

Monday 3 May

We may have Sundays off these days, the warm-downs having been knocked on the head after the Coventry defeat, but we still work hard. And there is no end-of-season feel about the club, even though we can't finish in the top four any more. It was Bank Holiday Monday but the boss still had us in for training, with the club now definitely going to enter the Intertoto Cup if we get the chance by finishing fifth.

It would mean matches against teams from Wales, Malta, Estonia and Finland and if we come through that series of games, we play off for a UEFA Cup place. Some of the lads are not keen, with games starting in July, but I don't mind. I am one of those who prefers playing to training.

In the evening I went to the AA meeting in London Colney again, which was useful. It's like starting all over again in recovery but with a bit more knowledge and self-knowledge this time. It's important that I keep going even if some nights I don't feel like it. They say that if you take your body, your mind will follow.

Wednesday 5 May

A running day at the club, with fitness tests to follow, measuring and monitoring our levels. It's probably to do with the end of the season and will be compared with the beginning to see what lessons there might be for next season. To me that makes sense. Though I like to keep busy, sometimes you have to save players from themselves – like kids who want to play all the time – and I think there have been times when we have worked too hard.

At Arsenal, Arsène Wenger is very much into recovery time and not overdoing things. And when I spoke to Bryan Robson about what we did, he thought we would burn ourselves out. He might have been right. I know I find it hard to strike the balance – but then I'm like that in life. I need proper guidance. Also, we do need to get a bit more scientific at Villa. Sometimes I think we're a bit Stone Age.

There have been more phone calls with Lorraine, trying to resolve problems. I don't suppose they will be until we have had a proper time away from each other to find out how we really feel, or until she has been to see a solicitor to discuss terms for a divorce. Most of the time I am playing football, snatching time with the boys, or sitting in the car. I know every song by heart on the zillions of CDs in the car. I am even beginning to remember the words of John's weird rap stuff, which is worrying.

Friday 7 May

I am in the team again for tomorrow's home game against Charlton Athletic, which is pleasing, but there is no Mark Bosnich once more.

When he arrived for his training, the outfield players were in a circle passing the ball and he came over. 'Morning Harry,' he said to Steve Harrison. 'Morning Ronald,' he said to another coach, Ross McClaren, who is nicknamed after Ronald McDonald because he is so fat. 'Morning coward,' he said to John Gregory. It looked like the boss was pretending not to hear but everyone else did. I told Bozzy afterwards that he was out of order.

After training, I went and put the deposit down on a two-bedroomed flat in Sutton Coldfield that I had been looking at. Colin Calderwood has bought one in the same block. It should come in useful for next season because I can stay there, rather than in hotels, when I am up during the week. Then it's easier for the boys to come and stay. It looks like I'm also going to need a new house down South where I can have them when it's my turn but until things with Lorraine are more clear-cut, I don't know how much I've got to spend on one.

I checked into a hotel at Leigh Marsden, with The Belfry being full, then went to the pictures to see *Message in a Bottle* with Kevin Costner, which was a mistake. Not because it was a bad film but because it was a love story. Afterwards I phoned Lorraine about five times. I was madly in love with her again. And I was hurting again.

I went back to the AA meeting in Tamworth in the evening. I was surprised last time how few of us there were and I thought there must surely be more drunks who don't want to drink than this in the town. Tonight there were a lot more there. I enjoyed it again and am beginning to feel at home at this meeting.

This time around, I am starting to look forward to meetings a bit more. Before they seemed like a bit of a chore and I found it hard to sit through them and concentrate, sometimes in smoky atmospheres. At least, those were the excuses I used to stop going. Now I feel more as if I want to go rather than just need to go.

Saturday 8 May
Aston Villa 3 Charlton Athletic 4

Lorraine was on the phone early this morning with some problem about money. I said that I couldn't sort it today, because I had a match but that I would on Monday if she still needed me to. It didn't bother me and I didn't let it upset me. It is amazing what being back on the AA programme can do. Five weeks ago today I drank on much less than that.

I do feel I am turning things around again and getting some self-esteem back. Even John has noticed a change in me. He says that I don't swear so much, that I'm not so angry and that I'm not just staring out of the car window all the time when we drive up to Birmingham. I still have fear and doubt, and a sadness about the way things are turning out with Lorraine, but I feel more able to cope.

It was an amazing game against Charlton. They would score, then we would. Gareth Barry put the ball into his own net, then redeemed himself at the other end. Clive Mendonca tucked one in, then Jockey equalised, John Robinson restored their lead then Jockey equalised again.

Near the end they had their goalkeeper Andy Petterson sent off and didn't have another on the bench, so put in an outfield player, Steve Brown. 'That's the sort of luck you get when you're at the bottom,' Mendonca said to me. 'Not over 36 games,' I said to him.

We thought we would go on to win from there but it

was Charlton who grabbed the winner through Danny Mills, who I really like as a right back. He's strong and he's quick and would be a good signing for somebody.

It wasn't until afterwards that I realised Charlton would have been relegated but for Mills's goal, with Southampton having won at Wimbledon. I think they will go down, though. They're just not a good enough side.

Nothing was said in our dressing room, which is typical of us. Our European place was going down the toilet as well and nobody says anything. After some of the things that had happened in the season, I didn't feel it was my place to speak out but in leaving Bozzy out, I think the boss had cut off his nose to spite his face.

We had our Player of the Year dinner at the club in the evening and had some time to kill. I had a chat with Gareth Southgate, who by his own admission had a poor game today. I feel for him. He takes responsibility for the whole club as captain and sometimes he forgets about himself. Nobody notices on a Saturday afternoon that he was doing well in talking to so-and-so on a Friday or that he has done well to organise something for the lads.

He had to nurse Gareth Barry through the season, and cope with Ugo Ehiogu being injured for half of it. He is tired. With the World Cup, he has played non-stop for two years and didn't even get a rest against Hull City in the FA Cup. He is a great lad and a natural captain but he deserves a rest. It may be a team game, I told him, but sometimes you've got to be selfish.

Jockey won the award, deservedly so. He has seen the boss bring in two strikers for £12 million, with another previously bought for £7 million already here, and he has been dropped several times but always kept his head up and bounced back, scoring 16 goals. He's a nice lad, a quiet lad and very quick. I think he could still work on his game, though, mainly in the timing and direction of his runs. Quickness is in the mind, too. I would like to see him now wanting to get in the England squad.

Afterwards I went with the lads to a place at Broad Street called the Mellow Bar, just for the company. A couple of them got paralytic, which is fine for them but not for me so I knew when it was time to leave.

Sunday 9 May

I took the kids to golf in the morning, swimming at Debbie and Marco's at lunchtime then to a wildlife park in the afternoon. The compulsive behaviour of an addict or what? I can't just do one thing sometimes, can I? I have to go for the full house.

I managed to sit down for a couple of hours and watch Manchester United win 1–0 at Middlesbrough and thought that now they would go on to win the title. That was their hardest game left, I reckon.

Monday 10 May

I spent my day off looking at houses, one at St Albans and one at Cheshunt. I can't prey on Debbie and Marco's hospitality for ever and besides, I have to have a big enough place down here near the boys' schools where I can have them to stay. Neither of the places really appealed to me, though. Anyway, it's still difficult for me to start making decisions yet because me and Lorraine are no closer to sorting out the money.

Lorraine has agreed that we should employ a nanny who can help me on the days when I have the boys, though it is difficult to find one who will work at weekends when I am playing football. We interviewed three in the evening and at least Lorraine and I talked in a civilised manner about it. Afterwards, I went and got an Indian take-away for us. I even missed watching Spurs v Chelsea on the box, so I suppose I'm getting my priorities right.

Tuesday 11 May
Cardiff City 1 Aston Villa 3

I asked John Gregory if I could play for as long as possible in the testimonial we were taking part in for Carl Dale, Cardiff's long-serving striker. The boss agreed and some of the boys were surprised I wanted to. Julian was playing 45 minutes and when I told him that I wanted to play the whole game, he looked baffled. 'Feel guilty now, don't you?' I said and he smiled.

I enjoyed the game and could even smile when some Cardiff fans starting singing at me: 'Where's your missus gone?' I didn't realise I was so big in Wales, that the ins and outs of my private life were so well known there. It was nice to score the third goal.

A lot of the lads are glad that the season is ending but to me now it is a shame. I am getting a buzz from my football again. It is a healthy drug for me. Some lads can play cards on the coach for money, some can have a drink. I have to concentrate on my game and get back to my best. I think I'm doing that right now, which bodes well for next season.

I heard that Arsenal had lost 1–0 at Leeds. If United get something from their game at Blackburn tomorrow, that will be it, as far as I am concerned. In fact, our game against Arsenal at Highbury on Sunday will mean more to us than them, with West Ham trying to nick that fifth place off us. I am looking forward to going back for the first time as a player – clear-headed.

Wednesday 12 May

I took in an AA meeting in St Albans at lunchtime. I am really feeling the benefit of going regularly again.

In the evening I watched United draw 0–0 at Blackburn, who are down now. That's despite doing the double over us this season. It is going to be interesting on Sunday, with Spurs going to Old Trafford and us going to Highbury. Even if they beat us, Arsenal have to hope that Spurs can get a point at least off United. I know George Graham would probably prefer his record of two titles to survive at Arsenal but he'll want to take something off United for sure. He is a professional and will want to prove that Spurs can be a force next season.

Thursday 13 May

We trained hard in the morning, going on till early afternoon, then I went and picked the boys up to play on the pitch-and-putt golf course. They want to play all the time these days. They think they're Tiger Woods now. From there it was back to Debbie and Marco's. There's a lot of banter in the house with them being big Arsenal fans. 'You score on Sunday and your gear will be out on the lawn,' they said.

Friday 14 May

We've had a couple of foreign players training with us but it doesn't look like the boss is going to take them on.

There has been Mondragon, the Colombian goalkeeper, who I reckon is ordinary, and Jose Dominguez, not the Spurs one but a lookalike from Paraguay. Do we really need another little left-sided player though?

After training, all the press wanted to talk to me about the game on Sunday, what with me returning to Highbury. I said I thought that it would be difficult for Arsenal after losing at Leeds because when it's out of your hands, you really are struggling.

Saturday 15 May

Had to travel up to the training ground again to join up with the team, then go down to the Royal Lancaster with them in the coach but this time I am all right with it. It's funny how things seem to piss you off less when you feel better about yourself. I was pissed off, mind, that the papers have interpreted what I said about the title race as being that Arsenal have no chance. That will only wind them and the fans up and leave me as a target.

In the afternoon I went shopping around New Bond Street with Steve Watson, Alan Thompson and Gareth Barry and bought some clothes. The boys went to the pictures in the evening at Marble Arch but there was nothing on I fancied.

Sunday 16 May
Arsenal 1 Aston Villa 0

I was up really early. That's another thing that's improved without the gambling or drinking again. I go to bed at a reasonable time, sleep well then get up instead of turning over and trying to nick another hour's sleep. Now I get into the day.

I wasn't nervous about going back to Highbury. I never am before a game when I am feeling OK within myself. I did get anxious just before I got dropped, when I was taking all my worries into football. I was playing with fear all the time. I was sure people would see how badly I was playing and would come to the conclusion that I must be drinking or gambling because no one could play this badly and be normal. Usually you can run around and at least look busy but I didn't even have that in me at the time.

I had breakfast with Paul Barron and Gareth Southgate and we discussed where we thought we had gone wrong during the season. It was funny. I had plenty of ideas but I couldn't say too much because to be honest, I was one of the things that had gone wrong during the season. There had been times looking back, when I messed up sessions big time by slowing things down or standing out on the wing sulking.

I wondered if I would get a bad reception when the coach pulled up outside the Arsenal reception in Avenell Road after what had been in the papers but the fans were great to me, chanting my name as we got off the bus, and the lads were well impressed. It was great walking through the marble hall and saying hello to everybody, including the Arsenal players. I had only ever been in the away dressing room to clean it as an apprentice.

The lads were out warming up but I was stretching in a corridor when Arsène Wenger walked past and asked me how I was. 'You are not warming up with the team?' he asked me in that clever, understated way of his that makes you feel guilty. He does have this way of making a point quietly; our boss is a bit like that, too. Sometimes, though, I do like a manager to have a go at you and the team, just to keep you on your toes. Sometimes with these quiet managers, you can kid yourself you're playing well.

We did all right in the game. Even though they had all the possession, I thought we had the better chances, including one for me. And I thought that if we had needed to get a point we could have done.

You could feel it going round the ground when Spurs scored at Old Trafford, and also when United scored twice to ensure that Kanu's goal would not be enough for Arsenal. It was a strange, subdued feeling at the end with them finishing second on the same number of points as won the title last season and us missing out on our place in the Intertoto Cup that West Ham took by beating Middlesbrough. It went unnoticed but it was a sickener for us.

Charlie, Ben and Sam had been watching the game with Debbie and Marco and with Lorraine being away in Spain with friends for the weekend, I took them back to St Albans for the night. After putting them to bed, I packed ready for a golf week in Florida with John, starting tomorrow.

I am shattered. It feels strange to think that the season is over. All the success and struggles are gone just like that.

Monday 17 May–Monday 24 May

It could hardly have been a better week. Golf every day, lots of sun. And plenty of AA meetings, four during the week in fact.

It's funny. I have been to Florida eight out of the past 10 years, and I was even here the same time last year during FA Cup week before meeting up with England, but I had never thought about going to meetings. There were times in years gone by, in fact, when I was on the phone back home half the time, placing bets and finding out how they were getting on. My hotel phone bills alone were usually around £1,200.

In England, meetings are anonymous and I do have trust that no one will say anything outside of the meetings about me. It's people I meet in bars who are likely to go to the papers, I have found out. Sometimes, though, to be honest, I am worried about what I say because some people know who I am. It is my problem, and me who is uncomfortable. I know it is something I will have to work on.

In the States, though, very few people know of me and I feel more relaxed and can just be myself. I can talk about my work and my relationship without any inhibition. It was just Paul and money and fame didn't enter into it, though one American amazingly recognised me in a shopping mall.

The meetings were going on all over Orlando at all sorts of times all through the day but the one that suited me took place at 3pm every afternoon, when there were about 10 people there. They were very positive and spiritual. John even came to an open meeting with me on the Sunday morning, at which there were about 50 people. It was a really uplifting experience.

The golf was great too, apart from one experience. On the Celebration course in Orlando, we were teeing off one evening when the starting marshall warned us not to go too near the lakes because of the alligators or the deep rough because of the snakes. Now we had played the same course the night before and never heard this as we hacked our way through undergrowth that said only 'Environmentally unsafe'. We thought it just meant not to trample the ground.

Anyway, on this night John and I were looking for a ball in the rough on the eighth hole when I suddenly saw a snake about as long as my leg slither through the grass. I jumped in the air, shouted to John and we both bolted back to the fairway. We packed it in on the ninth hole.

The only other time I felt threatened was one night when we decided to go out to a couple of bars. It was difficult to get into them and once we did, I wondered why I had bothered. What was the attraction if you are not drinking alcohol? It was just my illness taking over and the next day I had to get to a meeting. I knew straight away I was in the right place.

Wednesday 26 May

I had other priorities in Florida than watching Manchester United do the Double by beating Newcastle 2–0 in the FA Cup final. Like everyone else, though, I was gripped by them scoring twice in added time to win the European Cup by beating Bayern Munich in one of the most thrilling finishes to a game of all time, though I still reckon Arsenal's win at Liverpool in 1989 takes some beating.

It is strange to think that we led United in the Premiership for half the season, strange to think that they started the month beating us 2–1 and ended it with the same score to record a treble. They have done English football proud – even if they were a bit lucky against us. There's an adage in football that it's not how you start, it's how you finish that's important and United have shown it us again.

Watching it on TV after flying back from Florida, I was particularly pleased for Teddy Sheringham, who had tried to rescue me in the Titanic Bar that Saturday night in April and had now succeeded in rescuing United. He showed me there are a lot of people who care about me and I was touched.

It happened too when I got a letter from Shane Nicholson, the former West Bromwich Albion player who is now in recovery after being banned for taking drugs. He wrote to me after I had relapsed, encouraging me to get back on the AA programme and made me see how easy and dangerous it is to let it all slip. It was good of him.

Friday 28 May

Ted has deservedly found his way back into Kevin Keegan's England squad for the Euro 2000 qualifying match against Sweden at Wembley next Saturday. The manager says that his recall holds out hope for three Pauls – Ince, Gascoigne and Merson.

What a difference a year makes. This time last year, Ted was in disgrace for his few days in Portugal, Incey was a mainstay of the England team, Gazza was about to become an outcast in La Manga and I was about to be named for a World Cup.

It has, as they might say in AA, been a learning and growing year for me.

It certainly was with regard to Villa. I'm sure the manager absorbed lessons ready for our return to pre-season training on 2 July and I just hope the young players in particular don't waste the experience and are more able to take advantage if we get in this position again. You don't always have to work harder, just smarter sometimes.

What could I have said about the team and the club that Sunday morning over breakfast with Paul Barron and Gareth Southgate?

I thought we needed at least three new players. And I thought that as a team, we had to give up drinking. I know it is one of my hobbyhorses these days but if you want to be the best, you have to make sacrifices. The boss does it. Fair play to him, he stops drinking at the beginning of the season and doesn't touch a drop until the end because he wants to stay clear-headed. We should follow his example.

Also, too many players these days judge themselves by how good their car is and the size of their house, rather than the medals they have won. I see players who are rich after five years in the game but have never got close to winning anything. I can see people retiring at 25 in the future. The winning mentality, rather than the comfort zone, is what we need at Villa. I personally don't think that unless we change things we can get above fourth or fifth.

Too many of us were playing within ourselves sometimes, content to play in the comfort zone where it didn't hurt enough if we lost. We didn't expect to win some games but we should. We are a big club with a support as big and as passionate as anywhere. Sometimes I wonder if we care enough. I have never seen a cross word at training, let alone a punch-up. At Arsenal something kicked off every week.

We have to do more than just talk about signing players like Juninho, we have to do it – and keep it quiet while we do. I was also a bit surprised that the boss didn't throw some of the kids in for the last few games of the season. We have got some good ones and you never know if one or two of them might respond. When George Graham threw me in near the end of a season at Arsenal, I did, and he put off signing a centre-forward that summer.

From a personal playing point of view, the worst experience of the season was the game at Tottenham. It didn't feel like me playing. I had this weird feeling of not wanting to release the ball because I knew it was going to go astray. The gambling and the drinking around that time were crippling me and the fear factor had crept into my game.

It felt a bit like Patsy Fagan must have when he couldn't push the snooker cue or Eric Bristow when he couldn't release the dart. It was the equivalent of the golfing yips and it frightened me. I had never had that feeling before and I felt desperately low. The fans at Arsenal and Middlesbrough had always loved me and now they didn't at Villa and that hurt.

Usually I am not afraid to make mistakes because trying the unusual is what my game is all about but now I was paralysed. The reserve games turned me around, because I could get my confidence back without a crowd on my back. That and stopping drinking and gambling.

It was only after coming back from Florida in March and getting the drink out of my system that my attitude changed. And for next season I need to be one of the things that has to change. At times I didn't realise how much of a pain I was.

I know I can't change other people, only myself, and I know I can't take responsibility for everyone, but I do think I could make more effort with some of the younger players sometimes and help them with some advice. Take

Gareth Barry. I don't feel I got to know him as I should have because of being absorbed in myself at times. When I am well, I am more open to other people.

He is a nice lad, the best footballing centre half I think I have ever seen, but still needs to work on his defending. I hope I can get across to him that he has a chance to be one of the dominant players of his era, which is all any player can ever do. He's got to look after himself, though, and avoid the pitfalls. Same as Lee Hendrie.

During my bad times during the season, the price tag did worry me but then when I am feeling good about myself and playing well, it wouldn't matter if I cost £20 million and earned £50,000 a week. I would feel I was worth it. It did concern me during the season, as with Stan Collymore, that because you are a professional footballer and earn well, you are somehow immune from sadness and pain. Everybody has feelings and money doesn't stop those.

As for my disagreements with the boss, well they are usually more about me than him, I have come to see. In fact it is the same with everyone. If I am at ease with me, then I am at ease with everyone. If I don't get on with me, everyone gets on my nerves. It is all about me.

When I look back on the year, I have had three relapses, a £6.75 million transfer and played in the World Cup. That is more than happens to most people in a lifetime.

I feel now I have woken up a bit. I don't know if it is a spiritual awakening or what, but I have a new feeling about recovery. I did my best in treatment over four years ago after hitting rock bottom, getting honest and doing the programme to the best of my ability. But I think I took it too easily. I complied in treatment.

I can't afford to do that any longer. I have to keep going to meetings, keep reading the AA literature, stay in touch with people who are in recovery. I can't say how football will turn out, or how my relationship with Lorraine will pan out, but I do know that if I stay away from a bet, drink or drug one day at a time, things will work out as they are meant to.

Now I feel better for my experiences than I ever did in treatment. Perhaps I needed to be reminded of the pain by these relapses. It's funny, I've kept a diary of the 52 weeks and the best one has been the last.

Epilogue

Final Redemption

How long an English football season can be, how low are its troughs and high its peaks. After the season of relapse from my addictive illness that plumbed the depths, leading me to contemplate suicide at one point, I might have expected a quiet time in 1999/2000 with my life seeming more settled. Wrong.

It was a year that would see me out of the Aston Villa team for almost half the season, then reach the FA Cup final with them, winning the club's supporters' and players' Player of the Year awards on the way. At the end of it, though, I would be sad and surprised to discover that the Villa manager John Gregory was willing to sell me.

It was also a year that would see me finally accept that my marriage to Lorraine had finally run its course, along with my England playing career. But above all, and most important, it was a year clean and sober, free of gambling, alcohol and drugs, as I emerged through all these events having learned some painful but valuable lessons. Aston Villa may have tasted the bitter disappointment of losing the last Cup final at Wembley, but because I had managed to make a lot of personal progress despite the setbacks, I still felt victorious.

The first issue came in pre-season. Villa were playing a tournament in New York – it couldn't have had anything to do with the fact that Bruce Springsteen, John Gregory's hero, was playing a concert there at the time, could it? I was on the substitute's bench for the first game, against Ajax. I only played the last 10 minutes of a 2–2 draw and my bemusement at being left out of the starting line-up was compounded when I wasn't even named among the penalty-takers, one of my specialities as I had proved for England against Argentina in the World Cup. I was getting bad vibes already.

I was then shocked to be left out of the next game against Fiorentina and didn't even get on even though we were getting thrashed, eventually losing 4–0. When we got back to the hotel, the boss's assistant Steve Harrison asked me what I thought about it but I couldn't say anything more than: 'Don't ask me. I thought I knew something about football but if I can't get in this team, then obviously I don't.'

So it didn't really surprise me when I didn't make the starting line-up for the opening Premiership game against Newcastle. It was the first time in my career I had not started a season but I consoled myself with the knowledge that there was plenty of time and I needed to be patient. Gareth Barry, who would go on to win the club's Young Player of the Year award, was also left out and I remember saying to him not to worry, that nobody remembers the first game of the season.

With the team starting well, I had to wait for my chance, which came in the fifth game of the new campaign, at Watford, after the boys had just suffered their first defeat, against Chelsea. I tried to impress too much and didn't play my own game but the management seemed pleased enough with my work rate before I was subbed in the 1–0 win. It started a four-game run in the side but even though I set up a consolation goal for Julian Joachim in a 3–1 defeat at Arsenal, I found myself dropped again for the game against Bradford City.

I went to see John Gregory to ask him why. I thought it would be the type of match when I could unlock a defence that was not among the best in the Premiership. He said we needed to be solid and that it was a job for more defensive-minded players. I did get on as a sub, as I did several times over the next two months, but it wasn't until November that I got another start – due to injuries – at home to Southampton. Now the team was struggling for form, having slipped into the bottom half of the table.

I thought I did well enough but was dragged off with about a quarter of an hour to go, a decision which upset the Villa fans and I could hear the Holte End chanting: 'You don't know what you're doing', at John Gregory as I left the field. It was 0–0 when I went, and we lost 1–0, a result that provoked jeers all around the ground and led to the press questioning whether Doug Ellis might sack the manager.

After that, we had more than two weeks until our next game because of England's two-match Euro 2000 play-off against Scotland, and I was given permission to have a week off, so took Charlie, Ben and Sam to Florida. When I came back to discover that I would not be playing in the next game, at Coventry, I began to think that I might have played my last game for Villa. If I still couldn't get in the side when they were doing badly, what hope was there?

I was determined not to add to the manager's problems by seeking some sort of showdown because I knew he was under strain. He also had the Stan Collymore situation to deal with, having decided that Stan was not part of his plans. I stayed out of that, not taking sides, simply trying to be civil to Stan whenever we met at the training ground or played together for the reserves before he eventually went to Leicester.

Not that I thought John Gregory would get the sack. 'Deadly' Doug may have had a reputation for hiring and firing but he is not the sort who does what the press are saying he should do. He is definitely his own man. He had shown faith in John Gregory and, as Doug said, it is easy to sack a manager but not so easy to find a new one.

I just kept my head down, working hard in training and trying to accept the situation. I was feeling well in my recovery, through talking to fellow recovering addicts, going to AA meetings, reading my books and generally taking care of my well-being. By now I had bought a flat in Sutton Coldfield and was not travelling up and down from St Albans every day so was feeling more settled. I never thought about asking for a transfer – a loan, maybe, because I just wanted to play.

I remember thinking at the time that I wished I could accept my marriage break-up, which was still causing me a lot of anguish, as I could accept the way my football was going. I kept my enthusiasm by trying to give my all for the reserves. I even asked to play in a game against Loughborough University that I had no need to.

Things didn't always go well, mind. We were playing particularly badly against Barnsley one night and the reserve-team coach Kevin MacDonald had a real go at us at half-time. I felt he picked on me and said that he should bring me off if he thought I was that bad. So he did. It was all over the next day, though, when we apologised to each other. I have always got on well with Kevin.

It is usually the way in football that one man's misfortune is another's opportunity. The first team had just had a morale-boosting 4–0 win over Southampton in the Worthington Cup, when I was a sub again, and if Lee Hendrie had not got an ankle injury I am sure I would not have played against Darlington in the third round of the FA Cup in December.

People say that the club's fortunes changed when we were reinstated in the Worthington Cup after a quarter-final defeat at West Ham after they fielded an ineligible player in Manny Omoyimni, and we went on to win 3–1 after extra-time, but for me the Darlington game was a big turning point.

Any hopes we had of a top-three position and the Champions League had gone with a nine-game run without a league win, so the cups were looking like our only route to salvation. I felt a lot of pressure that day. Darlington came into the match relaxed, having lost in the second round but been drawn as the wild card after Manchester United's withdrawal from the competition, and represented a real banana skin. It was the kind of day when the fans look to a big player, an expensive signing, to show up the gap in class. I felt that player was me. I was worried, too, that you just can't turn it on immediately when you've been out of the side for so long.

But I thought I played well and the 2–1 margin of victory did not reflect our superiority. After that, I was off and running, as was the team, and I would play every game until the end of the season, except for an away match at Sheffield Wednesday in April when I was rested.

Our next game was against Wednesday, at home, and it marked our first Premiership win for three months. It also saw my first goal of the season, and one of my best, a curling 20-yard shot. Afterwards John Gregory said that it was a goal I wouldn't have scored had I not kept my fitness level so high during my period out of the team and I felt good about my football again, even though I also had a penalty saved in the game. What did mar the win was a freak accident to Dion Dublin, in which, we discovered a few days later, that he had broken his neck.

It was a 2–1 win at Leeds that really announced we were back. They were flying at the top of the table and I thought that it was about time we showed we could beat the big teams, rather than just the ones in the bottom third of the table. We really outplayed them and Gareth Southgate scored two rare goals, both world-class scrambles. It set us up nicely for another home FA Cup tie, against Southampton, and this time it was 1–0 in our favour with Gareth nodding home another of his brilliant goals from about a yard. They say they come in threes.

Thus we went into the fifth round, again at home, against Leeds, on a high despite a frustrating goalless Worthington Cup semi-final first leg at home to Leicester when they were without several key players and just packed their defence. What a game it was against Leeds at a packed Villa Park and for me, Benito Carbone produced one of the performances of the competition.

We were unlucky to be trailing 2–1, one of the Leeds goals a fantastic effort by Eirik Bakke, when Beni picked up a clearance about 35 yards out. Immediately he curled it past Nigel Martyn for a breathtaking equaliser. And from there, although Leeds's movement throughout the game had been good, I really felt we would go on to win.

So it proved. I got in a good run to the by-line on the left and managed to clip the ball in for Beni's winner. Not that I knew anything about it. I was laid out having got a kick in the face. I remember being on the treatment table having six stitches put in a cut on my forehead – I also had one on my nose but that wasn't stitched, leaving me with a scar – and asking to go back on but the doctor said I was concussed and couldn't. He also said that at least my last contribution to the game had been worth it, so I started to feel better.

Still, I shouldn't have played in the midweek second leg against Leicester as I was still feeling a bit groggy. They have become our bogey team and we rarely looked likely to win the game. After a lame 1–0 defeat I sat on the coach hoping that we would all remember this feeling for our developing FA Cup run, because I didn't want that gloom of being a semi-final loser again.

I felt better by the weekend and really enjoyed a 4–0 win over Watford, when I scored twice, once with a header and once with a chip. Then followed another 4–0 win, this time at Middlesbrough. I wasn't looking forward to going back to the club whose fans felt I had left under a cloud, but in the end the result silenced them.

The game was made memorable because of Paul Gascoigne's early blow to the chin of George Boateng – the one that broke Gazza's forearm. I thought it was a scandalous challenge and I'm sure Gazza regrets it. I'm also sure it was down to frustration at not being the player he once was, unable to impose himself on the game with his ability the way he once used to do.

An hour after the final whistle, on the team bus, my mobile rang. It was Gazza asking to speak to George to apologise. That's the sort of bloke he is, impetuous but with a sense of honour that sometimes gets overlooked. Gazza also phoned me the next day for a chat, perhaps a little bit envious of how I was doing in my recovery, but that was it. I didn't hear from him the rest of the season. He went off to New York for a while to escape – and there's a few of us who have done that. He has to find his own path, I suppose. Mind you, I had not been in the best of emotional health myself that night at the Riverside. I was angry at being subbed by John Gregory and told him so in graphic terms. He told me not to talk to him like that.

Perhaps it was the reason behind what happened at Everton six days later. The FA Cup quarter-finals took us to Goodison Park for what I thought would be an even more difficult tie than the one against Leeds. It turned out to be a tight, frantic game.

We struck an early blow with a short-corner routine that the gaffer talked about in the dressing room before the game, Steve Stone getting on the end of it as it worked a treat. Then, after Everton had equalised, I went on a mazy run just before half time, that ended with my shot being saved and Beni tapping in the rebound to restore our lead.

I was jubilant when we came into the dressing room for the interval, only to be told by John Gregory that he was hauling me off because he wanted to put on a more defensive player to hold the lead. Kevin MacDonald, knowing that the gaffer had missed us going ahead as he was on his way to the dressing room, asked him if he knew that I had set up the goal but I think the strategy was in the manager's mind even before the game if we were leading at half-time. This time I said nothing, knowing it would be disruptive, but I was not happy. It was the perfect scenario for me. The hard work had been done, Everton would have to chase the game, leaving me gaps to exploit. Was it payback for Middlesbrough?

Anyway, I have to say that the manager's thinking worked, that was the important thing, even if just trying to protect a lead is a risky tactic. We were through to the semi-finals, where we would play Bolton Wanderers. The draw had been made that afternoon – we were aware of it at half-time – and facing a First Division side had been a massive incentive to hold on.

It was around this time that England were playing a friendly against Argentina at Wembley and there had been talk that I might get back into the squad because I was playing well. In fact, I was disappointed about not being included and when I was asked about it by reporters, I said that I thought the time was ripe, with my 32nd birthday fast approaching, to retire from the international game. If I couldn't get in now, in this form, then I didn't think I would ever add to my 21 caps.

Regret is not a luxury I can allow myself these days, as I have to live in the now rather than in a past I can't change, but in hindsight I was probably a bit hasty. At the time, I don't think I had seen my kids for a while and was feeling a bit down. I thought that I needed to spend as much of the summer, when Euro 2000 was on, with them rather than just being a squad player for a month. It is a shame because I might have got in, though Kevin Keegan never phoned me to ask me to reconsider. I had hinted at retirement once before under Glenn Hoddle and he flew on to the phone to reassure me that I was still in his thinking.

So I concentrated on Villa and after our poor start, and the blow of the Worthington Cup defeat by Leicester, a promising end to the season was in prospect. One of the reasons that my own game picked up so much was that after a long period of soul-searching about whether we might get back together again, I had finally been forced to accept that my relationship with Lorraine was over. All the evidence of our separation and phone calls said that I could cling on to it no more. I once thought that it was the worst thing that could ever happen to me but when I surrendered to the inevitable, a huge relief came over me and I concentrated on getting on with my life and devoting all my energies to my football and my children. I've learned in recovery that the fear of something bad happening is usually worse than the something bad actually happening.

I was enjoying the responsibility of being the team's playmaker from a position behind the front two. I had revelled in the same role of being the creative heartbeat at Middlesbrough after being at Arsenal, who had plenty of quality attacking talent in players like Dennis Bergkamp and Ian Wright and could win a game from anywhere. Some players shrink when a burden is placed on them. I thrive on it.

Villa were now becoming a very hard team to beat, developing that knack of getting results even when we weren't firing on all cylinders. I scored again at Bradford City and with a diving header against Leicester as we lost only two of our last 21 Premiership games, a limp 2–0 at

Southampton and 1–0 at home to the champions Manchester United on the last day of the season, when I was presented with the supporters' Player of the Season trophy. The irony was not lost on me that I was standing there with a big bottle of champagne. I've had a lot of them, what with man-of-the-match awards, and I usually give them away to family and friends, or staff in the Villa lounges.

Eventually we would finish a creditable sixth in the Premiership but it was the FA Cup that was taking over the club and the city. Villa hadn't been in the final since 1957 and the semi-final against Bolton at Wembley represented a great chance to write a new chapter in the club's history, even if being favourites was not a position we were used to or particularly relished.

Actually, I shouldn't really have played. My back was giving me trouble in the week leading up to the tie and my hamstring had tightened up. But it was just too big a game to miss and I gave it a go, if not contributing as much as I hoped. Without being arrogant, I do believe that if I play well, then Villa play well. Neither I nor the team played well that day, though, in what must have been a poor game to watch.

We did improve after Mark Delaney got himself sent off because we just had to lift ourselves. Often when you have only 10 men you redouble your efforts. Then when Dean Holdsworth missed a gilt-edged chance, almost an open goal, for Bolton, I did get the feeling that it just had to be our day as the game went to penalties.

I was down to take our fifth but it didn't get that far. David James, who had had a great season rebuilding his confidence after his unhappy latter days at Liverpool, did his stuff in goal and Dion Dublin made it a fairytale story by scoring the fourth, having returned much earlier than expected after his broken neck. Lee Hendrie also deserved a lot of credit for coming on as a sub in extra-time and almost immediately scoring with his penalty. We may have scrambled it but I thought we deserved to win.

My mind went back to that opening day of the season when I had told Gareth Barry that nobody remembered the beginning, only the end. There's a saying in football that it's not how you start but how you finish that matters. Manchester United had been proving it for years. Now I and we were ending on a high.

People were saying that I was playing the best football of my career and I would probably agree. I felt the time was right now to talk to John Gregory about extending my contract, which had two years left to run. I was about to go through an expensive divorce and I wanted to get my life in order and make my future secure.

At a meeting with the gaffer, I told him my thinking. He suggested that I could see out my two years with Villa then maybe go to America to play in the Major Soccer League on a 'Bosman' free transfer for a final pay-day. I told him that I didn't want to do that because I had three kids who needed to live in England. I was a bit surprised by his attitude. I expected him to say that he wanted to keep me and that we could sort something out. He had told me, after all, when I first signed that he would look after me if things went well. And they had done. I know I was a pain in the neck that first season but now I was really doing it for him and the fans loved me.

I was worried that he had misunderstood me, perhaps believing that I was angling for a transfer, so about a week later I went to see him again and assured him that

I wanted to stay with the club and was willing to take a pay cut for that extra year I felt I had left in me and needed financially. Nobody expects a 34-year-old, as I would be in two years' time, to be on top money and I was realistic about that. He reacted as if he didn't want to hear it. This time he just changed the subject before telling me to wait to the end of the season before we sorted things out.

Although I was saddened by his response, I was willing to leave things at that but not long after I got a call from my agent, Steve Kutner, to say that the *News of the World* had been in touch with him to say that they had heard from a 'very, very good source' at Villa that I would be leaving at the end of the season. So I went to see the gaffer again. He told me to squash the rumour as the Cup final was coming up but that we could let it come out afterwards. I was shocked now. It seemed he really was willing to sell me.

I was determined not to let it unsettle me in the run-up to the final. This could have been my last big match at Wembley – it was certainly going to be the last final at the stadium with it being knocked down to be replaced by a new one – and if it was also going to be my last game for Villa, I wanted my swan song to be memorable.

Anyway, I was in such good spirits that nothing was really bothering me at that time. I had been working hard on my recovery through AA meetings, and after having built up a good new network of support around Birmingham since moving there, and having let go of Lorraine, I was reaping the benefits of feeling good about myself.

I've always believed that if my head's all right, I'm all right and so is my game. It is not a Cup final that lifts my spirits, it is the knowledge that I am doing the right things in being honest and telling people I trust how I am feeling. If I am OK with myself, then I could be playing in the Third Division and be happy. If my head's not right, then I could be somewhere nice, in the sun at Disneyworld for example, and be unhappy. The Cup final was a bonus to being right in myself.

It didn't worry me in the slightest that the gaffer had described me as a 'high-maintenance' player in a TV interview and in the *Sun,* who were serialising his own book in the week leading up to Wembley. I probably have been a problem for him at times but I like to think he was now getting his reward from me. He's probably learned a lot about management from having to deal with me. He discovered that there were days when I was not right and he left me alone, which was good.

I think he was a bit worried that some of his comments might have upset me, though. One morning at breakfast at the team's Cup final hotel in Harrow Weald, he saw me reading the book extracts in the paper and asked me what I thought. It was OK by me, I told him. I was in such a good mood at that time that he could have written anything he liked about me. It could have been a lot worse. That's another good thing. If my relationship with myself is good, then it is good with other people. I remember being asked at the Player of the Year dinner what had turned my season around. I said that Lorraine had done me a big favour by kicking me out. It forced me to move on with my life.

Despite the shock John Gregory had delivered to me, I didn't fall out with him. He has his job to do but I have also got to take care of myself. I had always had an honest, open relationship with him even if we had had our disagreements. And whenever I had been wrong, I apologised to him, as I had done at Liverpool that time the previous season when a 1–0 win proved him to be right about leaving me out.

That's the way it should be in football. It is an emotional, spontaneous game and you are bound to have run-ins with each other when you both feel so passionately about it. The important thing is not to bear grudges or carry resentments. The one thing that did concern me was that he had been talking about me a lot before the final. I have seen managers do that with other players before they sell them.

I simply resolved to do my best in the final, then have a word with Doug Ellis at our post-final party at the Grosvenor House Hotel in London to see where I stood with the club. Again we did not do ourselves justice at Wembley, though, in what was another disappointing spectacle.

Our final opponents Chelsea, the team I supported as a boy, are such a good passing side and we knew we had to be playing to our ultimate, hoping also that they weren't at theirs. For the first half we cancelled each other out, about our only half-chance a volley that I steered just wide, but we were pleased enough that we had stopped them playing at least.

But there comes a time when you have to kick on and win the game. Chelsea found the extra gear and we couldn't. We got a bit static and although we got in some good positions with set pieces, Frank Leboeuf and Marcel Desailly defended them well.

Everyone put their winner down to a mistake by David James and he was big enough to own up afterwards to taking his eye off the ball as Gianfranco Zola curled in a free-kick from the left. After David could only push it out, it hit Gareth Southgate before falling to Gustavo Poyet to smash home. Still, even though time was running out, I felt sure that we would get at least one chance. We had to open up and become more attacking, as we should have been earlier. Sure enough, we did get that chance, only for Beni Carbone to scuff his shot and Leboeuf to clear off the line. The real name of the game in tight matches at this level is taking the chance that falls. Chelsea took theirs and won the Cup.

In trying to make amends, David James surged upfield trying to grab a late equaliser, but in vain. When the final whistle went, I found myself next to him in the middle of the pitch. He just lay there, tears filling his eyes, and I tried to haul him to his feet. I told him that he had got us here, by saving the penalties in the semi-final. I said that he had had a great season and re-established himself as one of the best goalkeepers in the country. He was distraught, though. It's an unavoidable fact of the game that outfield players can make 10 mistakes in a match and get away with them. A keeper makes one and it can be crucial.

I walked over to Dion Dublin, who was also really down. I told him just to think back five months ago when he was lying in a hospital bed with a broken neck and that he had come a long way. I know I had. It was only just over a year ago that I had felt suicidal and had been using alcohol and gambling to try and feel better.

I did a couple of interviews and got back to the dressing room after the rest of the lads. It was very quiet and the gaffer looked especially gutted. I was one of the lucky ones, I realised. I had an FA Cup winner's medal with Arsenal. As I looked around at the young lads it occurred me that this could actually be a positive for them, if they reacted the right way and became even hungrier to win something.

My own opinion was that Chelsea had pointed up a difference in class. We were a good side but to become one capable of living with them, Arsenal and Manchester United consistently and to achieve a Champion's League place, we would need three or four players of top quality. I said it to the papers in my post-match interviews, and I don't think it made me too popular with some at the club, but it was honest and I reckoned anyone who knew football could see it. I said it for the best of motives.

Not surprisingly, the evening party was a subdued affair. I was in bed by midnight. I did get the chance to talk to the chairman though and he was surprised to hear that I might be leaving. 'You're like a son to me,' he said. 'Let me see what I can do.' But what could he do? If the manager has other ideas, in the end the chairman has to support him.

The story that the gaffer was willing to let me go came out on the Sunday and it made things tricky for me in Birmingham as we went on an open-top bus tour to say thank you to the Villa fans who had been so terrific. The gaffer, still in his own disappointment I think, didn't say anything to me, though he did describe the story as 'bollocks' on television. They had to bleep it out. I wasn't quite sure why he was denying it. Perhaps he was going to make me see out my contract without talking about the extra year.

I got talking to Tom Ross, the local radio reporter, on the bus for a while then was surprised when we started doing an interview and he said: 'You're not leaving are you? It's rubbish, isn't it?' I could only say again that I wanted to finish my career with Villa but that it wasn't up to me. I had a holiday booked in Florida starting the next day so I simply let go of it, leaving my agent to try and sort out the situation while I was away.

In the sumer, Wimbledon did come in for me but the move didn't feel right at the time. I resolved to start the season with Villa, try to play well again and perhaps earn the extra year on my contract that I was seeking so that I could finish my career with them, as I really wanted to do.

I had to get it all in perspective. The Cup final defeat was a massive disappointment and the prospect of moving on was one I would rather have avoided but after my nightmare season of 1998/99 I felt I had made great strides in my life. That is after all what will count when I finish playing – how well I can cope with life and all its challenges without the need for any mood-altering substance or compulsive behaviour.

It had been a year of growth. In 1993, I was a Wembley winner with Arsenal but now I look back uncomfortably at those pictures of me making a show of knocking back pints of lager. This time I may have stood under the twin towers, shattered, as a loser but the most important thing was that I believed, clean and sober for more than a year second time around, that I had won back my self-esteem. The worst was over, the best could be yet to come.